Knowledge & Existence

KNOWLEDGE & EXISTENCE

An Introduction to Philosophical Problems

Joseph Margolis

New York OXFORD UNIVERSITY PRESS *1973*

for Grove and Jennie,
Muffin and Fu—
the rest of the family

Copyright © 1973 by Oxford University Press, Inc.
Library of Congress Catalogue Card Number: 72-89399
Printed in the United States of America

PREFACE

The central theme of this book is that men—human persons—are cultural emergents, physically embodied but exhibiting attributes that cannot be characterized exclusively in physical
terms. In saying that they are physically embodied, moreover, I
wish to say that there is no reason to suppose that men are composed of anything but matter.

It is primarily in the pursuit of knowledge that men exhibit
their most distinctive traits, and it is there—and more narrowly
in their perceptual capacity, their use of language, their performance of actions, and their commitment to values—that the complexity and unifying force of the concept of a person are best appreciated. I begin, therefore, with the analysis of knowledge and
proceed systematically through a set of central philosophical problems that progressively expose considerations bearing on an adequate theory of persons. In fact, what is fascinating in philosophical analysis itself is just the respect in which the coherent admission of a wider and wider range of concepts—and the puzzles
traditionally associated with them—impose unforeseen constraints
on the admissibility of theories otherwise addressed to apparently
independent or small-scale questions. I have, throughout the book,
tried to draw attention to the remarkable interrelatedness of philosophical issues and arguments. I take this feature to point both to
the most promising condition for sound philosophical invention
as well as the firm need for philosophers to remain (to borrow a

v

term from professional medicine) generalists—without, I trust, having to lose a grip on the most advanced specialist work that is being done. For example, I try to show that the thesis that mental states are identical with physical states cannot be favorably received without an antecedent examination of what is entailed in treating states, processes, events, and similar conditions as entities of some sort—which issue is not, in itself, narrowly associated with the mind-body problem and is hardly ever raised in that context.

I have deliberately omitted nearly all mention of the views of particular philosophers. I believe I do not mention even Descartes by name; though, if I were to single out that thinker whose grasp of the issues most intimately has drawn my own ideas out, I'm sure I should have to say that it was Descartes. I certainly find his sense of philosophical puzzles—though, characteristically, not his solutions—to be remarkably contemporary in its penetration and pressure. It also seems to me that the history of modern Western philosophy is tirelessly absorbed with the puzzles that Descartes had set for himself. But I have tried to keep the issues clean and bare and to presuppose as little as possible—at least in the sense of doctrinal allusions—in addressing the attentive reader. My intention in this is to attract readers, either in agreement or disagreement, either amateurs or professionals, to attend to the issues without the sort of scholarly paraphernalia (important as they may be) that, more often than not, positively obscures arguments and generates illusions of same. Nevertheless, in composing the account, I have been conscious, at every turn, of the bearing of particular theses on a professional literature that is expanding at a rather frightening rate. I have also found that, however impressive piecemeal solutions to philosophical puzzles may be, the really telling contribution has most to do with the range and coherence of a conceptual system that is neither arbitrary nor bizarre nor merely contrived, that finds a place for everything that is familiar (though its constructions of the familiar may not be familiar), and that conveys a strong impression of being plausible, workable, memorable and, above all, fruitful.

I take it, also, that there is no single settled procedure for the resolution of philosophical problems. In fact, the nature of philosophical work has itself always formed a significant question for philosophers. It is, for instance, claimed by some that the methods of science and philosophy are essentially the same. But this might mean that the so-called empirical sciences are rather more complex than is generally supposed, that conceptual or theoretical adjustments in our view of the physical world cannot be directly confirmed like some straightforward hypothesis for which a crucial experiment may be constructed, and that science itself may ultimately rest on the seemingly more uncertain (and relatively inexplicit) procedures of philosophy. But it might also mean that, given certain canonical practices in the principal sciences, philosophy properly so called is viable just to the extent that it subscribes to such canons. The first view threatens to be subversive of science as traditionally understood; the second, procrustean about the scope of philosophy. Furthermore, it seems not unfair to hold that the solution of the very question of the relationship between science and philosophy cannot be provided by any obvious application of the most familiar procedures available to the empirical or formal sciences.

In fact, turning again to the mind-body issue, it is well-nigh impossible (and, increasingly, pointless) to try to say where scientific work leaves off and philosophy begins. Contributors to the issue are themselves impressively divided: one says it is flatly a scientific matter and philosophers ought not to tamper with it except to acknowledge the fact; another says, with equal conviction, that it is a scientific matter and philosophy ought to confine its own practice to the rewarding procedures of science; another says that it presents a scientific and a philosophical puzzle, that these are formulably distinct and must be jointly resolved to meet the problem; another says that the scientific issues are important but only to set the problem, since the philosophical question of mind-body identity is open to dispute precisely when the fullest scientific information is at hand; another says that it is a pseudo-problem anyway. I have not invented these alternative views: each may be drawn from well-known papers written within the last twenty years.

The source of the trouble here is quickly located. For, often, as with identities like 'Scott is the author of *Waverley*' or '$5 + 2 = 7$,' the facts to be ascertained do not in any obvious sense require initial philosophical clarification of the use of 'is' or ' $=$.' The same is true of such a statement as 'Lightning is a motion of electrical charges,' though it is somewhat different from the others mentioned. But when the statement, 'Consciousness is a process in the brain,' is put forward, disputes arise precisely about whether it can, in principle, be supported by means of science or philosophy. Where, then, a particular claim raises ulterior conceptual questions about its own proper characterization as an identity claim and about the very nature of its confirming grounds, the inquiry involved may fairly be said to be philosophical; the surface grammar of the sentences examined can hardly be appealed to to settle the matter.

It is also sometimes claimed that philosophy proceeds by making linguistic proposals that depart from ordinary usage and that philosophical statements that thus "violate" ordinary language usage are false. The trouble is that philosophers who proceed thus, by exposing such deviation, cannot be said to proceed by proposal themselves, for they possess—on their own view—a viable method for refuting their opponents. And, if traditional philosophy did actually proceed by proposal alone, then no method of refutation would be at all eligible, which seems anomalous. Furthermore, it is difficult to see in what sense philosophers who wittingly and for a purpose depart from prevailing usage can either be said to be making mere linguistic proposals (they themselves would claim that they are speaking about the properties of a certain sector of the world and are adjusting our concepts to such properties) or can be said, for that reason alone, to be mistaken in what they claim. More generously construed, the thesis that philosophy proceeds by proposal may be meant to signify the enormous variety of methods by which different philosophers have worked and the historical likelihood that even more novel methods are bound to evolve from established practice. The record shows that philosophers quite confidently attack and support doctrines they take to bear on relevant truths, and that they are prepared to work with, and to acknowledge, a significantly wide range of competing methods.

The methods philosophers have used in the past continue to be remembered and applied, and the limitations and strength of their practice are palpably open for all to consider. Consequently, the force of any newer methods of philosophical work that may be proposed can always be compared with the rigor and effectiveness of those already in use. These considerations justify speaking of the objectivity of philosophical practice even in its most revolutionary moments. But, since the procedures of philosophy are never quite as settled or as widely adopted as those of the empirical and formal sciences, there remains an ineradicable, and even characteristic, element of conceptual invention in most philosophical work. In fact, it is just the provision of a novel but recognizably forceful philosophical argument that obliges philosophers to attempt to formalize the properties of the "method" employed; but the informality of these so-called transcendental considerations is inescapable and suggests again the importance of the philosophical generalist.

To grasp the force of a philosophical theory is, perhaps, to instruct oneself in the historical development of a system of conceptual problems and to learn on what grounds one may responsibly subscribe to a method of solution by means of which to test (and retest) traditional, recent, and forthcoming solutions. To retell the history of philosophy from the point of view of a newly adopted method would be an enormous undertaking and would, of course, have to be paralleled by the vision of philosophers of differing persuasions. But philosophical solutions thus supported are not more immune to being toppled than direct solutions to currently favored questions that depend on a comparable (if sketchier) sense of the accumulating tradition.

In this respect, the discussions that follow have focussed on the unsatisfactory state of understanding of certain key issues and have done so in such a way that advanced readers will easily recognize allusions to the professional literature and less prepared readers may at least grasp the argument without the disconcerting pressure of having to shift from the issues posed to even the most casual research. Also, my effort here is to suggest fresh solutions for well-known problems and, thereby, to provide specimens of how one might arrive at a fresh solution of other problems. To have done so for the obvious gain is to have paid the price of an equally obvious economy.

Finally, I must say again that I have been very forcefully impressed, in preparing this account, with the way in which an unfolding problem simply drives one to explore topics that had not initially seemed so sensitively linked with one's opening concern. I have, in fact, deliberately tried to convey a clear sense of this developing linkage. I begin with an analysis of knowledge, that forces us at once to anticipate the need to admit a public world, our principal access to it, the nature of creatures capable of knowledge, and their primary way of expressing what they know. Hence, it seemed fair to proceed from a general account of knowledge (contrasted with belief) to perception (contrasted with other forms of sentience) to the boundaries of doubt and certainty regarding what we may know. In the interests of an enlarging coherence, I found myself obliged to distinguish between what is linguistically expressed and what we may convey by way of linguistic models without supposing an ability to use language (as in speaking of animal beliefs and expectations) or an actual use of language (as when beliefs are implied by one's actions); to distinguish between determining what is true (against the backdrop of a public world) and determining that there is a public world (given which, questions of truth and falsity arise); and to coordinate our analysis of perception (our principal access to the external world) with the admission of such a world, as by the use of the critical term 'exists.' Hence, the first three chapters afford a provisional sense of closure respecting knowledge—on the condition, that is, that the essential features of the world of which, presumably, we have knowledge would be disclosed. Accordingly, the fourth and fifth chapters explore the difference between what we can talk about and what, within that range, we say exists. There, we are forced to notice a threatening gap between what we admit exists (in accord with our principal means of access to the external world) and what we judge to be the nature of whatever there is in the world (the vexed question of the nature of metaphysics); and, since whatever there is is identical with itself, we are obliged to sort out the large variety of senses in which the verb 'to be' is used (including, now, the 'is' of existence and the 'is' of reference) in order to facilitate whatever we may say about whatever exists (distinguishing, say, the 'is' of identity, of spatiotemporal continuity, of present time, of composition, and of predication).

These distinctions raise further problems, oblige us for instance to decide whether we can refer to what does not exist and why it is that we cannot always say the same thing, under given linguistic circumstances, of what is self-identical. Here, we come to see the respect in which questions of identity, particularly where discontinuity and decomposition obtain, are resolved in informal ways and the sense in which the very meaning of identity is made difficult to explicate. Also, recognizing that the enterprise of pursuing knowledge is essentially the activity of men, chiefly by means of language, the next three chapters provide a natural sequel. There, we are drawn to examine the general nature of actions (contrasted with physical events), the nature of language (with emphasis on meaning and truth), and the nature of persons and creatures that have minds (contrasted with physical bodies). Given these considerations, we find ourselves obliged to specify a general rubric in terms of which culturally identified entities are embodied (actions in physical events, words and sentences in marks and sounds, persons in bodies); to clarify further the problems of existence and identity as they bear on cultural entities (for instance, the dependent status of actions and events, the difference between identifying persons and bodies, and the difference between what may be predicated of persons and bodies); and to explicate the heuristic status, with respect to language and knowledge, of propositions, facts, meanings, and concepts. The distinction of creatures having minds, it turns out, must be explored jointly in terms of sentience and other forms of awareness (which recalls the discussion of knowledge and perception) and in terms of the rulelike order of cultural life (which permits us to integrate the analysis of action, language, and persons). Also, in the interest of realism, that is, in the interest of understanding our knowledge of the external world, the meanings of such key terms as 'know,' 'exist,' 'real,' 'fact,' 'true,' and 'verify' must be suitably and defensibly coordinated. Finally, since the question of knowledge with which we began leads on to normative considerations and since reference to rulelike regularities confirms the importance of norms, the discussion turns, in the final chapter, to distinguishing fact and value.

The sense of closure that the entire account provides is, of course, provisional only. There's no doubt that each of the large issues explored would, if pursued, lead on to an enormous range of new puzzles. And that is as it should be. But I cannot imagine that any systematic account of our principal concepts would not admit as absolutely central all of those that I have been hinting at; and I cannot imagine any that are genuinely important to the whole conceptual fabric that have not found an important place in the account that follows—even if quarrels may justly arise about that assignment. In any case, I hope to have captured, by the way in which I have proceeded, the manner in which the strength and weakness of discrete philosophical theories and partisan schools of thought are testable in terms of the coherence, the fit, the scope of a single, unified theory shaped in accord with a sense of an unfolding, relatively unyielding mat of details that inexorably bear on one another. To grasp this feature of philosophical work is, I think, to grasp the principal educational benefit of philosophy itself.

ACKNOWLEDGMENTS

I wish to thank my friends Fraser Cowley, Hugues Leblanc, Peter Machamer, Harold Morick, Milton Munitz, and Jack Nelson for their kindness in reading portions of the manuscript and in offering improvements and corrections, which I've tried to incorporate. I also wish to thank Grace Stuart and Ruth Bray for the preparation of the manuscript through all its phases. I can't imagine that it would otherwise ever have seen the light of day. Portions of the argument, particularly in its preliminary stages, have been presented to a good many audiences and have benefited accordingly. I must, finally, reserve a special thanks for James Anderson of the Oxford staff, whose tact and trust I have strenuously tested but not yet plumbed.

Philadelphia, Pennsylvania   J.M.
August, 1972

CONTENTS

xiii

Knowledge & Existence

I

KNOWLEDGE & BELIEF

If we cannot say what it is to have knowledge, we call into doubt whatever we so designate. In particular, the large enterprises of science and philosophy presuppose our grasp of the sufficient conditions of knowledge. Like truth and existence, however, knowledge does not appear to lend itself to any familiar kind of inspection or introspection. Traditionally, the analysis of knowledge concedes that whatever is known must be true and that whatever one knows one also believes. These conditions are thought to be necessary but not sufficient for knowledge, and supplements have been alternatively proposed in order to provide both necessary and sufficient conditions. Such additions, however, may be shown either to be questionbegging or inadequate, in that they either presuppose an adequate criterion of knowledge or else generate anomalies they cannot themselves resolve. In particular, counterinstances are normally available that satisfy the set of conditions offered, not themselves admissible as constituting knowledge; and the logical relations that hold for propositions not prefixed by 'knows' or 'believes' can be shown not to be straightforwardly applicable to propositions that are thus prefixed.

But even the allegedly necessary conditions of truth and belief face serious difficulties. Thus, although it is impossible to hold that what is known need not be true, statements that, on some philosophical accounts, cannot be true, are readily admitted, in familiar contexts, to convey what is known—for instance, that Bellerophon rode Pegasus. In such cases, we are pressed to choose between two relatively powerful doctrines: the one, that whatever is known is true; the other, that we cannot refer to what does not exist (and that, accordingly, statements purporting to do so are false). The second is the weaker and must give way. And in this sense, our analysis of knowledge affects other seemingly independent conceptual issues. Again, the condition respecting belief seems not to hold, since ascriptions of knowledge are possible in the absence of corresponding beliefs and even in the presence, under certain circumstances, of disbelief.

If we examine the way in which ascriptions of knowledge are actually made, we cannot fail to notice an inherent informality that attends them. In fact, such ascriptions are relativized to our norms of expectation and competence regarding biographically distinctive candidates: the conditions we expect to be fulfilled by children, primitives, experts, and the like, in qualifying as knowing something or other, are decidedly variable. For this reason, we are drawn to consider whether or not there is some isomorphic relationship between belief and what is believed, and knowledge and what is known. Belief appears unquestionably to be a psychological state but knowledge appears to be characterizable as a certain normative status assignable to psychological states and skills. On this view, it seems reasonable to contrast the structure of sentences detailing belief and knowledge—which produces certain puzzles about the logical relationships between them. Thus, for instance, 'Duane believes that Washington crossed the Delaware' and 'Cedric knows that Washington crossed the Delaware' appear to have similar grammatical structures, in that we may say, 'Duane believes what Cedric knows' —that is, the same proposition. On the other hand, what Duane believes is the very content of his state of belief, not a statement that may perspicuously convey that content. Since we wish to speak in both ways—specifying a statement that Duane believes to be true and that Cedric knows to be true and admitting that what is known must be true but that what one believes is part of a psychological state and not a detachable statement—the structure of the relevant sentences must be suitably analyzed. The result is that sentences conveying belief and knowledge may be said not to have congruent structures. But if it is more plausible to construe ascriptions of knowledge as ascriptions of a certain status to given psychological states (conceding relevant skills) than it is to construe them as ascriptions of such states, then causal theories of knowledge will fall and the relevant ascriptions will depend on justifying reasons rather than on causal factors alone. To say so would not be to deny relevance to causal factors but only to resist the thesis that the necessary and sufficient conditions of knowledge can be formulated exclusively in causal terms. In fact, the effort to support the causal theory is characteristically questionbegging.

Given truth, then, ascriptions of knowledge are decidedly informal. But also, the matter of ascribing knowledge—once truth is ascertained—is a relatively subsidiary consideration: it is only that form of knowledge in which what is true is established as true that is decisive. But if this is the case, then the problem of justifying beliefs (that may not even be true) and of justifying knowledge claims (that, though sincerely advanced, may be extreme or wild) must be even more remote from the analysis of the conditions of human knowledge.

1. Ascriptions of Belief

To explain what knowledge is promises to be the central concern of philosophy simply because knowledge must be present or possible whenever explanation of any sort is attempted. Also, of course, to speak of knowledge is to speak, at the very least, of a certain favorable relationship between human beings and the external world. Hence, the concept of knowledge systematically focusses whatever we may say about the nature of the external world, about the nature of human agents, and about the way in which they act with respect to what they discriminate in the world, particularly by the use of language. It is hard to see how a sounder sense of unity could be so quickly imposed on the sprawling investigations of philosophy by attending to the problems associated with any other important concept. And yet, pressing the inquiry, ascriptions of knowledge recede in importance and other conceptual connections actually emerge to shape more decisively our largest theories. Our first concern, then, is, rightly, to understand what knowledge is and why, in general, ascriptions of knowledge may be assigned a relatively dependent role within any philosophical system.

It is perhaps because belief is generally taken to be a psychological state, and because knowledge is taken to parallel belief in so many ways, that knowledge is said to be a psychological state as well. But there are *prima facie* difficulties with this view. For, one supposes that he may scan his own beliefs by some introspective effort, perhaps even detect beliefs he did not know he had; but it seems wrong to suppose that one might, simply by scanning his inner states of mind, detect those among them that, as such, count as instances of knowledge. (Let us set aside, for the time being, cases of so-called direct knowledge, knowledge of self-intimating states.) It seems fair to suppose that a man, canvassing introspectively, comes to realize that he believes (or fears) that horses will attack him if he approaches; but it seems absurd to suppose that, by introspection, he may realize that his mental state is rather one of knowing that horses will attack him (even if it is true that they will and that he knows it).

There is, also, a decided informality involved in ascribing knowledge to people. For example, a boy who knows (because he has been taught the facts in school) the date of Hannibal's crossing of the Alps and the date of Washington's crossing of the Delaware is, characteristically, admitted to know that Hannibal crossed the Alps before Washington crossed the Delaware, though he has never thought of linking the events or had them relevantly linked in his lessons and experience. The inference involved is taken to be of such a simple order, well within the capacity of the boy as demonstrated in other comparable situations, that whether or not he is directly questioned about the two crossings, he will normally be admitted to know *what he has never even thought about* (which is not to deny, of course, that he could be tested). In any case, that he has the ability to answer correctly and, therefore, given the circumstances, is said to know which is the earlier crossing, is emphatically not to say that he is *disposed* to answer the relevant question properly; for, on the hypothesis, the question has not occurred to him at all. On the other hand, it may turn out that (in a legal setting, for instance) a man may be judged not to know or to have known that the butler, whom he knew to have been present in the house through a given interval, was in fact the only one who was present in that interval—when the old man was alleged to have been murdered—though it may be an equally simple inference from the various bits of information our man admits he knew. No simple and comprehensive rule for the ascription of knowledge, therefore, in circumstances calling for inference (as yet unperformed) seems forthcoming. Knowledge, it seems, is ascribable in the absence of corresponding thoughts and beliefs, on the condition of certain relevant skills rather than certain dispositions obtaining; and, in otherwise comparable situations, additional expectations and norms of a conventional sort may lead us to deny knowledge. There is, therefore, a certain informality, defying codification under closed rules, in ascriptions of knowledge; and such ascriptions appear to depend on considerations not altogether restricted to the causal conditions under which one's beliefs are generated and changed.

It is often supposed by those who would assign a stricter conceptual role to knowledge, that one must believe what one knows or that what one knows one also believes. But counterinstances abound, if, as we have seen, belief is construed as a determinate psychological state. In the schoolboy case given above, we obviously ascribe knowledge in the absence of belief and disbelief: our schoolboy is said to know about the relative timing of the crossings though, *ex hypothesi,* he had no thought or belief about it, though he had about the independent items. Also, a man may —however irrationally—have some doubts or hesitancy or lack of assurance amounting to some measure of disbelief of precisely what he is said to know. The famous case of the compulsive door-checker is all that needs to be mentioned: our man knows he has locked the front door but returns again and again to satisfy the nagging doubts that he has. Also, in this connection, a man may be said to know, say, the dates of the reigns of the English kings if, despite his uncertainty about remembering them or uncertainty about whether he ever learned them (they are the kind of thing that must have been learned), he gets them right on direct examination; or, he may be said to have some knowledge of the dates if he gets a sufficient number of them right. Hence, he may have some knowledge that he doubts he has.

The important consideration, of course, is this: one may be said to know that p because he believes that q (where he has no belief at all about p). Under the circumstances sketched, it would be flatly false to hold that he now had a determinate (psychological) disposition to answer certain questions in certain ways (though we may, knowing what we do about him, predict how he would behave). He need never have thought about p at all, need only have certain requisite skills and have thought about certain other relevant truths. But if this is so, then a man does not always believe what he knows; he may merely believe what is sufficiently closely connected (as by inference) to what we allege he knows. And here again, we may suppose that there is no formulable rule for determining whether the connections marked are or are not "sufficiently close." Everything depends on context and expectations (as the court setting suggests); but this would be impossible if knowledge were, in any straightforward sense, a psychological state.

Again, if a man may be said to believe that *p* just because he may be said to know that *p*, then belief will not be construed as a determinate psychological state (since, if it were absent, the thesis would be false) and, if it is construed as a necessary condition of knowing that *p*, it will not be able to serve as an independent condition or criterion (since it is itself identified, precisely, only relative to knowledge). On this view, if a man may be said to believe that *p* *if* he may be said to know that *p*, we should always deduce his believing from his knowing even if there were no determinate psychological state of belief that could relevantly—say, introspectively—have been ascribed to him. On the other hand, if we treat belief as a determinate psychological state—closely related to full-fledged cognitive claims and the like—we shall want to say either that someone believes that *p* if he can now introspectively report that he is in a certain occurrent mental state (he finds, say, that he is now thinking that *p* is probably true or that he is now inclined to claim or admit that *p* is true, should anyone ask, or to commit himself in effect, through relevant action, to *p*'s being true, should any appropriate objective concern him) or if we have adequate third-person grounds for supposing that he is determinately so disposed (even if, occurrently, he is not thinking about *p* at all or aware that he is so disposed). But it seems fair (as a *first* approximation to an adequate account) to insist that if anyone believes that *p* is true, there must be occurring or must have occurred some determinate episode in which he thinks or thought about (considers the truth of, entertains, weighs, favors, etc.) *p*. It is entirely reasonable to reject the view that one's knowledge is actually restricted to what one occurrently believes or thinks about —say, consciously; for, on that view, knowledge becomes incredibly restricted and incredibly intermittent. Still, it is useless to hold that one believes what he has never thought about occurrently at all or what is not actually entailed (independently of considerations of knowledge) by some occurrent action or incipient action of his or the like, *if* belief is to serve as an independent condition that must obtain if ascriptions of knowledge are to be justified. (One may have believed what he now no longer believes.)

It is, of course, entirely possible to parallel, for belief, the informalities already remarked that bear on knowledge. But this would require an adjustment in the use of 'belief,' in the sense that no determinate psychological state of a certain kind (usually introspectible) would then need to be independently adduced. Indeed, it would be necessary to parallel knowledge thus, *if* we held that knowledge that p entails belief that p (a concession that can only increase the informality with which ascriptions of knowledge are made).

The delicacy of the matter becomes clearer when we consider that equivocal ascriptions of belief may actually rest on construing a man's behavior as his having acted in a certain way (said to entail the belief that p). On that construction, we may infer that the agent believes that p from an appropriate characterization of his action, whether or not we have independent knowledge of any relevant occurrent beliefs of his and even if he lacks the relevant introspectible mental states. His so-called belief might merely be the interior, but shadow, counterpart of the alleged intention in terms of which his behavior is construed as an action; and his "intention" might merely correspond to conventional interpretations of behavior. The adjustment is necessary, particularly for animals, since they are not in a position to report introspectible mental states. But then, precisely, ascriptions of knowledge are made of animals by way of analogy and by conflating, under normal conditions, questions of belief and knowledge. Thus, a sheep dog may be said to believe (and know) that barking at a flock of sheep in a certain way will facilitate herding them correctly *if* the dog's barking may be fairly described as *trying* to herd them in a certain preferred way): to describe a bodily movement as an intentional action (in the sense in which the agent may be said to have a relevant intention) is, on this view, tantamount to ascribing to that agent a corresponding belief. But then, we do not actually ascribe a belief to the animal (or to a man, under similar circumstances) because, on independent grounds, it (or he) is said to have a certain intention in performing an action: characterizing its behavior as an action done with a certain intention already entails ascribing the relevant belief to it. There is, of course, no need to resist this way of speaking; it is enough to appreciate its bearing on the problem of formulating the necessary and sufficient conditions of knowledge. The informality is useful, because we are clearly not prepared to say that animals—lacking language and introspective capacities—are, for that reason, incapable of having beliefs. But, for all its usefulness in liberalizing ascriptions of knowledge and belief, this second sense leads the account away from the cognitively central cases of belief, namely, those with respect to which introspective reports are normally expected and forthcoming. Also, in such cases, one will be inclined to assign beliefs chiefly for the sake of preserving a semblance of rationality, whereas, with introspectible beliefs, considerations of rationality may be significantly muted and even waived.

Knowledge is not an introspectible mental state even if belief is; and ascribing belief without reference to introspectible mental states is best construed as an increasingly generous extension of usage beyond those cases in which propositions serve as *expressions* of belief (as in the act of expressing one's belief) or in which believing is itself an interior analogue (a so-called mental act) of affirming that such and such is the case. Furthermore, where beliefs are thought to be entailed by actions performed, it must be admitted that one may act against his beliefs and also that one may perform an action properly described in intentional terms without having the relevant intention—*a fortiori,* without having the relevant belief (a man may play to win though he believes he will lose and a man may inadvertently signal a left turn in his automobile). Also, a man may have a belief that is not relevantly linked to any action he is occurrently disposed to perform. Also, there are indefinitely many beliefs congruent with an action performed by an agent said to have a certain intention: hence, on the basis provided, we should not be able to distinguish between the belief the agent actually had and others plausibly imputed to him. *If* we are to say that, in performing an action, the agent acts with this or that belief, we are inevitably driven back to some linkage with determinate mental states. Thus, for instance, a man may occurrently believe or think about *q* and, because he performs action A in a certain way under certain circumstances (not caused by his occurrently believing that *p*), we often ascribe to him as well the belief that *p*. In short, ascriptions of belief are, under these circumstances, made in accord with a certain norm of coherence and rationality rather than with evidence of relevant introspectible or independently ascribable mental states.

In fact, if beliefs are normally expressed by making assertions, we must admit that assertions do not necessarily express one's actual beliefs. To say that S's asserting that *p* expresses S's belief that *p* is only to say that S asserted that *p* with or *in* the belief that *p*. To say that he asserted that *p* is true though he did not believe it, is not in the least self-contradictory: when I say (assert), *"P* is true" (though I believe it to be false), I mean to deceive or some such thing (which is not an incoherent thing to do); and when I say, *"P* is true, but I don't believe it," I have *acted* oddly, without contradicting myself (for the point of *saying* that something is so is to favor in some public way, or to support, or to appear to support, or to lend one's authority to, something's being so—for whatever reasons one may have—*and* to say that one does not believe it is to undermine the very commitment or impression one intends to convey). This shows, incidentally, an important respect in which linguistic acts form a species of action and are difficult to characterize without reference to larger social practices not, in any obvious sense, purely linguistic in nature.

Again, as in ascribing beliefs to animals, it is by no means necessary to suppose that if a dog expecting his master at the door may be said to be in a state of believing that his master will be coming through the door shortly, the animal must, in some sense, be entertaining or must have entertained some linguistically formulated sentence expressing the proposition in question. The sentence may perspicuously convey or, in a somewhat attenuated sense, describe the (propositional) content of the animal's belief. By the same token, not only infants but linguistically competent adults may be said to believe this or that without there ever having been formulated in the mind a suitable sentence expressing the imputed belief. On some occasions, perhaps, one's belief is so palpably conscious that one is, in effect, sub-vocally formulating the statement of his belief (as, for instance, in a sudden storm, a woman may be saying to herself: "I don't think I closed the windows!"). And clearly, if ascriptions of knowledge may depend on admitted skills and non-linguistically formulated but relevant beliefs, there is no reason to suppose that if, say, S knows that *p* is true, S must have the appropriate sentence before his mind, or must have had it once, or must be disposed to utter some relevant sentence under given circumstances.

It does seem reasonable to hold, however, that if a man knows this or that, he must have *some* relevant beliefs; even in our effort to relax the linkage between knowledge and belief, we have merely made the linkage as informal as possible—challenging any would-be rules governing necessary connections between the two "states." Even this linkage raises some difficulties—as in ascribing knowledge to certain computers, animals, and infants; for, in spite of the liberalization conceded, belief is normally analyzed in terms of a certain complex endowment—at least usually detailed in terms of a capacity to use language, to examine introspectively one's own mental states, to weigh alternative possibilities, to collect favorable and unfavorable evidence of a graded sort, to be emotionally or viscerally or attitudinally disposed to different alternatives of action on the basis of relevant evidence, to withhold evidence of, or to deceive with respect to, one's belief. Still, it would be anomalous to ascribe knowledge to entities said to be incapable of belief.

On the other hand, it is sometimes supposed that ascriptions of belief are every bit as normative as ascriptions of knowledge. This would not be to say that belief cannot be a psychological state, but it would be tantamount to saying that, in ascribing belief, we do not and need not always rely on independently identifiable and determinate states (of belief); it would be tantamount to permitting the ascription of belief in the absence of such states. On that view, given certain other determinate and psychologically relevant items (thoughts, desires, actions, for instance)—respecting the propositional content of which, questions of truth and falsity do not yet arise—we may ascribe belief if (or if and only if) such elements exhibit a certain relevant coherence with a system of beliefs admittedly held or a system of beliefs and desires and the like. The trouble is that it is entirely possible to hold inconsistent beliefs, even if it is rationally impossible to persist in doing so when the inconsistency is appreciated. Also, it is possible, as in hypnotic suggestion or in rote learning among children, to believe relatively isolated propositions that—wherever necessary—a rationally motivated agent will try to integrate with antecedent beliefs. The contrast with knowledge is palpable. A creature capable of belief must have a measure of rationality, but such a creature may also hold irrational beliefs: a purely normative model cannot account for this.

2. Asymmetries regarding Knowledge and Belief

The least vulnerable thesis about knowledge appears to be that which holds that what one knows must be true—that S knows that p implies that p. This also has been disputed, as by holding that knowledge is justified belief, where justification is construed in terms of the best available grounds for confirmation for a given culture at a given time. On such a basis, for instance, one would have to hold that the medievals knew that the world was "flat," even though it is "round." This would, of course, undermine the thesis that knowledge of p implies the truth of p, or else—what is conceptually intolerable—truth itself would have to be relativized to correspond with changing capacities of confirmation. But, in fact, even though knowledge is, as we shall see, relativized with respect to changing expectations and capacities of individuals and cultures, we can preserve this feature without at all giving up the crucial implication indicated. All that needs to be acknowledged are the differences between knowledge and claims to knowledge, knowledge and evidence of knowledge, knowledge and justification for one's claim to knowledge. These differences have important consequences, but, for the moment, we may merely observe that the medievals may have been entirely justified in claiming to know that the world was flat (and in believing it). One would not, of course, be justified in making the claim today (in one sense at least); and since it is false, neither they nor we, making the claim or believing it, could be said to know that the world is flat. It is, of course, quite possible to hold that the medievals *knew* a great deal about the conformation of the earth, in spite of the distortion of their theories and in spite of the falsity of certain of their beliefs. If we construe certain true propositions as suitably *embedded* in the body of their beliefs and theories, we may ascribe knowledge of these to the medievals without in the least relativizing truth. Surely we reason in a similar way about primitive people whose knowledge of medicine is embedded in a theory of demons—whether we regard that theory as utterly false or unconfirmed. Even in our own setting, ascriptions of truth are tensed, in the sense that the discovery of error does not entail the relativizing of truth itself but only the reversal of an ascription of truth made at some particular time.

It is, then, a necessary condition of knowledge that what one knows be true. But, if the foregoing arguments be sustained, it is emphatically not a necessary condition of knowledge that one believe what it is one knows—both in the sense that, under certain circumstances, one may positively, if only partially, disbelieve what one knows or doubt that one has learned what he must have learned and in the sense that one may know what he specifically has no beliefs about. Alternatively put, belief (belief that *p*), as a determinate introspectible state (or an appropriate disposition causally dependent on some relevant introspectible state or an appropriate analogue thereof), is a state the occurrence of which sort is only contingently (though regularly) connected with such occasions as one could correctly and relevantly ascribe knowledge (knowledge that *p*) to sentient beings. But, of course, if believing that *p* is not a necessary condition of one's having knowledge that *p*, neither is it, *a fortiori,* a necessary condition that, if one has knowledge that *p*, one has a *justified* belief that *p*. Knowledge, therefore, cannot be construed adequately as justified true belief. Also, the rejection of the thesis entails the rejection of certain forms of the causal theory of knowledge; for, on the theory, the satisfaction of certain necessary and sufficient causal conditions regarding belief that *p* is itself essential (and equivalent) to establishing that knowledge that *p* obtains. Alternatively put, if knowledge that *p* is said to entail belief that *p*, then the causal theory of knowledge cannot rely (as it is characteristically made to do) on the causal history of given beliefs that happen to be true.

Another relevant consideration is this. If knowledge entails the truth of what one knows, then if, say, Peter knows that Bellerophon rode Pegasus, it must be true that Bellerophon rode Pegasus. But, in that case, constraints will have to be placed on the analysis of 'Bellerophon rode Pegasus' such that, although it concerns fictitious entities, the statement is true and *true about them.* Otherwise, we should put in doubt what seems most certain about knowledge, namely, that knowledge that *p* entails the truth of *p*. Still, it is often maintained that statements like 'Bellerophon rode Pegasus' are false because the singular names given are said not to designate or denote anything since they cannot be said to denote (or to be used to refer) to anything that exists. But since it is utterly indefensible to suppose that what we know is false and since the sentence 'Peter knows that Bellerophon rode Pegasus' conveys an entirely familiar specimen instance of knowledge, the debatable thesis that we cannot refer to what does not exist and that sentences purportedly used to do so are therefore false must give way. (We shall return below to the question of referring to what does not exist.)

What we may say, in sum, is this. Knowledge entails the truth of what is known and belief is a psychological state whose *telos* is knowledge. Yet, only sentences or statements or propositions are true, and animals that lack language (or even linguistically competent creatures) may be said to know and believe what they are unable to formulate linguistically (or have actually not formulated in linguistic terms). Hence, belief cannot be essentially an act (of any kind) of assenting to some linguistic formulation. To say that a man or an intelligent creature has a belief is to say that he or it is in a certain psychological state suitably congruent with the act of assenting to a certain linguistically formulated proposition. What we have then is an interpretive (heuristic) model in terms of which given states are construed as belief-states; although, of course, one may express his belief occurrently and linguistically. The model act is actually one of assertion, with respect to which assent may be construed adverbially (asserting "assentingly" or sincerely)— which draws our attention usefully to necessary psychological conditions; hence, psychological states that are appropriate analogues of favoring or assenting may, interpreted in accord with the model, be construed as, or as entailing, so-called mental acts of assenting to a proposition, even where linguistic skills are lacking. This construction accommodates all of our puzzles about the conscious expression of belief, the complexity of occurrent and dispositional belief, and the important fact that linguistically competent creatures as well as those that cannot use language may be ascribed belief and knowledge in the absence of any acts of speech. It is worth mentioning also that iterations like 'S knows that he knows that *p*' and 'S believes that he believes that *p*' appear to have a use only for linguistically competent creatures and, in that sense, are not entailed by the truth of their counterparts, 'S knows that *p*' and 'S believes that *p*.'

Belief, however, has what is called an intentional nature: one cannot have so many mere beliefs; they must be beliefs *about* something; they must be "directed" upon some "object," whether that object exists or not, or upon some "proposition," whether it is true or not. That is, to specify what a belief is about, or what the content of a belief is, is to specify the belief itself more fully. A man who believes that the world is flat has this particular belief, namely, the belief-that-the-world-is-flat (that is, he is in the state-of-believing-that-the-world-is-flat). The intentional feature of the belief is, obviously, not eliminable in the context of epistemic claims and psychological reports since it is precisely the feature that distinguishes and individuates one belief from another; but it may conceivably be eliminable in the context of a would-be materialist reduction of belief-states to physical states. The analysis of belief, therefore—in epistemic and psychological contexts—cannot be more than a provisional and partial one. But, in those contexts, what one believes cannot straightforwardly be detached from one's belief, in the sense in which a statement whose truth one may be said to know can be detached from one's knowledge of it, or a tree that one actually sees may be said to exist independently of one's seeing it. (The normative model of belief, of course, facilitates detachment, but it does not *then* construe belief as a determinate psychological state.) The content of a belief (where a belief is a determinate psychological state) is an integral and indispensable part of the belief itself. It is *not* a statement (or proposition or sentence) though it may be perspicuously conveyed by a statement. In fact, in a sense, a belief has no parts at all and the content of a belief is the belief itself or is abstracted from a given psychological state. The point is important.

Perhaps only beliefs can be proper parts of (complex) beliefs, as when I believe that *A&B, A* is a part of my belief; but then '*A*' is an elliptical way of designating my belief-that-*A,* which has no parts. In any case, the conjunction of the propositions *A* and *B* cannot be equivalent to the conjunction (whatever that may mean) of the belief that *A* and the belief that *B* and *that* conjunction may or may not be usefully contrasted with the belief that *A&B*—depending, as it does, on intentional considerations. The reason for insisting on this feature of belief is, precisely, that it provides a substantial contrast with the "state" of knowledge. It is true that one cannot simply have knowledge, one must have knowledge of something, knowledge *that* something or other is the case. Nevertheless, if what has already been said is so, namely, that S knows that p implies that p, then p (being a statement) is detachable in a way in which the content of a belief is not: the statement that S knows to be true stands as an independent statement *which* S happens to know to be true (or, alternatively, the facts to which p corresponds); but the statement that *conveys* the content of a belief is not itself a psychological state or, like that content, an abstracted "part" of a psychological state. And the *content*—the psychological (or propositional) content, unlike the statement that conveys it —cannot stand independently of its being believed by someone. Alternatively put, if knowledge that p (Kp) implies p, then there is at least *this* truth-functional connection between knowledge and propositions known; but there is no corresponding truth-functional connection between the psychological state of believing that p (b_p) and p—the use of 'p' as a subscript suggests an equivocation on 'p' that we shall explore at once. 'p,' in the expression 'belief-that-p,' is itself part of an indissoluble, monadic, predicative expression whereas 'p,' in the expression 'knowledge that p,' designates a proposition that is part of a more complex proposition when preceded by the prefix 'K' (that does not itself have the form of a sentence). Again, when we speak of the *content* of a belief, we may mean either a certain proposition or statement that can be true or false and that, so identified, cannot in any sense be an actual feature or element of a psychological state, or a feature or element of a psychological state that, so identified, cannot in any sense be true or false. To speak of the content of a belief in the second sense is to speak only of being *in that state* or a state of that kind—indexed, so to say, by formulating a certain sentence. (I should also add here that important distinctions among such expressions as 'statement,' 'proposition,' 'sentence,' and the like are ignored here and will be explored more fully in another context.)

All the relevant puzzles are caught up in a familiar remark: one is always prepared to allow as intelligible and possibly true that, for instance, Duane believes what Cedric knows. But this means that if Cedric knows that Hannibal crossed the Alps (call this *p*), then the very statement *p* is what Duane believes. In that case, it looks as if *p* *is* detachable from both belief- and knowledge-formulas, in the sense in which, speaking about *p*, we say that Cedric knows it and Duane believes it. On the other hand, if the intentional nature of belief be admitted *and* if, unlike knowledge, belief is a psychological state—so that *p* is not a detachable *statement* relative to which Duane is in a state of belief but an internal part of the psychological belief itself (the belief-that-*p*)—then, '*p*' is being used in a syntactically equivocal way in saying that Duane believes that *p* and Cedric knows that *p*. Nevertheless, we wish, it seems, to preserve both ways of speaking. The paradox is a little like that (with important differences) generated by our being willing to say that Duane had a mental image of what Cedric perceived: if Cedric perceived my father, then Duane had a mental image of my father; but one cannot simply have a mental image —Duane must have had a mental-image-of-my-father—whereas my father, who exists independently of Cedric's perception of him, is what Cedric perceived. Consequently, 'my father' must be being used in a syntactically equivocal way. The issue (returning to knowledge and belief) cannot be resolved without sorting out semantical and syntactical equivocations respecting the use of '*p*' and the use of 'believe.' To anticipate what will be found, let me say at once that we speak of belief both as a psychological state of which statements (or sentences) cannot form a part and as a certain relationship between some particular statement and an agent capable of knowledge. Hence, we tend to confuse statements with the intentional content of belief states precisely because statements may be said to convey that content (suggestively but perhaps misleadingly characterized as "propositional"). But to stress the difference is to facilitate the analysis of the "state" of knowledge.

Let us, then, in order to uncover these equivocations, schematize what we normally say. The sentence, 'Duane believes that *p* and Cedric knows that *p*' (assuming belief to be a psychological state of some sort and assuming that 'p' is detachable for knowledge-formulas) may be schematized as '$b_p D$ & $K_c p$.' Here, 'b' is a predicate expression of some sort—belief being predicated of Duane—and 'p,' used as a subscript, signifies what is internal to what is predicated of Duane, a further specification of what is thus predicated. Consequently, 'p,' thus used, does not designate a statement at all, as it does in the formula '$K_c p$' ('Cedric knows that p'). Furthermore, the sentence, 'Duane believes what Cedric knows,' may be schematized as '$B_d p$ & $K_c p$,' where 'p'—to capture the sense intended—is used in a syntactically univocal way; but now 'B' (as yet unanalyzed) is made to replace 'b,' to accommodate the detachability of 'p'—which, so we have argued, is not possible when belief is construed as a psychological state. Whatever 'B' designates, then, is either not a psychological state or at least not a state like mere psychological belief. Consequently, we have pictured both the syntactical equivocation on 'p' and the semantical equivocation on 'believe.'

But we need to know further what it means to say that Duane believes what Cedric knows and what, precisely, knowledge is. The following proposal regarding belief seems at least promising (that is, regarding 'B'): Duane believes that p ($B_d p$) when Duane is in the (psychological) state of believing-that-p ($b_p D$) *and* in that state claims or asserts that p. The suggestion is too narrow, of course. Hence, in passing from the explicit act of assertion to the implicit mental act of assenting, we convert our heuristic model of belief into a literal analogue of (believed) assertion. *Otherwise, p* would *not* be detachable. But this shows that even when we affirm that Duane believes what Cedric knows—knowledge not being a psychological state—the formulas '$B_d p$' and '$K_c p$' cannot be convincingly construed in isomorphic ways; and *that* shows that no formal systematization of the so-called operators or prefixes 'B' and 'K' can possibly be developed along parallel lines or that, if it were developed along parallel lines, the resulting system could possibly be satisfactorily interpreted in terms of what we are prepared, independently, to say of knowledge and belief. The issue is not to provide a closed account of belief, for that would obviously depend on alternative liberalizations of the concept of belief; it is only to exhibit characteristic differences between knowledge and belief.

Our distinction has another important application. We may wish to say that Peter believes that Cicero denounced Cataline, at the same time denying that Peter believes that Tully denounced Cataline—even though Cicero and Tully are one and the same man. We should normally not disallow admitting that Paul, who believes that Brutus stabbed Caesar with his right hand, believes that Brutus stabbed Caesar. But we should most certainly not take it as settled by logic alone that Mary, who believes that Brutus stabbed Caesar, believes that Brutus stabbed Caesar or that Cicero denounced Cataline. The same is true of whether Margaret, who believes that an equilateral triangle is a triangle whose sides are of equal length, believes that an equilateral triangle is a triangle whose angles are equal; or of whether John, who believes that Samson had an enormous beard and head of hair, believes that Samson was hirsute. Now, it is a distinct advantage of the view that construes belief as a determinate psychological state at the same time that it recognizes an equivocation on 'belief,' in terms of which the detachability of propositions may be countenanced, that *what* we should allow as replaceable for the content of an ad-mitted belief that someone has should depend on the very psycho-logical state of the agent himself—and *not* merely on equivalences that may hold for propositions *outside* the context of belief. The predicate 'b_a' remains a one-place predicate, regardless of com-plexity, designating what, in the usual way, is ascribable to per-sons or other suitably endowed creatures; and the operator 'B' added to sentences forms two-place predicates relating persons and detachable sentences (paralleling the use of 'K'). We may, then, preserve whatever flexibility we require about paraphrasing the content of belief (appealing, for instance, to some suitable norm of rationality) at the same time, given the referential opacity of belief contexts, we make replacement depend on intentional factors. The two-place predicate will then be employed only on the assumption governing the use of '*B*,' namely, that the heuristic model may be read literally. In this way, we provide syntactically distinct formulas corresponding to belief-states and to acts of uttering one's beliefs (and then conflate them). The upshot is that where belief is construed in terms merely of an assertion-like model, in order to preserve as far as possible the symmetry of contexts involving knowledge and belief—so that what is believed may be detached as a distinct proposition—psychological considerations are ignored or need to be independently added; and where belief is psychologically construed, detachability is inappropriate. The first construction treats belief dyadically, and the second, monadically; and any attempt to combine the two betrays the fundamental asymmetry between relevantly paired sentences conveying belief and knowledge.

Again, we must distinguish between *sentences* in which '. . . believes that' functions as a prefix by which some simpler, well-formed sentence is incorporated into a more complex sentence and *predicates* like 'believing-that . . .' that designate psychological properties that may be ascribed to suitably endowed creatures. This, then, provides another basis for insisting that '*b*' forms an indissoluble monadic predicate and the use of '*B*' permits the detachability of '*p*' only on the assumption that what is designated thereby includes an assertion or assertion-like force with respect to *p*.

We may now summarize our distinctions in a somewhat more compendious way. Beliefs *have* content in the sense that, as psychological states, they are designated by monadic predicates. Creatures *have* beliefs in the sense in which suitably endowed beings are matched, for predication, with suitably selected attributes. Creatures *have* knowledge in the sense that selected beliefs selected creatures have may, on appraisal, be graded as constituting knowledge. Beliefs are intentional, then, in the sense of being individuated in terms of propositional content. They are psychological states, in the sense, being thus individuated, of being attributable only to a selected range of entities. And talk of knowledge is sim-

ply talk of a certain favorable congruence between belief states
and the conditions under which relevant truths may be established.

3. The Justification of Beliefs and Claims

We have thus far provided grounds for holding that knowledge
and belief are not "states" of a similar sort, that belief is a psychological state, and that certain characteristic equivocations—
both syntactical and semantical—affect our discourse about belief
and knowledge. We must, however, say more about the nature of
knowledge, its relation to belief, its relation to justified belief, and
its relation to claims to knowledge.

The signal consideration is this: Duane cannot be said to know
that p unless p is true; knowledge that p entails the truth of p (because it presupposes it) is normally taken to be the least uncertain
axiom that we have respecting the nature of knowledge. But one
may believe that p is true when p is false; one may even justifiably
believe that p is true when p is false; and one may most certainly
justifiably claim to know that p is true when p is false. If these
considerations be admitted, then knowledge cannot possibly be reduced to belief, to justified belief, to making a claim to knowledge,
or to any combination of these conditions. Possibly only the thesis
that knowledge is justified belief (or justified true belief) is remotely plausible among these alternatives, but the slightest reflection shows that it is as untenable as the others. The issue repays
attention.

Trivially, if one knows that p, one's belief that p would be just-
tified; and equally trivially, if one knows that p, one would be justified in claiming that p. But the justifiability of one's belief and of
one's claim also arise—in non-trivial ways—under weaker circumstances, namely, when either p is false or when the truth or
falsity of p may be ignored. Here, the important difference to bear
in mind is this, that belief is a psychological state and a claim to
know is an act that some agent performs or may perform; consequently, to justify the act of claiming to know that p is to justify

the *doing* of something and to justify the belief state one is in is to favor the *congruity* between that state and whatever (more happily) would have counted as being in a "state" of knowledge. Clearly, then, the justification involved is of two quite different sorts. We may schematize this very simply by introducing a distinction—with respect to which one may easily, and often does, equivocate—respecting the justifiability or reasonableness of the two sorts given. Let us say that a man is justified in his belief— reasonable $_{val}$ —if the supporting grounds for his belief conform significantly to (while possibly falling short of) whatever would validate the truth of what he believes. And let us say that a man is justified in claiming to know that *p*—reasonable $_{bel}$ —if he believes he has supporting grounds (even though he may not) for validating *p*. It is easy to see that both senses of 'reasonable' require that justification be extremely informal and only informally connected with whatever validates the truth of one's belief or claim and with whatever would establish that some believer or claimant actually possessed knowledge of what he believed or claimed to be true; and it is equally easy to see that the kinds of justification involved are of distinctly different sorts and that the justification for making a claim to knowledge is, if anything, even more informal and more informally connected with whatever bears on validation and knowledge than the justification for holding the beliefs one does. One is said to be reasonable $_{val}$ if the reasons on the strength of which he believes that *p* is true are relevant to the validation of *p* and carry some force favoring such validation; such reasons normally do not entail either the truth of *p* or the believer's knowing that *p* is true. *How* close such reasons must be to validating *p* cannot be completely formalized, for the very simple reason that, however strong they are, it is admissible that one may be justified in his belief even when what he believes is *not* true. But then, it can only be a courtesy—however important socially or practically or morally it may be to decide the matter—to determine that one's belief is justified. The serious conceptual issue concerns rather what would be sufficient to validate one's belief;

but saying so implies, in effect, that the important conceptual matter does not concern belief at all or even justified belief but the truth of propositions (that one may happen to believe) and their validation. And this *is* so, so far as the theory of knowledge is concerned. It is also important, however, in the context of analyzing psychological concepts, to have a satisfactory account of the nature of belief; and it is instructive (in order to escape misunderstanding) to grasp the subsidiary role of belief and justified belief for the central issues regarding knowledge.

Correspondingly, one is said to be reasonable $_{bel}$ if the reasons on the strength of which one claims to know that p is true are reasons that one believes are relevant to the validation of p and adequate for validating p; again, such reasons normally do not entail either the truth of p or that the claimant knows that p. Furthermore, they have no clear connection with whatever might properly serve to validate, or to contribute to the validation of, p. In this sense, the reasonableness of someone's claiming to know that p is even more remotely connected with the truth of p and knowledge of p than is the reasonableness of someone's believing that p. Consequently, the question of justifying one's claiming to know that p has nothing whatsoever to contribute to the analysis of knowledge. It is an entirely derivative—and decidedly remote—matter; although, once again, it is quite important, as far as the analysis of linguistic expressions is concerned (as opposed to the issues of the theory of knowledge), to take adequate notice of the obviously asymmetrical use of expressions like 'I know,' used to put forward a claim to knowledge (which, of course, is not to deny them a reporting use as well). Since, as has been remarked, claims are acts of a certain sort, one may perform them in one's proper person where another may only report or describe their occurrence or endorse or justify their having been made. Otherwise, the analysis of claims to know bears on the analysis of knowledge in that sense in which, understanding their nature, one realizes that the analysis of knowledge must move along entirely different lines. In a word, a man may be entirely justified in claiming to know that p when his reasons are quite outrageous, provided only he believes that they satisfactorily ground his claim.

Here, perhaps, an additional remark will be useful. If a man's confidence regarding such reasons is shaken by some consideration that another mentions, whether plausibly or not, why then our man is no longer justified in claiming to know that p is true. So it must be the case that the justification of one's making a claim to knowledge is entirely relative to the state of belief he happens to be in at any given time; but not to be justified in claiming to know that p is true, in one state of belief, does not at all establish that one is not justified relative to another state of belief at another time and may not even establish, as we have seen, that one does not know that p. To admit this, however, is to confirm the remoteness of the issue from the issues of truth and knowledge. It is, indeed, to make the justification of claims to knowledge a relative matter. And, of course, if it is the case that one may even be justified in believing that p or in claiming to know that p when one is not prepared to put forward (or is not thought even obliged to put forward) supporting reasons—in accord with some theory of how we come to know certain relatively simple matters—then, given the foregoing arguments, the inherent informality of justifying belief and of justifying making claims to knowledge is placed beyond dispute. It is also worth noting that, given the difference posited between knowledge and belief, anomalies are bound to arise if knowledge were construed—as is often the case—as justified true belief. These may be avoided at a stroke, if, grasping the special informalities of epistemic logic, we realize that it is not at all obvious that if one is justified in believing $p,$ one is invariably justified in believing q—which one correctly deduces from p. For instance, if I am justified in believing that Jones will be hired for a given job and that Jones has ten coins in his pocket, I am not, for that reason, justified in believing that *someone* will get the job who has ten coins in his pocket (which, *per accidens,* may be true of Smith). I should only be justified here (trivially) in believing that someone *who is* Jones will be hired. Similar considerations show that if I am justified in believing *p*, it does not follow that I am justified in believing the disjunction *p or q*, unless I am independently justified in believing *q* (or the disjunction). The rules of epistemic logic governing the use of sentential connectives and quantification cannot convincingly be said to correspond straightforwardly with the rules of the corresponding calculus in nonmodal contexts. And, in every case, one cannot be said to know that something is so on the basis of evidence that is merely or wholly false. The constraints that operate on what one is justified in believing—in the sense either of what is reasonable$_{bel}$ or reasonable$_{val}$—depend on the context in which what one believes (in the sense of being in a determinate psychological state) is related to the circumstances under which one has come to believe what he does more than it depends on formal connections that hold between the propositions given *when detached* from the belief context. This confirms, also, the advantage of carefully contrasting states of belief and "states" of knowledge.

About knowledge itself, the following consideration is probably the most important. If we are talking about public matters, that is, about matters that different persons may be said to have knowledge of, *and* which they may be said to have come to know by the same cognitive means (as by seeing or hearing), then knowledge cannot be determined by any introspective effort whatsoever. For the truth of whatever it is alleged one knows is entirely independent of whatever means one takes to determine its truth and it itself is a condition that must, logically, be satisfied before the question of someone's knowledge of it can be intelligibly raised at all. Thus, quite simply, if one wonders (I myself, perhaps) whether I know that James has seven brothers, it must—antecedently to any question of confirming *my knowledge*—be true and capable of being validated that James has seven brothers. So that, even if knowledge did involve psychological states, being in a "state" of knowledge cannot be established merely by attending to psychological states: the satisfaction of an independent, non-psychological condition is absolutely necessary to one's being in that "state."

Now, then, in the least controversial case possible, if someone establishes or proves that p is true, he must be admitted to know that p is true. In this sense, the ascription of knowledge presupposes a solution to the question of validating a given proposition; it is, to that extent, a dependent and subsidiary question and, if one reflects on it, a question that allows for its own characteristically informal distinctions. That is, the ascription of knowledge is essentially a biographical matter, a biographically adjusted application of whatever is required for the validation of any cognitive claim. Given that a particular claim (or would-be claim) is validated, someone or other may be said to have knowledge if selected biographical details put him in a certain favorable position vis-à-vis the validation of the claim. Even so, what he may be admitted to know as grounds for holding that he knows a certain proposition to be true need not entail the truth of the proposition in question or an ability on his part to establish its truth, though that proposition (contrary to what merely obtains for justified claims to know) must of course be true. (By a further liberalization, it may be enough that true propositions be suitably embedded in a body of beliefs, as in speaking of primitive science.) If we recall the instance regarding the schoolboy's knowledge of the relative timing of Hannibal's crossing the Alps and Washington's crossing the Delaware, the inherent informality of ascriptions of knowledge cannot be denied; and if the reasonableness of an ascription of knowledge of p need not suppose a belief that p (but perhaps only a belief that q, where q is "significantly" related to p), the informality may be expected to apply as well to the biographical details of any candidate knower. In fact, our requirements respecting candidates, given the truth of what is alleged to be known, are characteristically relativized in terms of our expectations of the competence of children, professionals, people of different cultures and of cultures in different epochs. A child, for instance, may be admitted to know that $3 \times 3 = 9$; but it is fair to ask how much competence regarding mathematics a child must command in order to be said to know that $3 \times 3 = 9$, or how much

competence in chemistry a West Indian must command in order
to be said to know that curare paralyzes the system. Clearly, unless we hold that only if one can actually prove or establish that
some claim is true can he be supposed to have knowledge of its
truth, the ascription will regularly be made on grounds weaker
than whatever would entail the truth of that and other claims. But
if this is so, then it very much looks as if the ascription of
knowledge—that is, the confirmation that someone has a set of
beliefs that is quite favorably related to whatever would validate p
(though beliefs that need not be logically strong enough to entail
the truth of p)—is essentially an honorific matter, regardless of its
practical and social and professional importance. To say that
someone knows that p is to grade his set of beliefs favorably.
Hence it is that knowledge, though it involves psychological states,
is not itself a psychological state at all. It may be construed,
rather, as a certain normative status that someone's psychological
states have been assigned. And it is for this reason that causal
questions of knowledge are entirely out of order, unless in the
proxy sense of accounting for the psychological states (beliefs) *that
are appraised* as constituting knowledge.

4. Causal Conditions and Evidence

On the view given, nothing may strictly be said to *cause* one to
know, though the cause of one's beliefs, on the basis of which an
ascription of knowledge may be justified, is entirely eligible and, indeed, useful: we may offer *reasons* only (in accord with some
rulelike—rather than lawlike—regularity) in virtue of which
someone is said to know. (Consequently, *if* to perceive is to know
by sensory means, then a causal theory of perception must be inherently inadequate, even if it is the case that, in perception, phenomena of a certain sort must occur and must be caused to occur,
in virtue of which one may be said to perceive something, that is,
to know it by sensory means.) Also, of course, a person may be
said to know that p, even though he has not reasoned that p (for

instance, he may simply have witnessed something). Again, a person may be said to know that p, even though *he* has no reasons for believing p (for instance, he may believe q, which is suitably related epistemically to p). Again, a person may be said to know that p even if the justifying reasons for ascribing knowledge to him are not reasons that he has, in any causally relevant sense of 'have' (for instance, if a person may be said to know that p because he believes that q—where q is suitably related epistemically to p—then, on the hypothesis, no relevantly conclusive causal sequence even obtains). Finally, consider that if a schoolboy may be said to know that $3 \times 3 = 9$ and if his belief that this is so is causally due to his having been so told by someone serving as his schoolteacher, whose authority he has never questioned, it seems obviously remote to suggest that there is some relevant causal principle by which the necessary and sufficient conditions of knowledge would capture just such a connection.

In any case, if someone is caused to believe that p by some set of circumstances, P, such that if p is true and it is claimed thereupon that he knows that p is true, it remains problematic *what* the proper relationship between p and P must be—for the one is, or is conveyed by, a proposition and the other is not a proposition (or a fact) at all; and it remains problematic *whether* the causal sequence linking P and the belief that p, that admittedly obtains, appropriately obtains or can be assessed as so obtaining, on antecedently formulable (causal) criteria. But this is simply to say that causal theories of knowledge cannot avoid the threat of circularity, in precisely the same sense in which justified beliefs that happen to be true may yet exhibit some anomalous feature (not affecting justifiability) in virtue of which we should deny that they were indeed instances of knowledge. Knowledge claims appear to be defeasible and no determinate causal connection appears to be immune to such anomaly. Alternatively put, no one can deny that beliefs are caused, but to provide a causal theory of knowledge is to hold that causal connections *of a certain sort* constitute the necessary and sufficient conditions on which one's (true) beliefs may rightly be taken as knowledge. The theory is vacuous without a detailed specification of the conditions required; also, it is always possible to provide ad hoc a causal version of any otherwise adequate theory of knowledge, simply because beliefs are caused. Finally, it must be borne in mind that it is by no means pertinent to the resolution of the issue to specify whatever may actually be the necessary and sufficient causal conditions of one's (true) beliefs; for, presumably, even if one's (true) beliefs did not constitute knowledge, such causal conditions could, in principle, be supplied. What is needed rather is an *explanatory* model of the causal sort —which shows at once why it is merely questionbegging to say that the conditions required are just those that "standardly" obtain when we have knowledge. At this point, however, the argument may fairly be left in an inconclusive state. The general kind of difficulty confronting the causal theorist is clear enough; the burden of proof lies with him, of course, and further, detailed difficulties may be held in store for the more promising versions of the theory —in particular, for perceptual versions. For, the causal theory could not have any force at all if it did not propose to identify conditions for specifically perceptual or inferential knowledge or the like; otherwise, as we have seen, there is no prospect of escaping an obvious circularity.

More pertinent, however, is the informality of ascriptions of knowledge. For, for one thing, if knowledge that p does not entail belief that p, then, trivially, certainty (that is, psychological certainty or conviction that p is true) cannot be a necessary condition of knowledge. But also, ascriptions of knowledge do not, and could not, require a strict accounting of the background beliefs against which putative knowledge is to be appraised—in the sense in which if S claims that p is true, the set of background beliefs that S holds (more or less relevant to the claim in question) need only be favorably congruent with the conditions for validating p, need not satisfy any antecedently formulable set of necessary and sufficient conditions for validating p (or even for congruence with such conditions). On the concession, either certainty is irrelevant or tantamount to the denial of doubts specifically relevant to chal-

lenging the ascription of knowledge or merely an excessively stringent condition incompatible with the informality indicated.

Again, if knowledge were, on some grounds, identified with certainty, so that no one could be said to know anything if he were
not "entirely certain" or "sure"—where we may allow, for the
purposes of the argument, the psychological and epistemically relevant aspects of that condition to remain relatively unspecified—
paradoxes would result. For, imagine that a primitive is "certain"
in the required way about, say, the treatment of a given disorder.
A modern physician, aware of an enormous range of possible
error and the like, may be less certain with respect to the same
matter than the naive primitive, to whom relevant doubts will not
even have occurred or been weighed or set aside as unlikely; yet,
without a doubt, the physician may be said, with more justice or
at least equal justice, to know about the treatment of the disorder
in question. Also, the very certainty of the primitive may, under
the circumstances, count to some extent against his having knowledge; or, if it is allowed because relativized to *his* cultural setting,
assessing the relative certainty of the modern physician may, at an
even later stage of science, be similarly affected. It is easy to see
that the thesis that links knowledge and certainty is inclined to
posit a limit of absolute certainty to which, through time, men approximate in different ways and to different degrees; and hence,
the thesis tends to lead to a deeper, but altogether unnecessary,
skepticism about the possibility of knowledge itself.

Also, non-inferential knowledge could not, then, be markedly
different, in the required respects, from inferential knowledge:
knowledge that p, even in the presence of belief that p, could not
then be vindicated by reference to further necessary and sufficient
beliefs (background beliefs), $q_1 . . . q_k$: such beliefs could not but
reflect merely idiosyncratic biographies. Nevertheless, it would be
excessive, on such grounds alone, to support the skeptical view
that men know nothing or very little; for, the honorific ascription
of knowledge itself presupposes the very availability of grounds
confirming the truth or falsity of particular statements.

Also, of course, ascriptions of knowledge that p cannot be made to depend on formal conditions of one's having evidence. For, for one thing, not all knowledge may be said to depend on evidence (as of pain or simple colors)—unless, quite misleadingly or trivially, by supposing that the facts corresponding to the knowledge alleged, serve as evidence. For another, *any* belief not incompatible with what is putatively known and not strong enough to entail what is known may, by some circuitous route, be construed as evidence. Again, if knowledge that p need not entail belief that p, then there can be no formally adequate connection between the belief that q and knowledge that p (suitably had by S) if, on the hypothesis, S has no belief about p. Again, if S must know that some belief of his, q, is evidence for p, in order to qualify as having knowledge that p, then we should be caught in a vicious regress in order to establish that S knows that p. The informalities already noted run through all alternative accounts.

We earlier set aside, it may be remembered, so-called cases of direct knowledge, knowledge of self-intimating states. These, usually taken to include beliefs, thoughts, sensations, intentions, attitudes, feelings, emotions, moods, mental images, and the like, are puzzling because first-person avowals or reports of such states and occurrences are taken to be incorrigible. To press these cases may be supposed to lend some credence to the thesis that knowledge *is* (at least for this range of cases) a psychological state. But, actually, this need not be admitted, regardless of one's theory of these (allegedly) incorrigibly intimated or self-intimating states (not necessarily equivalent notions). For, on any view, it is not knowledge as such that may be introspectively spotted but rather these states, the knowledge of which constitutes knowledge of a special or privileged sort. The upshot is, then, that, even here, knowledge is rightly construed as a question of the status of one's beliefs, avowals, and the like rather than a question of particular psychological and similar biographical data. The two issues are, understandably, often telescoped. But, apart from *what* we are said to have knowledge of in the range of cases in question and apart from *whether* such alleged knowledge is incorrigible, the question of having knowledge remains essentially an evaluative question concerning the assignable status, on a scale of ignorance-knowledge, of the particular psychological states and other biographical data characterizing some particular person. It may, perhaps, be usefully added that the positive appraisal—that someone knows that *p*—is an all-or-nothing affair; this is not true, be it noted, of such psychological states as beliefs: one may half-believe, half-disbelieve. Once the threshold question of whether S knows that p is settled, S's knowledge may be graded against the *knowledge* of others; but this has to do with how what S is conceded to know fits into a system of other true statements that S may or may not know. And this also explains, favorably, why it is that we can afford to relativize ascriptions of knowledge.

If the foregoing arguments are conceded, then the sorts of informality acknowledged may be seen, in the context of questions regarding truth, knowledge, justified belief, belief, claims to knowledge, to remove us gradually but inexorably from the central questions of the theory of knowledge—that is, from the question of truth and of the validation of what is true. The primary issues here concern what is the case and how this is determined: distributing the honor of being sufficiently closely related to these in order to qualify as knowing what is the case is, obviously, an entirely parasitic matter. Also, although knowledge cannot be construed as an act of any sort, knowledge presupposes processes of thought and belief and, in that sense, may be said to presuppose mental acts of considering and weighing and favoring alternative propositions (or suitable analogues of these, as among animals). But then, although knowledge is not action, patterns particularly adjusted to explaining action are—and are understandably—applicable as well to explaining the fact that S knows that *p*. In particular, to explain how it is that one knows that *p* is to redescribe his relevant beliefs (for which suitable causal accounts may be rendered and required) in accord with the conventions and practices of a society by which belief, meeting normative qualifications, is counted as determinate knowledge. Just as events are construed as actions by reference to governing norms, institutions, conventions, and the like, so too, beliefs, thoughts, mental operations, behavior are construed, by reference to similar norms and conventions, as, or as entailing, a state of knowledge. The analysis of such explanatory patterns requires a fresh start. But to have demonstrated, by way of contrasting knowledge and belief, that what it is to have knowledge essentially depends on the rulelike or rule-governed practices of human societies is to have taken a significant step in the direction of one kind of philosophical system rather than another.

II

PERCEPTION & SENSATION

Perception is the most fundamental source of our knowledge of the external world as well as the most fundamental form of such knowledge. We take it for granted that what we perceive exists independently of its being perceived and that, in perceiving, we perceive what and the actual properties of what thus exists. But there are difficulties with this view. For one thing, the admission of causal connections between external objects and the excitation of the physiological senses entails a temporal lag between what is alleged to be perceived and what causes our perception—which obliges us to consider what actually is perceived and how to characterize it. For another, experiences as of hallucinations, dreams, mental images, and the like distinctly resemble at times what we experience when we say we perceive what exists independently of being thus experienced—which obliges us to consider whether there is some more basic form of sensory discrimination on which so-called perception itself depends. And for a third, our perceptual judgments, on which our knowledge of the external world is alleged to depend, especially our science, are notoriously open to doubt and error

*because of the variable appearances of things and the resemblance
between perceptual experience and hallucination and the like—
which obliges us to consider whether or not we are capable of a
form of sensory discrimination that ensures indubitable knowledge, on which our science may reliably depend. These considerations are thought to be serviced by any of a variety of theories
about what we are "directly" aware of in sensory experience
(sense-data). If, however, the discrimination of what is thus "directly" given proves to be a restricted range of whatever we are
normally admitted to perceive, the theory in question will not escape the difficulties already collected. Otherwise, these theories
(so-called sense-datum theories) advance linguistic proposals for
the systematic replacement of sentences about physical objects
that we say we perceive, by sentences about sense-data, that we
theorize we are directly aware of in perception; or else, they advance the view that perception is an interpretation of some sort
of what we are directly aware of in sensory experience—that,
characteristically, is private to each of us and has whatever qualities it apparently has in such experience. The linguistic versions
of these theories typically insist on the equivalence or near-equiv-
alence of the paraphrases provided; but then, they are more cum-
bersome, difficult to provide, less familiar and less easily grasped,
and without any clear advantage over a well-established idiom.
Otherwise, they propose replacements that are not equivalent and
thereby fail for the reason that no sentences about perceived
physical objects entail any particular set of sentences about
sense-data and that no set of sense-datum sentences entails sentences about perceived physical objects; also, matching the appropriate sentences of each sort presupposes an independent use
for perceptual sentences. Those theories that hold that we are, in
sensory experience, directly aware of sense-data risk our reliance
on perception as the principal source and form of our knowledge
of the external world, for they force us to attempt to build our
account of a public world on the strength of allegedly private
sensory discriminations. In the interest of avoiding incoherence,*

such a maneuver is to be resisted. Also, the mere admission of awareness of sense-data, like the admission of dreams and hallucinations, does not as such bear on the analysis of perception proper.

If we distinguish true perception from those forms of experience that resemble perception but are not actually forms of perception—for instance, hallucinations, dreams, mental images, and the like—then, apart from relevant causal distinctions, the principal basis for contrasting the two depends on the theoretical consideration that whatever we perceive exists independently of being perceived—which, in the nature of the case, cannot be determined by mere sensory discrimination of any sort. But since identical sentences or sentences having the same apparent grammatical structure may be used to report or describe what is discriminated both perceptually and in these other forms of experience (in which what is experienced does not, as such, exist independently of being experienced), we must be able to specify relevant differences in sentences so used, so that the contrast regarding existence is seen to be reflected in their structure. Also, as it turns out, there are other forms of sentient experience, such as of pains, aches, tickles, twinges, and the like, that do not resemble perception in the way in which, say, hallucinations do. Nevertheless, pains do not exist independently of being felt any more than do hallucinations. So we are obliged to register the systematic differences between sentences reporting and describing experiences of these two general sorts as well. The entire range of sensory or sentient experience may, then, be rounded out by considering what characteristic perceptual senses we have, what their appropriate objects are, and what kinds of mistakes we may make or what ignorance we may exhibit consistent with actually perceiving something. The problem here is to ensure the internal coherence of an account of perception that preserves the independent existence of what is perceived and accommodates all puzzles of the sort sketched. Finally, since perception is a form of knowledge, we must consider in detail whether the necessary and suffi-

cient conditions of having knowledge by perceptual means can be given in merely causal terms: on inspection, it proves to be the case that theories of this sort are inherently questionbegging.

1. Perception and Sense-datum Theories

The complexity of perception cannot be evaded—is, moreover, troublesome, since perception is obviously fundamental to our knowledge of the external world. Merely to admit that sight, for instance, is causally dependent on the presence of external objects and physiological processes that require time to occur, raises questions about the proper characterization of the objects and nature of perception. The same conclusion strikes us reflecting on the nature and limitations of the organs of sense themselves: light passes through the eye and vibrations in air and water strike the ear, and yet we speak of seeing and hearing complex physical objects that cannot, in any obvious sense, be reduced to light and such vibrations—though, given the temporal lag implicit in the relevant causal sequences, whether we even see light and hear such vibrations may be made quite as puzzling. Compound these reflections by considering that dreams, hallucinations, sensory delusions, and mental images may all, at times, either be phenomenally confused with veridical perception or at least noticeably resemble such perception—in respects casually detailed by using a common perceptual vocabulary—and one begins to wonder whether there is not some range of sentient discriminations more restricted than those of full-blown perception (or more fundamental) that may be specified. Additional and independent yearnings for incorrigible sensory knowledge, or at least for sensory knowledge that is not freighted with the obvious theoretical baggage of the concept of a physical object (what is often construed as providing an "interpretation" of whatever is discriminated in the barest sense imaginable by the senses alone), lead us to attempt to sort out what is *sensed* and what is *perceived*. Also, more significantly in speaking of perception than of knowledge, we are tempted to ascribe the sensory processes that we call sight, hearing, and the like to the functioning parts of certain physical bodies; and yet, if sensory perception is a form of knowledge (though the contributing sensory processes need not be), we are bound, at least provisionally, to ascribe perception to persons and sentient creatures. The puzzle is worth noting here, though its resolution will have to be postponed.

It is sometimes supposed that the distinction between what is sensed and what is perceived can be made out by careful or exceptional attention to what we admit we perceive; but this seems naive for at least the reason that, if the implications of the causal issue be admitted, a discrepancy between what there is to be sensed and what we say we sense (what is sometimes said to be "immediately perceived" or what we are said to be "directly aware" of) can be pressed as well: the causal thesis is plainly capable of supporting an embarrassing regress. There are other difficulties, as we shall see. So the most promising way of proceeding is probably to favor whatever theories may ensure the most coherent and comprehensive account of the modes of sentience (perception, dreaming, hallucination, sensory delusion, sensation, and the like) consistent with our having knowledge of the external world. That is, since our puzzles concern, precisely, what it is we perceive and sense, it is a dubious strategy that advises us that the required distinctions are themselves simply of a perceptual or sensory sort, of a sort that can be made out by the mere exercise of our sentient skills. The nature of these is just what baffles us.

In fact, the most important questions respecting perception and the other sensory-like modes may be said to concern the existence of what is discriminated and the systematic differences and similarities among the various modes. But, surely, existence is not, as such, a sensory quality; and, since, by hypothesis, hallucination and perceptual delusion for instance may be phenomenally confused with true perception (whether frequently or not is not important), the differences among them cannot possibly rest with mere sensory distinctions. This means, of course, that whatever distinction may profitably be said to hold between perceiving and sensing will have to be made out in terms of the comparative coherence and power of alternative theories; but if this is so, then the attraction of pristine, basic, theoretically uninterpreted sensory discriminations must be an idle one and the usefulness of the distinction (between perceiving and sensing) must lie in another quarter. All sensory discourse must be theoretically freighted and the classification of the various modes of sentience must be based on such considerations as of alternative physiological (causal) processes differentially underlying what may well, on occasion, be phenomenally indistinguishable; in particular, they must be based on considerations of existential import and on the conditions of knowledge.

There are any number of different advantages that may attract the partisans of immediate sensing, though, by and large, their accounts are of two distinct sorts. Either they propose a linguistic theory—that whatever may be said in the perceptual idiom may be more perspicuously said in a sense-datum idiom (that is, by replacing talk about perceived objects by talk about objects sensed or "immediately perceived"); or they propose a phenomenal theory—that, in the actual perception of physical objects, there may be discriminated what we sense (or "immediately perceive"), that is, sense-data. Proponents of the linguistic theory often hold that there is an extensional equivalence between strings (obviously, very complex strings) of sense-datum statements and statements in the perceptual mode (what are often called statements about material objects); and sometimes, they hold that sense-datum statements may justifiably replace the others, though they are not strictly equivalent. Proponents of the phenomenal theory usually hold that the perception of the proper objects of perception entails the sensing of sense-data, which, presumably, may be sorted out in an appropriate way for particular perceptual episodes. Sometimes, they hold that perception is simply an "interpretation" of sensing proper and that, correspondingly, so-called physical objects are postulated or "constructed" in order to provide a coherent causal picture of the streams of sense-data of which we are directly and primarily aware (or of the orderly possibilities of having such sense-data).

The difficulties of the linguistic theory all depend on the fact that the meaning of the sensory terms employed vis-à-vis sense-data is inevitably drawn from the meaning of the sensory terms employed in the material-object language and that the specification of sense-datum statements allegedly equivalent to perceptual statements (or only relevantly connected to them) cannot be freed from the use of referring devices addressed to the very material objects (including perceivers) to be replaced, in principle, by sense-data. Thus, if I am said to be perceiving a certain dog directly in front of me, I may be said, on the hypothesis, to be sensing certain canoid patches and the like. But *which* sense-data answer to which perceptual object cannot be identified, as by way of correlations between the two, simply because there is no plausible limit on occasioned sense-data and there are no particular sense-data that serve as necessary or sufficient conditions for the perception in question. If I see a piece of blue cloth, I may well have (or not have) a green or even a red sense-datum; and if I have a green or red sense-datum, I may well be seeing (or not seeing) a piece of blue cloth (or anything else). How should I collect the sense-data that are probably associated with a given perceptual object except (granting this much) by collecting my sense-data *as* occasioned by that object (where, normally, the object is itself independently identified by perceptual means)? But if this be granted, the prospect of replacing the material-object language by the sense-datum language (often called the thesis of phenomenalism) is doomed. Also, if the meaning of the sensory terms of the sense-datum language is either the same as the meaning of the sensory terms of the material-object language, or a restriction of the meaning of the latter, then it becomes problematic whether the intended replacement can be freed from the theoretical presuppositions of the latter or from alternative presuppositions; but in that case, we could not be assured that the intended objective of the sense-datum replacement had been achieved or what it would mean to claim that it had. Also, since there are no formulably necessary or sufficient conditions respecting sense-data relevant to the replacement of a material-object statement, would-be replacements cannot but be infinite strings of sense-datum statements; alternatively put, perception may be said to entail (determinable) sense-data but not any determinate sense-data (which is contrary to the point of the proposed paraphrase) and no string of statements of determinate sense-data entails any material-object statement at all (which again is contrary to the apparent purpose of the paraphrase). Also, no sense-datum reduction of percipients themselves seems remotely viable, since—speaking in terms of *sentience*—it appears that sense-data must, minimally, be *had* (or sensed) by entities of an appropriately complex sort.

The phenomenal theory, for its part, characteristically takes two quite different forms—which, as it happens, are easily and regularly confused with one another; indeed, there are versions of the theory that combine the claims of the two. The motivation behind them, however, is distinctly different. On the one hand, proponents wish to drive as far as possible toward incorrigible or indubitable sensory knowledge; and on the other, they wish to distinguish two quite different modes of sentience (however related)—independently of whether incorrigibility or indubitability claims can be defended. Consider, for instance, that dreaming and perceiving are distinct modes of sentience (without raising the question of incorrigibility for either mode). To grant this much is to admit a relevant (though only partial) analogue of the second version of the phenomenal theory. The first may be dispatched in a summary way. For, consider the following series of seemingly progressively reduced claims:

    a) I see a dog;
    b) I see what seems to be a dog;
    c) I see what seems to me now to be a dog;
    d) I seem to see what seems to me now to be a dog.

Whatever else may be said, it is clear that, in moving from a) to d), any increase in apparent certainty is simply the obverse side of the increased hedging of what one is claiming—increasing, in fact, in such a way that it verges on vacuity. Hence, with respect to perceptual claims, the reduced claims instanced cannot be said to bring us closer and closer to incorrigibly true (basic or protocol) statements, on which the edifice of science may be confidently erected. b) allows us to hedge by permitting the perception of both dogs and non-dogs (by way of resemblances not yet specified!) to validate the claim. And d) allows us to hedge by actually permitting both perceiving and not perceiving to validate the claim! Only a very strange sort of confidence and incorrigibility can be extracted here. Any stronger claim respecting the relevant use of 'seems' and 'appears' and cognate terms—such that questions of doubt and denial do not obtain at all (in one sense at least)—must rest on the independent fate of the concepts of logical indubitability and logical incorrigibility (and of the sense-datum idiom). We may here note that, without an independent defense of the applicability of these concepts in cognitive contexts, the prospect of redeeming relevant phenomenal theories is entirely idle. (Let it be merely announced, for the moment, that cognitive indubitability and incorrigibility are, for demonstrable reasons, untenable.)

If sense-datum statements were construed on the model, say, of c) or d), that is, merely as members of a set of perceptual statements, with respect to which questions of doubt are, by hypothesis, entirely inadmissible, they could be said to be indubitable only in the sense that they had already accommodated all the doubts that could relevantly be raised. And if, instead, sense-datum statements were construed as quite different—say, like:

c') I see$_s$-what-seems$_s$-to-me-now-to-be-a-dog,

then both the verb of sentience and the description of what is sensed (flagged by the subscript 's' and the hyphenation) must have a sense quite different from that which belongs to the counterpart perceptual verbs and descriptive phrases in the material-object language.

That is, 'seems,' in c'), is part of an expression designating sentient
discrimination of a sort utterly different from what may be said to
be perceptually discriminated. The introduction of 'seems' in c')
need not, of course, bear directly on the issue of incorrigibility or
indubitability. But what distinguishes c') from a)-d) is just that the
expression 'see$_s$-what-seems$_s$-to-me-now-to-be-a-dog' designates a
monadic attribute and not a relationship. Hence, it is an expression used to characterize a kind of experience, and its internal
structure marks a certain conceptual linkage (by way of phenomenal resemblance) between seeing$_s$ and full-blooded perception.
Perceptual statements, by contrast, predicate a certain relationship
between percipient and perceived. 'Seems,' therefore, registers,
with respect to the perceptual relationship, a certain cognitively
relevant hedging; but it may also register, as by the use of the subscript, the content of a distinct form of sentience (properly internal to "seeing$_s$"); and it *may* also register the content of sentient
experience (of whatever mode it may be) without regard to its
proper mode—hence, by way of retreating to an indissoluble
monadic characterization that entails no commitment about what
(perceptually) would be affirmed to exist or (as in confirming hallucination) would be denied to exist. In this sense, reports of mere
sentient experience are truncated reports regarding the various
modes of sentience, not reports of a cognitively more fundamental
stratum of sentience. They facilitate shifting—not necessarily
equivocating—between perception and such sentient modes as
hallucination. Thus d), above, *may* be taken to report an *experience* and, therefore, 'seems' need not be construed as conveying
doubt or denial; it will convey a kind of hedging, as by truncating
a full claim of one sort or another with respect to which existence
or attributes ascribed may be challenged. The "reduction"
achieved by c'), then, does not belong in the series a)-d) *unless*
one links the drive toward incorrigibility and the elimination of legitimate doubt to a shift from one mode of sentience to another.
Claims of incorrigibility, as has been hinted, are open to independent challenge—that is, without special reference to perceptual

contexts at all—and the particular form of the incorrigibility claim here encountered is patently trivial. It remains to be considered whether the alternative theory fares any better.

Here, a number of distinctions will allow us to canvass more systematically all of the usually acknowledged modes of sentience. We may safely ignore the usual designations of 'perception' and 'sensation'; for, we quite regularly speak of tactile sensations, when we wish to speak of perceiving by means of the sense of touch; and we quite regularly allow the use of perceptual verbs and perceptual descriptions in the contexts of dreaming, sensory delusion, mental images, and the like, even where the reporter is aware that he is dreaming, suffering delusion, attending to mental images, and not perceiving. That is, the ordinary distinctions between perception and sensation do not promise to follow whatever theoretically useful distinctions may be made among the various modes of sentience. It is, in fact, characteristic that when we speak of sensations, we often mean to signify only that there is a particularly intimate connection between what is discriminated and the discrimination of changes in the body itself; thus it is more usual to speak of tactile sensations than of visual sensations. If so, it is confusing either to insist on or to resist the use of the term 'sensation,' in the present context of discussion, without clarifying the import of the maneuver.

2. Transitive and Intransitive Modes of Sentience

The distinction required here is that between what we may call transitive and intransitive modes of sentience. Any sentient mode (whether termed perception or sensation) is transitive if what is veridically discriminated in accord with that mode exists independently of, or may be predicated of what exists independently of, such discrimination. And any sentient mode is intransitive if what is veridically discriminated in accord with that mode does not exist independently of such discrimination. It is entirely possible that the modes that we ordinarily take to be (implicitly) transitive (or intransitive) may, by some speculative innovations, be alternatively construed as intransitive (or transitive). But such speculations aside, we normally admit that pains are the "objects" of intransitive discrimination and that chairs and tables, or their shapes, textures, and colors, are the objects of transitive discrimination. Now, perception—that is, seeing, hearing, tasting, smelling, feeling by touch, and the like—are the very paradigms of transitive sentience. This means that statements true of what is perceived, inherently have a certain existential import: 'S perceives O' entails 'O exists.' On the other hand, 'S is dreaming about O' (or, taking a minor liberty, 'S is dreaming O' or, 'S perceives O in a dream') does not entail 'O exists.'

This is an arguable matter, to be sure. I am not here saying that it is logically impossible to hold that the entailment of existential import obtains for dreaming (or hallucination or delusion or the like) or that it is impossible to deny that it holds for veridical perception—only that it is conceptually inconvenient, counterintuitive, and, possibly, philosophically anomalous or indefensible. Thus, to affirm the entailment for dreaming, hallucination, delusion, and the like itself entails an equivocation on 'exists'; for, on any reasonable view, *what* one dreams (the content of one's dream), what one has an hallucination of, and so on, cannot be said to exist in the same sense in which what is veridically perceived exists. And to deny the entailment for veridical perception itself entails an equivocation on 'perceives' and its cognates ('sees,' 'hears,' and so on); for, although it is not at all deviant to use the perceptual verbs when reporting what one discriminates sentiently in any of these modes, whether wittingly or not (say, whether one realizes or not that he is having an hallucination), it is implausible —as, for example, in speaking both of dreaming that one sees something and of veridically seeing something—to hold that we may be said to see something, in these cases, in the same sense of 'see.' The principal consideration is this: we cannot eliminate the possibility of phenomenal confusion among these related modes of sentience either by equivocating on 'exists' or by equivocating on 'perceives' (and its cognates). There is, therefore, no use in holding, for instance, that 'A perceives X' does not entail that X exists, if (for hallucination, say) 'A perceives X' does not entail that X exists but only, say, that X *perceptually exists* rather than really exists. Similarly, there is no use in holding that 'A perceives X' is true either when A veridically perceives X (by sight, say) or when A has a dream of X, if, for dreaming, we mean to say only that A *dream-sees* X rather than sees X (or sees X by the use of sight).

The supreme benefit of admitting the existential import of veridical perception is its provision, in an epistemic context, of a public world—hence, its implicit utility against the conceptual difficulties of both skepticism and solipsism. It is possible, of course, to argue that skepticism and solipsism are defensible positions, in which case the alleged benefit may be dispensable; but what needs to be noted here are only the dialectical possibilities, not the arguments themselves. Failing such a defense, the provision of existential import ensures a public world. Any sense-datum theory, therefore, that rejects the thesis risks the difficulties of skepticism and solipsism. But, of course, *if* perception were construed as an interpretation of sensing *and* if sensing were construed as an *intransitive* mode of sentience, then precisely those difficulties would arise. On the other hand, if sensing were construed transitively, given the semantic problems already raised, it would be difficult —probably impossible—to distinguish sensing from perception proper. We may, consequently, pose a provisional dilemma for all sense-datum theories of the phenomenal sort: either they are ineligible unless solipsism is a tenable and viable theory or else they concern, in a philosophically innocuous sense, a subordinate distinction within the perceptual modes themselves.

The second horn of the dilemma is decisive. If sensing is simply reduced perceiving (or sense-datum claims are simply reduced perceptual claims—in accord, for example, with the proposed reductions of a)-d) already given), then whatever conceptual problems may be posed for perception will obviously be able to be posed for sensing as well; on that thesis, sensing cannot serve to expli-

cate the nature of perception. The first horn is provisional because
the threat of skepticism and solipsism is provisional.

Consider, then, that the admission of dreaming, hallucination,
sensory delusion, mental images, and the like does not, as such,
entail skepticism or solipsism. If sensing were to be construed as
an analogue of these, then, doubtless, the threat might be turned.
But if sensing were so construed *and* perception were construed as
an interpretation, in some sense, of whatever (and only of whatever) is discriminated by sensing, then solipsism would be an un-
avoidable prospect. On the other hand, it is implausible that dreaming, sensory delusion, and the like—which may fairly be regarded
as intransitive modes of sentience—are, or could be, the source of
those primary sensory discriminations that are alleged to be interpreted, in speaking of full-blooded perception. If, therefore, sensing were construed as a full analogue of such modes as dreaming
and sensory delusion, we should merely have enlarged our classification of alternative modes of intransitive sentience (that may
well be phenomenally confused with perception), without any attention at all to the relationship between sensing and perceiving
that we sought to clarify. These considerations lead to a second dilemma: if sensing, intransitively construed, is taken as the primary
mode of sentience on which perception depends (in that perception interprets the data provided by sensing), we are inexorably
faced with the threat of solipsism; and if it is taken as a mode of
sentience distinct from other intransitive modes, it will, as such,
also be distinguishable from the transitive mode of perception,
from which these other modes are distinguishable. If the force of
the two dilemmas posed be admitted, then sense-datum theories
(of the sorts identified) are either redundant or irrelevant or their
defense presupposes a defense of solipsism. That is, even the admission that we *do* sense sense-data is indecisive unless it can be
shown, on independent grounds, that whenever we perceive we
sense sense-data; and *that* cannot be shown by appealing to perceptual reporting itself but only on the strength of some theory
competing among alternative theories of perception—which,
under the circumstances, would lead directly to solipsism.

The following alternatives, then, confront sense-datum theories of the phenomenal sort. They may construe having sense-data as a suitably restricted form of sensory perception (as when one wonders whether sense-data are part of the surface of perceivable objects); but then, perception cannot be made to depend on having sense-data in the relevant sense and reports of sense-data will depend on the same concepts and show the same corrigibility as full-blooded perception. Or, they may construe having sense-data as a distinctive mode of sentience (like having images or dreams); but then, the admission has as such no bearing at all on the analysis of perception. Or, they may construe having sense-data as a distinctive mode of sentience (sometimes called "immediate" or "direct" perception), on which ordinary perception depends as by interpreting sense-data and with respect to which the use of 'seems' and its cognates conveying doubt and denial (with respect to perception) fails to capture the distinctively descriptive use intended; but then, since phenomenal resemblance is not decisive, the defense of the *theory* that perception is so grounded must depend on its systematic advantages over competing views—which prove to be nil. What needs to be stressed is that neither does the admission of such phenomena as illusion or perceptual delusion entail the admission of sense-data nor does the admission of sense-data entail the relevant dependence of perception on such sentience.

3. Varieties of Intransitive Sentience

Let us, then, examine the intransitive modes of sentience more carefully. These may be usefully sorted into two collections: those that may be phenomenally confused with veridical perception (or resemble it, in that our perceptual vocabulary may be directly applied to discriminations made by means of these modes) and those modes that are not thus confused or thus resemble perception. In the first are to be found hallucination, sensory delusion, dreams, mental images, and the kind of (apparently) sensory memory that obtains in epilepsy and during certain selective probings of the cerebral cortex; in the second are to be found pains, aches, tickles, tingles, twinges, and the like. It is important to note here that certain relevant phenomena have not been classified—in particular, illusions, mirages, the variable appearances of things, double vision, proprioception, and interoception. The reason is quite simple: these are all distinctions to be made with respect to perception proper. Consequently, if the account can be sustained coherently and plausibly for the range intended, it will exhibit considerable systematic power.

(Perhaps the chief lines of inquiry, regarding perception, that would need to be explored are of two sorts: one concerns the so-called proper objects of the distinct senses; and the other concerns the distinction of proprioception and interoception. The latter is important because it provides knockdown evidence that, even in perceptual contexts [contexts in which veridical perception obtains], we must admit a form of *logically* privileged access without necessarily admitting incorrigibility, indubitability, or infallibly self-intimating states; we have access to states of our own bodies by perceptual means not available to another with respect to one's own body—which is not to say, of course, that we have logically privileged information. The former is important because it obliges us to grasp the theory-laden nature of the concept of perception itself and to consider that the principal senses do not behave in parallel ways in cognitively important respects: crucially, where tautological accusatives having a clear and antecedently established extension ['sounds,' 'tastes,' 'odors'] may be assigned to 'hear,' 'taste,' and 'smell,' it is impossible to assign such accusatives, *on a uniform principle,* to 'see,' and 'feel' [by touch]—try 'colors' or 'textures'; again, for seeing and touching, 'of,' used in constructions involving proper objects [that are not internal or tautological accusatives], is never or never merely what may be called the productive or causative 'of'—always, rather, what may be called the predicative and proprietary 'of'—whereas, for hearing, tasting, and smelling, it *may* [as when sensory reports and statements are restricted to proper objects corresponding to the internal accusa-

tives] be the causative 'of' alone. One has only to remind himself
of expressions like 'the color of the house' and 'the sound of the
trumpet.' The difference between the two senses of 'of' lies simply
in the fact that the objects of the causative 'of,' but not of the proprietary 'of,' enjoy a presumptive status as distinct entities. The
difference is not conclusive, of course, though it is a difference
that must be confronted: we do speak of shadows, rays of light,
and bolts of ligntning, and an analysis of sounds and tastes and
odors may incline us to speak of them, ulteriorly, in predicative
terms.)

The distinction of the first sort of intransitive modes, is, precisely, that the perceptual vocabulary normally reserved for a
transitive mode of sentience is directly applicable to these modes.
It is applicable because of phenomenal resemblances, but in being
thus applicable, certain considerations of the theoretical import
of sensorily descriptive terms are either waived or altered. This is
not to say that these terms are applied in a theory-free manner
(which suggests again the appeal of sense-datum theories) but
rather that they are applied on the strength of quite restricted sensory similarities, without clear regard to dislocations in theory.
For instance, a man who knows he is suffering a visual delusion
(perhaps, because he is experimenting with particular drugs) may
still describe his experience in visual terms. If I say I see (or saw)
a white swan in my dream, the theoretical differences between actual swans and "dream-swans" and between the actual color white
and "dream-white" will be waived in so speaking. The terms
'white' and 'swan' will be used in a way that implicitly restricts
their sense to certain selected phenomenal resemblances. There
may, therefore, be certain semantical constraints that obtain in
shifting our perceptual vocabulary between perception proper and
certain intransitive modes with which it may be phenomenally
confused; or, our perceptual vocabulary may be construed as singling out phenomenal features in sentient experience in a way that
is relatively indifferent to the theoretical differences between the
objects of transitive and intransitive sentience, that is, to the issues

of existential import and of selected properties of relevant kinds
of (actually existing) things. Here, the theory of perceptual discourse leads on to the formulation of so-called proper objects of
the distinct senses. Should we, for instance, say that the direction-
ality of sound is a proper object of hearing or only, on some
theory, inferred from what is "properly" heard? There are difficulties with such accounts, but the objective is clear and lends a
provisional justification to counterpart phenomenal restrictions respecting the intransitive modes in question. This way of speaking
has the important and added advantage of not requiring us to say
that the meaning of our perceptual vocabulary changes with every
change respecting which mode of sentience is involved. And indeed, locutions like 'In my dream, I saw . . . ,' 'In my delusion, I
seemed to see . . .' flag the fact that the descriptions that follow
do not convey the existential import of veridical perception itself
and, therefore, of any of the usual theoretically relevant freight respecting whatever could be said to exist and to be perceived.

The signal change affecting our discourse here must be syntactical, with the possibly single important exception of the meaning of
the verbs of sentience themselves. If it is part of the meaning of
'see,' 'hear,' and the like that whatever is said to be seen or heard
exists, then locutions like 'In my dream, I saw . . .' convey a contradiction. That is, if the verbs are transitive, in the sense proposed (not merely grammatically), we shall have to accommodate
the equivocation of common usage in a distinctive way. What we
may say is that the use of prefatory phrases like 'In my dream
. . .' or the sense, in context, that such phrases are indicated, has
the effect of denying existential import, converting the description
or report that follows into a description or report of the intransitive sort, and justifies ascribing to the sentences so used whatever
syntactical adjustments are congruent with such descriptions and
reports. But this, precisely, is the model of sentences like c') introduced earlier on for the sense-datum idiom. If, on dreaming, I describe my dream, saying "I saw a white swan," we may construe
what is said as follows:

p') In my dream, I saw a white swan; or

p") I dreamt-I-saw-a-white-swan.

p") suggests that the equivocation on 'see' may be resolved by construing 'see' (relative to dreams or relative to hallucinations and the like) as an ellipsis for 'dream . . . see' and the like. (I mean, of course, to use the hyphenation of p") to signify the determinate mental state of dreaming of seeing a white swan— paralleling determinate states of belief.) But p') and p") both have the force of replacing terms designating a transitive mode with terms designating an intransitive mode. And p'), as opposed to p"), with which it is equivalent, serves to explain how it is that precisely the same perceptual vocabulary and precisely the same surface grammar may obtain in discourse bearing on transitive and intransitive modes of sentience. The reason this liberty is needed, it will be remembered, is just that discriminations within certain intransitive modes of sentience may be phenomenally confused with those of veridical perception. There is also the additional and extremely important advantage gained that p')—but not p")—permits us to qualify the "objects" of our dreams (as opposed to qualifying the state of dreaming itself) in whatever convenient way we may qualify the objects of veridical perception. (There are, in fact, similar devices used in discourse about other matters—about actions and events, for instance.) Also, of course, the analysis of p') and p") does not preclude admitting other distinctions, as for instance between dream-seeing white swans and dream-seeing oneself seeing white swans.

If, then, we follow the intransitivity of dreaming, sensory delusion, and the like, we may say—by way of parity with the primary senses themselves—that the only things that we can dream (can discriminate in dreaming) are dreams, the only things we can discriminate in delusions are delusions, and so on. But if these (so-called) internal accusatives of dreaming, delusion, hallucination, having mental images, and the like are to be construed intransitively, then what purports to be a sensory description of the *objects* of these modes of sentience is a detailing, in sensory terms, of the very *process* (or occurrence) of dreaming and the like. In describing these "objects" (so-called intentional objects, since, *qua* dreamed and the like, they do not [and, in other contexts, at least need not] exist), we are merely specifying the content of certain sentient episodes. But this is to say that, in p''), 'dreamt-I-saw-a-white-swan' designates what is being *predicated* of the subject, a mental state of some sort; whereas, in speaking of veridical perception, to say that I see a dog is not, as such, to predicate some monadic sentient state of me but to make a cognitive claim having existential import—hence, to predicate a certain relationship between my sentience and an independent existent. (In this respect, too, the linguistic behavior of 'I see' [or, 'I hear'] and 'He sees' [or, 'He hears'] corresponds precisely with the behavior of 'I know' and 'He knows,' except that—what is extremely important and distinctive—the mode of sentience that is cognitively relevant has been identified.) Also, of course, a sense will be needed by which—paralleling belief and knowledge—to concede that Cedric dreams of what Duane actually sees; but this would require only syntactical adjustments, not assigning existential import to statements about dreams, that is, not entailing that the objects of dreams, *qua* dreamed, exist. The meaning of 'exists' will have to be examined apart (we shall return to this), in order to strengthen the proposal here pursued, namely, that transitive—but not intransitive—sentience entails existential import.

The critical difference between these intransitive modes (like dreaming and hallucination) and those that concern feeling pains, aches, tickles, and the like is simply that the latter are never confused with (or phenomenally resemble) perception though they may be fused with perception. What I mean is that feeling a pain is never like seeing a visual object, hearing an auditory object, and so on, though in any particular sentient experience—as, for instance, in feeling heat—one may be discriminating at one and the same time what is perceptually (transitively) available (palpable heat) and what can only be intransitively felt (pain caused by such

palpable heat); or, again—as in staring at a very bright light—
one may discriminate the light and the pain in one's eyes. There
are, furthermore, additional differences between what we may call
intransitive sensation (feeling pain is the well-worked paradigm)
and the intransitive perception-like modes (of which dreaming or
sensory delusion may be taken as fair specimens). For, we may
describe the pains we feel but we do not specify the *content* of our
pains, in the sense of specifying the intentional objects of our
pains (and whatever may be descriptively true of them); whereas
not only do we describe our dreams in the sense of describing the
process of dreaming or what it is we are dreaming of, but we describe our dreams by specifying their content in intentional terms.
I may say of my dream that it lasted for several minutes—which
is a non-intentional description of the process of dreaming (in
which respect it may behave as do pains); I may say that it was
frightening—which is an intentional (or quasi-intentional) description of the process of dreaming (again paralleling what we may
say of pains). But I must say something about what the dream is
of, what the dream is "directed" on, without regard to the existence or non-existence of its object—which is to give an intentional account of the content of the dream (and in which respect it
is utterly unlike pains). So, although in speaking of a dream, one
is predicating dreaming of a subject, and in speaking of pain, one
is predicating having or feeling pain of a subject, the predications
involved are of quite different sorts; for, in the first, intentional
objects must be specified in well-formed predicates (one cannot
merely be dreaming; one must be dreaming *of* something), and in
the second, no intentional objects are relevant to the appropriate
predicates (if one has a pain or an ache or a tingle, one has a pain
or ache or tingle of some determinate description, but the description does not require reference to intentional objects). 'Of,' then,
is syntatically equivocal here: with respect to dreams, it introduces
intentional objects; and with respect to pains, it introduces determinate sentient descriptions of the occasioned sentience.

Of course, we must concede as well that insofar as they are construed in cognitively relevant terms, all episodes of dreaming, feeling pain, perceiving, and the like are intentional in nature, in the sense in which linguistic distinctions or rulelike conceptual distinctions (whether involving language or not) are in some sense applied to the brute world and to one's own brute sensitivities—as in judgment and in other so-called mental acts. Here, the usual marks of intentionality are inadequate; the world we refer to is the intelligible world, the world as it is perceived and considered through our conceptual network; and the admission of these so-called mental acts presupposes certain explanatory but sentiently quite inaccessible processes by reference to which we theorize about the various modes of sentience. That is, the intentionality of cognitive states concerns the propositional content of such states, that they are "about" what purportedly is the case (where intentionality or "aboutness" is a property of such states), consistently with given states being or not being intentional—in the further sense in which feeling pain is cognitively "about" one's pain but pain itself is not "about" or "directed to" any intentional object at all. Intentionality in the first sense presupposes that we are already engaged with a world rendered intelligible through our categories. Intentionality in the second sense is an essential property (or, better, a family of properties) of certain mental states.

What we see, then, is this. Intransitive perception-like modes *borrow* the sensory vocabulary of veridical perception and, in place of the existential import of the transitive modes, they substitute the specification of intentional objects; they are then able to employ the descriptive vocabulary in a direct way—without any adjustment in surface grammar but, inevitably, with a deeper syntactical transformation. And intransitive sensation *derives* a descriptive vocabulary addressed to pains, aches, and the like that depends (largely) on causal and other regularities that obtain among whatever may be perceptually discriminated. Thus, when I dream, I say that *I see a swan;* but when I have a pain, I say that *I feel a pain, as if a pin were pricking my hand.* Were the latter to be construed transitively, then, if nothing were touching my hand, the report would be false; but intransitively construed, it is solely a question of a correct description of a psychological state. Questions of indubitability, incorrigibility, infallibility, and the like are neutral to this matter and may be independently considered. Also, it is quite easy to confuse the notions of the intransitive sentient discrimination of pain and of one's awareness of what is painful, in the sense of awareness of what one is disposed to avoid or turn from. It is entirely contingent (witness masochists) whether a felt pain is painful in the sense given; and it is only the latter that must be construed in intentional terms (in the relevant sense of 'intentional'). It may be usefully added as well that there are modes of sentience, like those in which we speak of feeling warmth, that have both a transitive and an intransitive form —where the intransitive form does not require intentional objects. It is the existential import of veridical perception that provides the conceptual basis for a public idiom regarding dreams (and similar modes) and pains (and similar modes). The privacy, in the proprietary sense, of these intransitive modes does not entail either a private language or solipsism or radical skepticism.

There is an additional advantage to our account. Not only are radical skepticism and solipsism obviated, but also first-person reports of interior mental states are vindicated. For, the perceptual idiom in which we may hedge about existential import (as distinct from devices for hedging about predications regarding what exists) itself entails the eligibility of first-person reports of those intransitive states that may be phenomenally confused with perception. Thus, if I may make a perceptual report, then I must, in principle, be able to make a report of an hallucination or the like: if, on the basis of actual sentient experience of some sort, I may report that I seem to see a dagger before me, then, acknowledging that there is no dagger to be seen, I may persist in my *report*—now suitably changed syntactically. And if it is conceptually defensible to speak of first-person reports and statements regarding certain mental states, it cannot be ineligible to speak thus of other mental states—sensations, emotions, moods, thoughts, intentions, and the like—solely on the grounds that they are interior states and events.

Finally, we may catch up an extremely valuable distinction embedded in our contrast between transitive and intransitive modes of sentience. Veridical perception (or, alternatively, a sentence used to report veridical perception) is not intentional on the usual criteria of intentionality. For, veridical perception entails the existence of what is perceived; and, if the perception is conveyed by a sentence like 'Peter sees a bear' (rather than 'Peter sees that there is a bear in front of him'), the truth of the relevant report will not involve us in difficulties regarding the substitutability of equivalent sentences for sentences prefixed by so-called propositional operators: any codesignative term may be substituted for 'bear,' *salve veritate*. We are often misled here because of the admittedly intentional properties of such sentences as 'Peter sees that there is a bear in front of him' (which may also convey veridical perception) and 'Peter seems to see a bear in front of him' (which does not). Similarly—and perhaps surprisingly—*if* pains and the like are not thought to be existent objects of some sort, then sentences like 'Robert feels pain in his tooth' (or, taking a verbal—but illuminating—liberty, 'Robert pains' or 'Robert's tooth pains') is not intentional either. These considerations bear directly on any theory of the nature of mental and psychological conditions.

But to have distinguished between such sentient modes as dreaming and feeling pain as we have is already to have avoided, provisionally, the dangers of skepticism and solipsism—insofar as these depend on mapping the interconnections between such modes and veridical perception. For, if dreaming (and its allied modes) borrow their descriptive vocabulary from perception and if feeling pain (and its allied modes) derive their descriptive vocabulary from causal and other regularities that hold among perceptible objects, then a suitable conceptual connection has been forged between the intransitive discrimination of psychological states and the transitive discriminations of perception, which ensures our re-

liance on a common public world. This is the single most important matter affecting our theory of the various modes of sentience.

4. Perceptual Distinctions and Existential Import

It remains to turn briefly to a range of distinctions within perception proper, those that concern the variable appearances of things,
perceptual illusions, mirages, and the like. We may proceed easily
here if we attend to an array of claims like the following:

- h) I see a piece of blue cloth;
- i) I see a piece of blue cloth that looks green in this light;
- j) I see what looks like a piece of green cloth;
- k) I see what looks to me like a piece of green cloth.

It is obvious that, considering h) and i), one may see a piece of
blue cloth and yet not see cloth that looks blue. Again, considering i) and j), one may see blue cloth that looks green and one may
mistake the green look of the cloth's color for its actual color.
Again, considering i) and k), the green look of blue cloth may be
due to the light in which it is seen and it may be due to the nature
or condition of the eyes (or creature) by which it is seen. These alternatives pretty well capture the range of distinctions that are required. For, the only indispensable element in a perceptual claim,
following the foregoing arguments, is the existential element: if
one sees something, that something must exist; if this is given up,
we are forced to turn, as we have seen, to some perception-like intransitive mode (perceptual delusion, for example). Otherwise, we
have only to account for the variable appearances of things that
are perceived; and this requires only that norms and criteria be
specifiable (which will be based on both causal and non-causal
considerations) in terms of which what it is to perceive the actual
perceptible attributes of a thing (including the way in which it actually looks) may be formulated. A thing may appear to possess

certain attributes that it does not possess and it may possess what it does not appear to possess. And this may be so for two quite different sorts of reasons. The conditions under which the thing may be perceived may be such as to affect the appearance it will exhibit: a piece of blue cloth in a green light may actually appear green; if the discrepancy is very striking—as for instance when light and heat over a road produce the appearance of water—we speak of mirages and illusions, but these are distinctive only in their persistence for normal percipients and because of the remarkable discrepancy between what is perceived and how it actually appears (think of magical or optical illusions). Thus, we often speak informally of the existence of mirages and after-images—in a way not altogether unlike, but not altogether similar to, the way in which we speak of the existence of shadows. On the other hand, the appearance a thing exhibits may be affected by the sensory organs or psychological state of the percipient: a piece of blue cloth may appear green to someone who is color-blind; or a piece of blue cloth may appear to have remarkably altered colors to someone under the influence of drugs (or even under the influence of some persistent belief). So the appearances of things may be due, we may say, to objective or subjective factors. But, on any account, the various adjustments possible will preserve the existential import of perceptual claims. Also, to insist on this is to point to the coherence and systematic connections among all the different kinds of sentience that are normally admitted to be available and to do so without the provision of sense-data at all.

It is the existential import of statements of veridical perception that is decisive; for, the intransitive modes of sentience that may be phenomenally confused with perception lack such import *and* those modes are distinguished among themselves, on this very condition, by reference to further, causal conditions under which relevant episodes occur. That one is asleep, for instance, is decisive for dreaming; that the image maintains a relatively constant position within a visual field serves to distinguish after-images from other persistent phenomena like mirages. But it is also because veridical perception entails the actual existence of what is perceived that our ultimate conception of the nature of the world depends irrevocably on our perceptual access. Consequently, revisions in our theory of the nature of the entities of the world depend, epistemically, on what we may coherently admit *we* perceive; and talk of what it is possible to perceive is incoherent unless it is rendered in terms of what is perceptually compatible with what a given sentient agent actually does perceive in some set of perceptual occasions. In fact, characteristically, to speak of what it *possibly* is that one is perceiving is simply to hedge—in cognitively relevant ways—about what one is actually perceiving or about what one believes he is actually perceiving. If, however, "possible perceivings" are sentiently discriminated as a basis for, or as evidence for, perceptual claims, we are simply driven back to sense-data in a new guise. Again, attention to the existential import of veridical perception confirms the irreducibly theory-laden nature of perceptual discourse. For, if we distinguish "sensing" from "perceiving" (that, on some hypothesis, interprets "sensing"), there are no formulably necessary, sufficient, or necessary and sufficient "sensed" discriminations that can be made to provide a cognitive basis for affirming the existence, the identity, the spatio-temporal continuity, of whatever may be individuated in perception; and existence, self-identity, and the like cannot, on any remotely plausible thesis, be said to be mere sensory discriminations themselves.

Several final observations are in order. For one thing, theories of sensing may be introduced to explain perception, without postulating a special sentience or awareness. For instance, the pupil of the eye is sensitive to light independently of one's being perceptually aware of light, and the musculature of the body responds, maintaining equilibrium, to changes within the labyrinth of the ear, independently of awareness. That is, what may fairly be regarded as sensory information may be processed by the sensory organs without being consciously discriminated by the sentient creature; in this sense, it is entirely possible to construe perception as an "interpretation" (as a coding of the import) of what is "sensed." But this is a theory of a radically different sort from that of classical sense-datum theories, that posit some form of "immediate awareness."

Interpretations of what is admittedly perceived (as in representational or symbolic art) cannot be said to concern the use of the term 'interpret' in the same sense in which perception is itself viewed as an "interpretation" of what is ulteriorly "sensed" (of what may be directly avowed or reported or of what one may be said to be directly aware of, in some cognitively relevant respect). And explanations of perception, in terms of physiological and other causal factors affecting sentience itself, are simply not of the same sort as explanations of what it is merely to perceive, e.g., to "interpret" what is "sensed." For the causal explanation obliges us to introduce some *non-epistemically* relevant form of sensitivity entailed *in* perception taken in the full (epistemic) sense of knowing by sensory means. This identifies the context, for instance, in which we sometimes say that Peter *saw* the dog before him (though he did not *see that* there was a dog before him), because though the dog was in his visual field (and, therefore, affected his ocular apparatus in a way causally relevant for seeing [in the cognitive sense], he did not actually see [wasn't aware of] the dog in this sense [and may not even have believed he saw anything that, relevantly, could be said to be that dog]). But, of course, *if* this usage be allowed, then whatever *perceptually* available distinctions are assigned to what Peter saw (in the non-epistemic sense) are invariably conceptually dependent on whatever we admit a man may know by sensory means. Our theory may affect what we admit may be seen, but the dependence of assigning "discrimination" to sensitivities below the level of awareness remains unchanged. For, consider what it would mean to say, for instance, that a bee (having sight) saw a *bear* or a *coin*. The identification of what the bee saw involves not merely the physical sensibilities we assign to bees but also the range of discriminating objects and properties and the like compatible with those sensibilities *and* extrapolated, by way of comparing the capacities and behavior of bees with those of men, from the (epistemically relevant) perception of men. The specification of both the epistemically relevant perception of creatures other than man and the non-epistemic perception of men and other creatures depends on the categories in terms of which the (epistemically relevant) perceptual distinctions of men are themselves made—which is not to say that ascriptions of perceptual abilities to bees need be anthropomorphic.

5. The Causal Theory of Perception

Having said this much, I should say as well that causal theories of perception (as, indeed, of other forms of knowledge) appear incapable of escaping or resolving a certain vicious circle. No one, it may be fairly said, would deny that perceiving, inferring, grasping the meaning of, or the like entails causal conditions—perhaps we are even in a position to formulate necessary conditions; but a causal theory of perception requires that we be able to formulate sufficient conditions *of the causal sort* for perceptual knowledge.

Let us concede that only when objects of a certain sort are in one's visual field (which may be true when one does not perceive what is there or even when one does not have any beliefs about what is there), and only when one's eyes are activated by whatever is in one's visual field in whatever way is causally like what is involved in sight (which may be true without prejudice to whether one is perceiving or not), and only when one's beliefs about what one is perceiving are causally linked to the presence of certain objects in one's visual field and linked to the relevant activation of one's eyes (without prejudice to whether such beliefs entail perception or constitute perceptual knowledge), can the question of perceiving legitimately arise. What this concession says is that there are characteristic causal linkages—perhaps linkages involving even necessary conditions—that connect physiological and psychological states with perceptual knowledge, knowledge by perceptual means, or bare perception. The question remains: granting this much, how are such causal conditions to be converted or amplified into conditions *sufficient* for perceptual knowledge or perception?

We could say that the way in which the conditions mentioned obtain is *just the way* in which when I look at my hand in a good light, my hand is causally responsible for my eyes being appropriately activated and my beliefs being appropriately induced *when I do perceive* (or know by perceptual means) that a (my) hand is before me. But this is surely circular. Doubtless, we may allow a certain informality in specifying sufficient conditions for different perceptual situations when we are reasonably clear about the causal condition sufficient for some paradigmatic instances of perception or perceptual knowledge. But it looks very much as if we decide that a person perceives a given object by assessing whether, given certain minimal causal conditions, his beliefs conform to certain informal (but non-causal) norms for ascribing such knowledge or such perception, where further causal details may defeat but not confirm the ascription.

For instance, a man claims that he sees a moose at a distance. In fact, there is an elk in his visual field. He made a mistake about what it is he saw; but in construing this as an error about *what he saw,* we imply that he did indeed see the elk: he mistook the elk's appearance for the appearance of a moose. That is, the relationship between what he judges he saw and what was there to be seen cannot possibly be explicated, relative to ascriptions of perceiving or knowing by perceptual means, in purely causal terms: the issue, rather, is whether we would allow the discrepancy to disqualify ascribing perception. Again, a man claims that he sees a moose at a distance. In fact, there is a moose in his visual field, but he is at a distance at which it is unlikely that he could visually discriminate between a moose and an elk; he has, also, antecedent information that there is a moose in the vicinity and he hears a moose call coming from the general direction of what he takes to be a moose. Surely, given his background and collateral information, the congruence between his belief and what is in his visual field qualifies or does not qualify his belief as perceptual knowledge, in terms of the appraisive norms of such knowledge and not merely in terms of causal considerations; for, given the relevant causal considerations, the question appears always to remain. Again, a man claims to see a moose when, somewhat as before, there is a wooden elk in his visual field. He specifies, under questioning, that he sees at least a certain large animal-like form with horns on its head, something—perhaps a creature—that resembles a moose or an elk or the like; and he gives further specifications that are true of the wooden elk, in addition to what he says that is false (as presupposing a living creature). He cannot be said to know (by perception) that there is a wooden elk in his visual field, though it may be claimed that he sees the wooden elk or that he sees or perhaps even knows that there is a certain bulky animal form of a more-or-less determinate sort in his visual field. But here, precisely, we are obliged to evaluate whether and to what extent his true beliefs are justified and whether and of *what* his beliefs so justified may be said to constitute perceptual knowledge or to entail perception. Once relevantly so judged, the question of sufficient causal conditions may be raised and answered.

Alternatively put, when certain characteristic or necessary conditions of perception obtain, *if* we ascribe perception or perceptual knowledge to someone on the basis of his beliefs, we may "causalize" our account by holding that the sufficient (though unspecified, even unspecifiable) conditions of perception also (necessarily) obtain—where the ascription is defeasible (still) by reference to further causal details. Any claim that the perceptual beliefs that are held are caused *in just the way* they must be caused in order to count as knowledge is utterly vacuous.

The best that we may expect in this regard, *given* perception or perceptual knowledge, is that causal conditions necessary and sufficient for the beliefs judged to entail perception or to constitute knowledge by perceptual means may be specified. *If* beliefs may be causally accounted for, then there is no reason to deny that sufficient causal conditions may, in principle, be specified for any

given belief; but *whether* such beliefs entail perceiving or constitute perceptual knowledge depends, surely, on the justification for
so counting them. And that is a question concerning justificatory
reasons and not causal conditions. So, a causal theory of perception is trivially available, in the sense that whatever enters into
perception, *that is caused,* may be causally explained (which is not
to say that a causal account of *such* factors is trivial). But *if*
knowledge, whether by perceptual or other means, concerns the
normative status or significance of our beliefs (which are caused in
some way or other), and if the relevant norms are themselves inherently informal and changeable in accord with prevailing interests governing the ascriptions in question, then it is hopeless to attempt to provide a causal theory of knowledge. Another way of
putting the point (whose force we shall assume here) is that whatever causes S's perceptual beliefs does so under any description or
designation of the cause and belief involved; but whatever conditions, C, that rationalize (or justify characterizing) S's belief as
perception or as perceptual knowledge, do so only under some appropriate description or designation of S's belief. Thus, S's belief
that he sees an elk on the hill, under conditions including there
being an elk on the hill and the elk's being in S's visual field and
the like, may, relative to C, be rationalized as perceptual know-
edge under the designation 'belief that he sees an elk on the hill'
but not under the designation 'belief that he sees an animal of the
same kind Jack shot last winter.' Causal contexts are extensional,
but contexts of rationalization (or justification) are not, are non-
extensional. (I should add at once that causal contexts—*not* contexts of causal explanation—are extensional: that is, '*a* because *b,*'
where 'because' signifies a causal connection, is extensional; but
'*a* because *b*' where 'because' signifies that the causal connection
perspicuously conforms to norms of causal explanation, is neither
extensional nor truth-functional—and, of course, '*a*' and '*b*' here
designate sentences or facts, not events or the like). Were this not
so, and were it possible to substitute causal accounts for rationali-
zations or justifications, one might even have offered a causal

theory of justice on the grounds that human behavior is open to causal influence.

The causal theory of perception, in fact, takes two characteristic forms that are easily conflated. Consider a schematic visual situation, to fix our ideas. On one view, *light,* reflected from external objects, causes certain beliefs in a percipient. Here, belief may be construed as a disposition to behave in a certain complex way, and perception may be *identified* as belief (sometimes called "perceptual belief" to signify its causal source). On the alternative view, something's *looking* a certain way to a percipient (itself antecedently caused) *causes* the percipient to acquire beliefs *about* the phenomenal experience. Here, belief may also be construed dispositionally and called "perceptual belief," but, now, it is clearly distinct from the phenomenal experience itself. It may causally affect further phenomenal experience, and antecedent beliefs (emotions, desires, and the like) may affect the phenomenal experience given. But if it is causally connected with the experience, it cannot, in the relevant sense, be constitutive of, or identified with, it; and if it is identified with it, it cannot be causally linked to it. (We shall examine identity and composition more closely later.) Now, the identity thesis (just given) appears to eliminate phenomenal experience altogether—which, by analogy with the difference between sensations of pain and behavior that serves as criteria of the occurrence of pain, is utterly unconvincing. And the causal thesis, though it is, in the form given, altogether plausible, has nothing directly to do with vindicating the causal theory of perception and is, indeed, compatible with a great variety of alternative theories that concede *some* causal influences on perception and phenomenal experience. If one's beliefs, desires, emotions, even linguistic dispositions may affect one's perception—and *these* cannot normally be linked in a causal way to the external object that presumably triggers the causal chain leading to veridical perception—then it is clear that ascriptions of perception and perceptual knowledge must depend on normative considerations that cannot be adequately construed in the way the causal theory requires. We may add, also, that illusions like the Ames chair persists in looking a certain way to normal percipients in spite of learning (in a causally qualified way) and of knowing that they are illusions and even knowing how they are constructed—that is, the Ames chair does not change its look as our beliefs become more and more veridical. Other phenomena confirm the distinction as well. But also, and more fundamentally, perception could not possibly be adequately analyzed in terms of beliefs caused, for perception is transitive and belief is intentional. On any view, then, norms of justification will be required.

A last consideration is this: sentience by no means exhausts the available cognitive modes. There are obvious non-sentient modes of cognition, requiring an altogether different analysis, that range over thoughts, beliefs, intentions, wishes, emotions, moods, attitudes, and the like. These are often quite complex, sometimes involve sentience, and may be expected not to lend themselves to an entirely uniform analysis. They are distinguished in that what is discriminated must be described in intentional terms, also in that there are no antecedent limits—short of the limits of conception itself—on the eligible intentional objects of these modes.

The principal benefit of our account, then, is systematic. For, in canvassing all forms of sentience, we have—conditionally, on the assumption that transitive sentience is epistemically more fundamental than intransitive sentience—analyzed the systematic distinctions among the various modes of sentience at the same time we have shown that perception exhibits all the distinctive features of knowledge and that the transitivity of perception (the matter of existential import) accounts for our access to a public world. It has also been briefly remarked that perception (as well as the other modes of sentience) must be ascribed to entities capable of perception—which leads us on to deeper questions. But within the restricted context of cognitive considerations, it remains to eliminate the conditional assumption regarding the relationship between knowledge of what is public and what is private.

III

DOUBT & CERTAINTY

Doubt and certainty are psychological states. But, in the context of analyzing knowledge, the question naturally arises whether particular states of doubt and certainty are relevant to what we believe and know, in the sense that objections, evidence, grounds, and similar considerations properly bearing on the truth and on determining the truth of what we believe or purportedly know inform our particular doubts and states of certainty. We wonder whether we have any knowledge that is altogether free of the possibility of doubt thus informed and whether what we know we may know with certainty—perhaps even infallibly —also thus suitably informed.

To be relevant to appraising the justifiability of our beliefs and the justifiability of ascribing knowledge to us, doubts must be formulable as quite particular challenges to the truth of what we believe and to our being in a favorable position to know what happens to be true. Certainty, on the other hand, can only be assessed on the basis of an entire range of possible grounds for doubt. Conceding that men are not omniscient, we are obliged to admit that ascriptions of certainty are, necessarily, informal and

71

depend—very much as do ascriptions of knowledge—on the normative expectations of a given society. It has often been argued, however, that men have indubitable knowledge of their own mental states and of certain other selected truths, as for instance of what is said to be conveyed by the assertion 'I exist.' It turns out, on inspection, that the alleged indubitability of the first sort entails anomalies, including the consequence that no one can then even be said to understand what another is saying about his own private mental states. Arguments of the second sort prove to be unique, to have no bearing on any other claims of indubitability whatsoever, and to depend, in any case, on the analysis of assertions whose apparent content does not exceed whatever is merely entailed by making any assertion at all or by doing anything at all. Men are also sometimes said to know whatever is true about their own mental states; but the claim fails since it is not even possible to say, antecedently and exhaustively, what the appropriate ways are in which we may describe our own mental states. To defeat doctrines of these sorts, however, is by no means to deny that we have privileged access of some sort to our own mental states and that we are characteristically certain and entitled to be certain about our reports and descriptions of them. In fact, a similarly privileged access obtains even in perceptual contexts, as for instance in speaking of the proprioceptive senses (as of balance) and of the interoceptive senses (as of feeling the weight of food in the stomach).

Finally, doubt proves to be a more complex notion than certainty, both because certainty presupposes the resolution of relevant doubts or the fixing of the inappropriateness of would-be doubts and because the conditions on which doubts themselves are relevantly formulated presuppose a public world whose own existence cannot coherently be open to doubt—even though, of course, we can doubt in a piecemeal way whatever is said to be true about the particular details and features of the things of the world.

1. The Asymmetry of Doubt and Certainty

Imagine that someone wonders whether (or doubts that) there is a cactus plant in the room next door—wonders in fact whether there is one just at the very moment of doubting. Clearly, whether the doubt can be met fairly depends on the admissibility of certain theoretical considerations. Are there, for instance, physical objects like cactus plants? And do they exist unperceived? And is there some evidential connection between observations made now of a given cactus plant and its alleged existence during an earlier unobserved interval? Such considerations as these are quite obviously controversial in themselves; hence, it is difficult not only to put legitimate doubts to rest but also to determine the legitimate grounds on which legitimate doubts may be put to rest. In this sense, doubt and certainty are not merely psychological matters but conceptual or logical matters. We wonder not merely whether certain mental states can be avoided or sustained but also whether our cognitive beliefs can be justified and relevantly freed from challenge. The question profoundly infects all human efforts at knowledge and so draws us on to the extraordinary complexity of the relationship between doubt and certainty, on the one hand, and knowledge and belief, on the other.

Men have always wondered whether they could ever *justifiably* escape doubt or achieve certainty regarding their beliefs. Let us, with an eye to promising answers, distinguish among a) psychological doubt and psychological certainty; b) logical doubt and logical certainty; and c) empirical doubt and empirical certainty. Psychological doubt and psychological certainty are distinct mental states at least nominally relevant to some proposition given—in the sense that, if p is a given proposition, then one may be in a state of utter uncertainty that p is true or in a state of complete confidence that p is true or in some distinct state between these two extremes. It must be asked concerning such states whether they *rele-*

vantly accompany or qualify the beliefs that we hold. I may for instance doubt or be confident about *p* for the wildest possible reasons, and though this may be clinically interesting it will bear not at all on the truth or falsity of *p* or on my right to be said to know that *p* or to be justified in my belief that *p*. From these considerations, we may conclude that the principal forms of doubt and certainty affecting cognitive matters may be said to be propositional, in the sense in which what we are said to doubt or to be certain of, is the proposition *that p* (is true); and that psychological doubt and certainty, construed as mere mental states that accompany or qualify our beliefs that *p,* are pathological phenomena of no interest in themselves for cognitive matters. There may be no way of answering wild doubts but there may be a way of treating them; the same is true of certainty. Consequently, the mental states of doubt and certainty must exhibit additional features of some sort beyond the merely nominal linkage to propositions—in that *p* is the (intentional) object of a given mental state (or that *p* most perspicuously conveys that object, not itself a proposition) —in order that their analysis bear on the prospects of human knowledge and justified belief. We may also note that the mental states of doubt and certainty may be linked with skills and abilities rather than directly with propositions—as when we say that one doubts or is certain about his ability to play a given piece of music. But if behavioral manifestations and the like may be said to express such doubt and certainty, then the relevant states may be construed fairly as having a certain propositional import as well. And, though the states of doubt and certainty may be explored in ways that bear on other interesting questions of conduct and commitment and the like (e.g., as in saying that one believes in his country or in God or in his own genius), it will always be possible to formulate propositions as perspicuously corresponding to, or conveying, the proper objects of such states whenever doubt and certainty are taken to bear relevantly on cognitive matters.

Logical doubt and logical certainty are, by way of contrast, what may be called logical or functional states, in the sense in which they need not be psychologically embodied to be relevant to the truth of a given proposition p or to be cognitively relevant to the belief that p is true. Assuming that we have a comprehensive theory of evidence and of justificatory grounds for believing any proposition, we should find provision within this theory for justifying doubt and certainty relative to any belief. If p may be true and known to be true then, in general, doubts bearing on the truth and knowledge of p must relevantly be capable of being raised and put to rest. So logical doubt and certainty are possible states of mind that, within the scope of our theory of knowledge, relevantly bear on the truth of any proposition or the standing of any agent alleged to know or justifiably to believe that proposition. Clearly, therefore, psychological doubt is cognitively relevant if and only if it embodies states of logical doubt. Let us simply christen such psychological states states of empirical doubt. (Adjustments are needed, as we shall see, for certainty.) To say this much, however, is not, it should be emphasized, to restrict doubt and certainty to empirical propositions; for, it is entirely possible to doubt in a relevant sense (to be in a state of empirical doubt) the truth of an arithmetic proposition—that, say, $7 + 5 = 12$—which we suppose to be necessarily true. Also, it is not to say that cognitive theory is concerned merely to relieve empirical doubt or to achieve empirical certainty; for, it is entirely possible that logical doubts may be formulated that no human agent actually embodies as empirical doubts or actually embodies within a given interval of time.

Consequently, an account of doubt and certainty will have to attend bifocally to the possible resolution of empirical doubt and of logical doubt and to the possible achievement of empirical certainty and of logical certainty. The distinction has significant ramifications. For, if, with respect to any proposition p, logical doubts cannot be exhausted or answered, we shall not be able to escape a form of skepticism with respect to the truth of p; and, in particular, if we are unable to escape such doubts with regard to propositions bearing on the existence of a public world or with regard to any and all propositions, we shall be unable to escape a form of radical skepticism or of solipsism.

To return, however, to the distinction of empirical states of

doubt and certainty, we must concede an asymmetry regarding the
scope of the very concepts of doubt and certainty. For, if logical
doubt concerns cognitively eligible challenges to the truth of *p or*
to one's knowing that *p* is true or to one's justifiably believing that
p is true, it is debatable whether we could plausibly hold logical
certainty to be the state in which no possibility of logical doubt
arises regarding the truth of *p or* regarding one's knowing or
justifiably believing that *p* is true. If this were the construction
preferred, then a state of logical certainty would be tantamount to
a state of infallibility with respect to any proposition given; and,
in particular, if the claim were allowed for any and all propositions, logical certainty would be tantamount to omniscience. Presumably, God would be the only cognitive agent of whom such a
state could be convincingly predicated; therefore, a useful concept
(logical certainty) would, by such a constraint, have been effectively deprived of application in the context of human cognition
—though, it must be admitted that, seen in this extreme way, it
does provide a certain global range for the questions of doubt and
certainty.

We may take note also of the following. If a proposition is necessarily true, it may still be open to logical doubt, in the sense that
one may justifiably doubt that a proposition that is necessarily
true is necessarily true. *A fortiori,* any proposition that is contingently true is open to logical doubt. On the other hand, if a proposition that is necessarily true is known to be necessarily true or at
least justifiably believed to be necessarily true, then it is fair to say
that the agent who is in such a state of knowledge or belief is in a
state of certainty—that is, that he has satisfied a certain range of
logically relevant doubts respecting the proposition. Now,
if he has satisfied his *empirical* doubts—and we may understand
by this, that whoever raises logically relevant doubts regarding his
belief thereby obliges him to adopt these doubts (as a rational
agent)—it is fair to say that he is *empirically* certain. But if we
say so, we shall not be able, paralleling the definition of empirical
doubt, to say that empirical certainty embodies states of logical

certainty—where, by the latter notion, we wish to speak of infallibility or omniscience. The reason is instructive. In speaking of
logical doubt, we are really speaking of distributive challenges to
the ascription (to some agent) of states of knowledge or justified
belief. Whenever it is logically relevant to doubt the truth of p or
some agent's knowledge of p, we can withhold the ascription of
logical certainty. But if we were to ascribe logical certainty to
some agent in terms of infallibility or omniscience, we should do
so because, collectively and exhaustively, there are no possible
grounds for doubt. Consequently, in speaking of human agents, we
can do no more than hold that an agent is logically certain when a
sufficient range of logical doubts have been met; and, in particular, when all empirical doubts have been met, the agent is at least
empirically certain. If, then, the required psychologically embodied form of logical certainty may be specified—in some way paralleling our account of logical doubt—then logical certainty itself
(or logical certainty suitably embodied empirically) can be said to
obtain when a certain sufficient range of logical doubts, not necessarily exhausting all logically possible doubts, have been met. The
relevant range will be set by the practice of inquiry. Logical doubt
and empirical doubt, thus, will be assignable on a distributive
basis; and logical certainty and empirical certainty will be assignable on a collective basis only. Also, of course no doubts can be
said to be met unless they are formulated; in this sense, we are (as
rational agents) confined to empirical doubts.

What is important, clearly, is that logical certainty is a somewhat relaxed notion—corresponding to the relaxed notion of
knowledge itself—and that the ascription to a cognitive agent of
states of logical certainty depends on normative considerations
bearing on ascriptions of justified belief and knowledge. If, for instance, I have put appropriately to rest all of my empirical doubts
regarding p, then I am certain that p is true. It is entirely possible
that p be false or that I am not justified in claiming (believing)
that p is true, since I may not have canvassed all of a set of normatively relevant logical doubts regarding p or regarding my cog-

nitive position regarding *p*. Hence, it is possible to be empirically certain that *p* and yet not actually know that *p* is true (because it is false or because my grounds for believing *p* to be true do not meet whatever may be the standards of knowledge or justified belief). When, therefore, my empirical certainty meets either the conditions of knowledge or the conditions of justified belief, I may be said to be logically certain. Hence, we see the need for the asymmetry between the notions of logical doubt and logical certainty (and, correspondingly, between empirical doubt and empirical certainty). A convenient way of summarizing the distinction is to draw attention to the fact that empirical doubt (distributively) embodies logical doubt and that empirical certainty (collectively) must conform to norms of knowledge or justified belief in order to embody logical certainty; alternatively put, empirical certainty (descriptively construed) is merely the state that obtains when all of one's empirical doubts are resolved and empirical certainty (normatively construed) is the state that obtains when a certain sufficient range of logical doubts have been resolved in resolving one's empirical doubts.

These apparent quibbles may be seen to have considerable importance if we consider whether there are any propositions that one may assert of which one may be said to have incorrigible or indubitable knowledge. If we think of doubt in terms of logical and empirical doubt, then so-called incorrigible and indubitable knowledge come to the same thing; for, if what is said to be known is incorrigibly known, then there are no cognitively relevant doubts that can be formulated and all doubt is pathological; and if what is said to be known is indubitably known, then there are no formulable grounds on which to correct what is said to be known. It is, of course, quite possible to claim that one's *beliefs* (say, about inner mental states) are incorrigible *simpliciter*. On this view, incorrigibility and indubitability must be carefully distinguished. For, logical incorrigibility signifies there not being a basis for correcting a given avowal or belief, and logical indubitability signifies there not being a basis for relevantly querying the truth of a given belief or claim or report or the like. But then, incorrigibility entails a quasi-performative interpretation of beliefs and avowals such that independent questions of truth and falsity do not arise at all. In that case, the interesting question of whether, conceding that one may have beliefs about inner mental states, one may also make assertions, statements, reports about them and thus be said to have *knowledge* of such states, is ruled out: the mere avowal or say-so of someone (even if restricted in terms of sincerity and the like) decides the matter but forces an equivocation on 'knowledge.' The question remains whether there is indubitable knowledge.

2. Indubitability, Self-intimating States, and Privileged Access

We have already noticed that necessarily true propositions (*a fortiori,* contingent propositions) are open to logical doubt, simply because it is logically possible and cognitively relevant to doubt that a necessarily true proposition is necessarily true. If there are any indubitable propositions, then, we shall have to look in another quarter. Historically, candidates have been chiefly drawn from introspection regarding mental states and from such would-be specimens as the assertion 'I exist.' And these deserve careful scrutiny. But if the thesis that there are logically indubitable propositions can be made out, it appears—since logically necessary propositions are insufficient—that ascriptions of logical indubitability must be relativized, for given propositions, *to the agents who believe them;* and this is just the promise of the specimens we are to examine.

Consider, therefore, that some agent S believes that *p;* we may say that, in so believing, S "says in his heart" that *p* is true—meaning not that belief is interior speech but that belief is tantamount to interior speech, that it is as if S did assert that *p,* that the structure of a belief-state is here best rendered as an analogue of an assertion. Let us suppose, further, that S believes something regarding some mental state of his, something we concede he may be aware of in a directly introspective sense, something that another can have knowledge of only by way of public criteria. Now, there is no question that S will normally be empirically certain of what he believes: he will normally have no doubts and will normally be unable to formulate any doubts regarding his beliefs, his thoughts, his images, his pains, and the like. The question remains whether, in being empirically certain that p, S may, conceivably, be said to have logically indubitable knowledge that p. (In this context, we may even raise the question whether S may be infallible with respect to p.) In any case, a decisive answer can be given: S cannot have logically indubitable knowledge that p even when p concerns certain introspectively accessible mental states. The argument bears in an unexpected way on the threat of radical skepticism and solipsism.

A standard objection against the admission of indubitable knowledge holds that there is a difference between a state of affairs, any state of affairs, and the correct characterization of that state of affairs; in particular, then, it is held that there is a difference between being in a certain mental state and knowing that one is in that mental state. Given the difference (so it is argued), it is always possible that one may fail to characterize a given state correctly and, therefore, that any such characterization is open to logical doubt. The argument is normally allowed for all states open to public discrimination and so, for instance, perceptual judgments are normally not taken to be indubitable. But, precisely, the partisans of indubitable knowledge will argue that indubitable knowledge of mental states obtains in spite of the distinction. Since the mere difference between the occurrence of a given state and the correct characterization of that state does not entail the denial of indubitable knowledge, the argument comes to a stalemate (quite apart from the question of whether occurrent psychological states —pains, beliefs, thoughts, and the like—may, intelligibly, be said to obtain without the patient's being aware of, or having some propositional attitude toward, such states). A more powerful maneuver will be needed.

Consider that, although there is a certain cognitively relevant asymmetry between first-person and third-person knowledge of mental states, it is possible to make both first- and third-person reference to the same mental states. This means that, although I may be directly aware of my pains, my beliefs, my feelings, my thoughts, my images, and the like—although I need not rely upon, or use, "outward" criteria or external signs, of my own mental states—you may, in spite of the fact that you *do* rely, must rely, on outward criteria, relevantly have beliefs about my mental states and come to doubt and be certain about the nature of my mental states. If this be conceded, the counterargument is absurdly simple. For, if you may empirically doubt that I am in a certain mental state, *then your doubts are logically relevant to my beliefs about my own mental states;* and if this is the case, then, although I may be empirically certain (in the descriptive sense) about my own mental states—and even logically certain (in the normative but relaxed sense stipulated)—I cannot be said to have indubitable knowledge of my mental states. The only condition, *per impossible,* on which I could be said to have logically indubitable knowledge would entail that *your* doubts about my states of mind were always and necessarily pathological; but this would mean that one could never refer to, or have beliefs about, another's mental state; and it would mean as well that another could never be said to understand what one is speaking about in asserting that he is in this or that mental state. In short, to insist on the logical indubitability of first-person beliefs or assertions about mental states is, in effect, to deny that anyone can meaningfully be said (by another) to have such (particular) first-person beliefs or can meaningfully be said to make such (particular) first-person assertions; and, in that case, questions of knowledge become irrelevant —*a fortiori,* questions of indubitable knowledge. It may be entirely fair to hold that first-person knowledge of mental states enjoys some privilege or other over third-person knowledge of mental states—for instance, that it is rather implausible to hold that empirical certainty regarding states of belief and feeling and the like can be regularly challenged by third-person doubts—but this has nothing to do with the prospects of logical indubitability. The upshot is that, formulated for introspective knowledge of mental states, the claim of logical indubitability entails some form of solipsism or an appeal to an utterly private language; contrariwise, the admission of public discourse regarding inner or private mental states itself entails the denial of logical indubitability. The alternative possibilities—either unacceptable or inadequate—are these: if I can know with certainty that you believe you are in a certain mental state, then (on the hypothesis) I also may have logically indubitable knowledge of your mental state; if I can justifiably believe with certainty that you believe you are in a certain mental state, then I may have a logically indubitable belief about your mental state; if you can have indubitable knowledge of your own mental state and my doubts are necessarily pathological, then solipsism obtains; and if I can know or relevantly believe what your current mental state is, though my doubts do not undermine the logical indubitability with which you know what you do, then your apparent indubitability will have to be construed in terms of avowals and quasi-performative utterances—in which case, the usual questions of knowledge, belief, and indubitability (associated with privileged access) will become quite irrelevant.

The argument favoring indubitability is sometimes reversed. One may hold, thus, that if one has a certain mental state, then one must believe that that mental state obtains; that is, that p's being true logically implies that S believes that p is true. This is the thesis that mental states are "self-intimating" or "self-evident" or "directly evident." Together with the former argument, it forms the doctrine of "the perfectly transparent mind." But it is clearly false. For, if it is conceded that there are indefinitely many correct characterizations of any state of affairs—they may vary, after all, in intension or in terms of alternative emphasis and the like—then it is a foregone conclusion that if a certain state of affairs obtains, that may be identified under some preferred description, it is not necessarily the case that S will believe that the state *as identified under that description* obtains. Since there are not determinately many descriptions that may hold for any state of affairs, it is not even possible to formulate a closed set of descriptions from which S's belief about his own mental state must make a selection, conformably with the thesis. Consequently, the argument for indubitability and self-intimating states falls. But this is not to deny that, in the first-person setting, one is in a position of logically privileged access with respect to his own mental states; on the contrary, if the asymmetry conceded regarding first- and third-person knowledge of mental states be sustained, then it is impossible to deny privileged access. What *is* important to note, however, is that the doctrine does not in itself entail indubitability or self-intimating states; that is, even first-person empirical doubts are entirely possible, psychologically. It is in fact, the doctrine of privileged access that explains the plausibility of admitting that empirical certainty characteristically attends first-person beliefs regarding inner mental states; and it is in terms of this doctrine (applicable in the *perceptual* context as well) that we may move from a consideration of first-person propositions and reports to a consideration of doubt and certainty vis-à-vis inner mental states. For, *logically* privileged access may be admitted for the sensory modes known as interoception and proprioception, in the sense that each of us has access, through these modes, only to his own body; but, though this is true, relevant perceptual claims and reports are not, for that reason, indubitable. Hence, the mere admission of privileged access to pains, beliefs, and the like does not entail indubitable knowledge of such states.

The argument regarding the perhaps unique assertion 'I exist' proceeds along rather different lines. It is argued that, if I assert that I exist, then what I assert is necessarily true (though 'I exist' is not a necessary truth) and, understanding what I assert, I must have indubitable knowledge of what it is I assert to be true. My existence may be contingent, but a necessary condition for my asserting that I exist (though not a presupposition of mine, in so asserting) is that I in fact exist; consequently, understanding the meaning of my assertion (that I have made the assertion—any assertion), I must have indubitable knowledge of my existence. This is, of course, not to say or to deny that the conditional statement, 'If I do X (assert that I exist, do anything) then I exist,' is necessarily true; it is to say, rather, that the assertion 'I exist' is, when asserted, necessarily true and necessarily true in such a way that when I assert it, I have (according to the argument) indubitable knowledge. (That is, 'I exist,' when asserted, is necessarily true, but it is not analytically true.) The trouble is that the assertion is, if it is conceded to be an assertion, a degenerate one. For, *if I do anything,* then I exist. If I assert that I do not exist (which, understanding what I say, I cannot sincerely assert), then necessarily I exist: I do not necessarily exist but, on the condition *that I have asserted something,* then, necessarily, I exist. What makes the assertion necessarily true, *when asserted,* is that the assertion ('I exist') appears to affirm no more than whatever minimally is entailed by actually making the assertion or any assertion or doing anything at all. (Hence, if I *understand* that I am making an assertion—in particular, understand *my* assertion 'I exist'—then I know that necessarily I exist [though my existence is contingent].) This is the sense in which the proposition is a degenerate proposition and *sui generis.* The trouble is that both 'I' and 'exist' are used in such a way that no determinate predicates may be incorporated in one's assertion, while preserving the alleged indubitability. For, if I say anything about myself or my existence, I shall jeopardize indubitability. 'I' is a reflexive pronoun that may properly be used by indefinitely many persons; and 'exists' is, if construed predicatively, consistent with any and all logically possible properties of things that may be ascribed self-referentially; or, construed quantificationally, it belongs to a truncated generalization from some other singular statement that is not itself open to the ascription of indubitability. Under the circumstances, therefore, it makes little difference whether we honor the assertion as indubitable or not; it is *sui generis* in any case and cannot provide any foundation for other allegedly indubitable truths involving determinate predications of some sort; others, in fact—as the philosophical tradition attests—are themselves always to be counted among beliefs or assertions about one's mental states, which we have already considered.

Perhaps it should be stressed again that, in admitting 'I exist' to be, when asserted, necessarily true, its being necessarily true does not in the least depend on the analyticity of the sentence 'I exist.' Of course, it is not analytically true. But then, if we allow that everything is necessarily self-identical, we can see that identities like 'Cicero = Tully' are, when true, necessarily true—though such identities, employing only proper names, cannot be plausibly construed as analytically true. Their truth—hence, their being necessarily true—depends exclusively on sameness of reference. In short, neither 'I exist' nor 'Cicero = Tully' may be said to be necessarily true for either syntactical or semantical reasons: the one depends on the condition of someone's asserting it; and the other depends on considerations of reference.

3. Radical and Methodological Doubt

If we think of doubt and certainty as the polar limits of a continuum, we shall find ourselves obliged to admit that logical certainty that conforms to infallibility, omniscience, or indubitability, for whatever variable scope may be claimed for it, cannot convincingly be attributed to men. The question arises whether, at the other extreme, logical doubt can ever be overcome. And that issue turns out to be decidedly different.

The usual argument against radical doubt, that is, doubt that is logically relevant to a given (or any given) belief but that cannot, in principle, be satisfactorily answered or resolved, is simply that any logical doubt—precisely in being relevant to the truth of p or to the status of S's knowledge or justified belief that p—must be conceptually linked with formulable grounds for removing that doubt. Doubts arise, as has been said, distributively and, we may add, determinately. The general complaint that "it is possible that we may yet be wrong" when no determinate basis for doubt may be provided is either a pathological doubt or else not a doubt at all but a reminder (perhaps) that the belief in question concerns a contingent state of affairs or registers some similar consideration. When, therefore, all of S's determinate empirical doubts are satisfactorily resolved, S is in a state of empirical certainty. Now, of course, it is entirely possible that S be in a state of empirical certainty regarding p, at time t, and that S be in a state of empirical doubt regarding p, at time t' (later than t). This merely means that an additional logical doubt has occurred or has been presented to S at t'. To the extent to which it is impossible to formulate all logically relevant doubts regarding p, it is impossible to foreclose on S's being in a state of empirical doubt regarding p at any t' later than t (when S is in a state of empirical certainty regarding p). But, surely, we can never, at any given time, be logically certain (infallibly, or in the sense of omniscience) that all relevant logical doubts bearing on p or on one's grounds for believing that p have been collected. At best, we can only be certain that the empirical doubts that are collected form a sufficient range (given the normative preferences of a community of inquirers) with respect to which belief may be tested, in order to qualify as knowledge or justified belief. Since infallibility and omniscience are impossible, we cannot eliminate a certain informality in speaking of logical certainty—just as we cannot eliminate a corresponding informality in speaking of knowledge and justified belief. This means, of course, that if we speak of logical certainty's being ascribable to agents, then, as has been said, such a state is fully compatible with the agent's being in a state of doubt both before and after being certain—with regard to the same belief.

We had already noted, at the outset, that doubt and certainty, in any sense in which they relevantly bear on cognitive claims, must be informed by our theories of what serve as adequate grounds for ascribing knowledge and for justifying beliefs. They are, therefore, significantly theory-laden notions, constrained by larger conceptual commitments regarding the limits of knowledge. What we can doubt and what we can be certain of, fall, on pain of incoherence,

within the boundaries of possible knowledge. Hence, the presuppositions of knowledge are the presuppositions as well of logical
doubt and logical certainty. For example, the admission of a public world, both a world that we can share by means of a common
language (and common concepts) and a language that we can share
in order jointly to make reference to the same features of the
world, is a presupposition of our being capable of doubt and certainty respecting what we believe to be true of the world; for, it is
a presupposition of having knowledge or justified beliefs regarding
the world and of understanding that one or another may have such
knowledge or belief. Consequently, we cannot coherently doubt
whether there is a public world or whether we share a public language in terms of which we can make reference to whatever is in
the world, characterize it, and come to have knowledge of it. Our
doubts, I must insist again, appear only distributively and with respect to quite particular beliefs. That is, the very intelligibility of
doubt itself presupposes our public world and our public language.

There is, however, an exercise that need not reduce to mere
pathological doubt, that concerns precisely what is presupposed by
our being able to admit and to assess cognitive claims. We may
raise perfectly bona fide empirical doubts about what is presupposed by cognition itself. We fall into incoherence only when we
doubt what is actually presupposed by any cognitive endeavor—
minimally, by doubting that we share a public world and a public
language. But where the issue is itself controversial, it is hopeless
to deny that legitimate doubts may be raised. Here, however, the
test of legitimacy lies with the very coherence of admitting cognition together with alternative theories of the conditions under
which cognition is alleged to be possible. Thus, for instance, it is
less obvious that some particular ontology must be embraced in
order to provide for cognitive inquiry than that there must be a
public world that we share and can have knowledge of. This
means, therefore, that solipsism appears to be incoherent on the
admission of knowledge of the world, whereas it is arguable only
on more remote grounds that idealism or dualism or materialism

is incompatible with the admission that we have knowledge of the world. We may doubt the truth of determinate ontologies, but we cannot (coherently) be said to doubt that we share a determinate world.

Also, we must be careful not to mingle doubts of the two sorts indicated. It is one thing to doubt, for determinate reasons, whether something is the case—assuming that knowledge is possible; it is quite another to "doubt" whether knowledge is possible. The first marks a bona fide doubt; the second does not. The second is incoherent, since it presupposes that the question itself can be understood and thus grasped as an item of knowledge. Here is the clue to defeating radical skepticism; for the very formulation of the alleged radical doubt, when grasped, provides a counterinstance to its own query. On the other hand, doubts may be raised about the conditions under which knowledge is possible—without casting the very possibility of knowledge into doubt—and these form a distinct and profound inquiry. If, following historical precedent, we speak here of methodological doubt, we shall have to admit that it is incoherent to raise a question as to whether we (one—for the issue requires a solipsistic form) are not always deceived by an Evil Demon; otherwise—and harmlessly—we may merely christen our public world a Deception, preferring to speak of ulterior realities, which, ironically, cannot be understood save on the condition of admitting our language and our world.

We may conclude, then, that neither radical certainty (in the sense of infallibility and omniscience) nor radical doubt are logical states ascribable to human agents. But the arguments sustaining these findings are of noticeably different sorts. For, with respect to certainty, we need ask ourselves only whether there are any eligible instances of knowledge for which there are no conceivable grounds for doubt; and, with respect to doubt, we must ask ourselves what the conditions are on which knowledge itself is possible. In this sense, doubt is the deeper matter. And, in fact, denying infallibility and omniscience, we have found it necessary to construe certainty in terms of norms governing the resolution of determinate doubts. Justifying certainty presupposes cognitively accessible procedures for determining what is the case and what is not; but eliminating (radical) doubt cannot, coherently, be made to rest on distributively employed cognitive procedures: it is to explicate what, ontologically, is entailed in cognition itself—*a fortiori,* in the putatively intelligible doubt in question. Alternatively put, the objection to the radical skeptic is a transcendental argument that takes both a categorical and a dialectical form. Categorically, the skeptic is defeated in that the intelligibility of his thesis presupposes *some* determinate form of cognition with respect to a public world that is determinately there; dialectically, the skeptic is defeated just to the extent that whatever he challenges as being not verifiable or confirmable (as, for instance, that physical objects exist, or that they exist unperceived) proves, on inspection and relative to the conceptual system he challenges and wishes to modify, to be actually presupposed by the intelligibility of his own maneuver. There seem to be no other grounds for a possible counter-challenge. Thus, the issues of doubt and certainty serve to inform us of the underlying interdependence of our inquiries into the nature of knowledge (and of our principal cognitive sources), of existence, and of linguistically informed psychological states; and, in doing so, they confirm the sense in which philosophical theories proposed in one sector of inquiry may be assessed in terms of their compatibility and convergence with whatever is required or may most promisingly be proposed for seemingly independent inquiries.

IV

EXISTENCE & REALITY

The puzzle about what we mean when we speak of something's existence quite naturally arises when we consider that existence does not appear to be a property of any familiar sort —so that the difference, say, between actual and imaginary hundred dollar bills cannot be supposed to depend on the possession or absence of some particular property (existence); imaginary and actual hundred dollar bills are surely not merely different species of hundred dollar bills (comparable, say, to different species of dogs). Again, not only is it difficult to think of existence as a property of this sort but also we should find it difficult to specify a faculty (like the senses, perhaps) by the use of which we could reliably decide the presence or absence of such a property. But we need to be clear about the meaning of 'exists' for at least the reason that every coherent account of knowledge presupposes that we are in touch, by means of the senses or otherwise, with one, common world and presupposes that what belongs to that world exists.

The things we talk about, the things designated by the terms of our language, the things we refer to, are impressively diverse.

Notably, we speak about physical objects, numbers, impossibilities, imaginary persons, mental states, qualities, and the like. And in so speaking, we are inclined to say both that we cannot refer to what does not exist at all and that, though we refer to them, many of the things we refer to (centaurs, for instance) do not exist and never have existed. This suggests an equivocation on 'exists' and its cognate expressions, the explication of which confirms that sentences like 'Santa Claus does not exist' or 'There was at least one person who was loyal to Don Quixote but neither he nor Quixote ever existed' are not self-contradictory. In short, we use 'exists' and its cognates (including the quantifiers of formal logic) to convey mere reference—trivially, what we are talking about exists in the sense that we are talking about it ('exists$_1$')— and yet what we are talking about need not actually exist, need not actually be able to be found in the real world ('exists$_2$'). Once having made this distinction, constraints of different sorts may be placed on what we should admit we refer to and what we should admit is real or actually exists. So, for instance, it is reasonable to hold that we cannot refer to what is logically impossible (square circles, for instance) and that nothing can be said actually to exist that is logically impossible. Clearly, whatever actually exists must be capable of being referred to, but it is dubious to insist, in the face of widespread practice, that we cannot refer to what does not actually exist: there appear to be no obvious grammatical differences between sentences about the actual kings of France and sentences about the mythical heroes of ancient Greece.

Furthermore, in speaking of what actually exists, we should insist that what exists exists in the same sense of 'exists,' exists in the same real world. But this requires that, for whatever we admit exists, we shall have to distinguish between the sense of 'exists' and the criteria by reference to which the existence of different kinds of things may be established. Thus, for instance, if perceivable things are said to exist precisely in that they are perceivable, things that are in principle imperceptible—if such be admitted —cannot be confirmed as existing, on perceptual grounds. And when we consider whether, say, numbers exist, we find that our criteria must be of quite different kinds, since if numbers are said to exist they cannot be supposed to be found in this or that sector of the world, however temporally or spatially identified, can at best only be said to be or to be real. There is, therefore, a difference—that bears in an important way on the special claims of ontology—between expressions like 'is (to be found) in the room' and 'is real' that obliges us to distinguish between criteria normally used in confirming perceptual claims or other claims that depend on the use of faculties by which what exists in some sector of the world is ascertained and those criteria (so-called ontic or ontological criteria) by the use of which we claim to ascertain what there is in the world, what is simply real. Inquiries of this second sort inevitably infect those of the first but they may be distinguished relative to whatever is admitted to be true respecting those of the first sort; also, different ontologies, different accounts of what is simply real, may be fitted to whatever is said to be true about things identified in this or that sector of the world.

These distinctions once provided, it proves to be both plausible and defensible to hold that existence—in the sense of actual existence—is a predicate of some sort. On analysis, it proves to be a relational predicate of a special nature, whose use depends on satisfying the condition that whatever we refer to and whatever properties may be ascribed to what we refer to are also able to be known to be true of what exists. (We need not suppose this characterization to be circular.) The criteria we prefer, by which this formal condition may be made effective, are, minimally, those that yield coherence and adequate scope for all our discourse about the public world we share and, maximally, those that accord with variable ontological tastes.

1. Referents and Existents

One of the most strategic and much-misunderstood questions in the philosophical armory asks whether or not we ought to construe 'exists' as a predicate. It is not a question that can be answered merely Yes or No, for there is no obviously straightforward way in which the question can be met. Answers are bound to be proposals rather, that justify themselves in terms of certain large-scale economies and the avoidance of avoidable distortion in the handling of central considerations. The question, I should say, is emphatically not to be taken in the sense in which one might wonder whether real hundred dollar bills and imaginary hundred dollar bills are species of a common genus and, therefore, share the essential properties of hundred dollar bills or may share some additional non-essential property (for instance, being torn or being worn) but differ in that the one species possesses the additional property of existing and the other lacks it. 'Real' and 'imaginary' do not, in any obvious sense, designate distinctive properties of this sort—perceivable properties, for example, that may be selectively attributed—for, for any *such* property (excluding the putative properties of being real and being imaginary or others that may be said to entail or preclude existence), one may conceive that a real hundred dollar bill and an imaginary hundred dollar bill may be said to have *it,* and imaginary hundred dollar bills are not a *kind* of hundred dollar bill (marked by the differentia of being imaginary) but only the absence or non-existence of hundred dollar bills (having whatever determinate properties we may assign). But even this naive reading of the question focusses attention correctly on the extraordinary difficulty of specifying the sense in which, speaking of what we conceive to have these or those properties, we ask whether it exists or not or whether there exists something conforming to our conception.

The following, I think, are among the most general considerations affecting our question. For one thing, any solution may be judged to be relatively strong if it is consistent with a rock-bottom principle of philosophical sanity, namely, that we are all in touch with one, common world primarily by way of sentient experience; hence, if possible, we should opt for a univocal sense of 'exists' that answers to this consideration. Secondly, the question of existence is inseparable from the analysis of the use of singular refer-

ring expressions, which are, *par excellence,* devices for indicating
what does exist, and of the use of general terms that are taken to
designate classes of existent things. Thirdly, the question should
be explored in such a way that its resolution can accommodate coherently and naturally whatever independent findings may be collected respecting how we determine what things actually exist;
here, the semantic analysis of 'exists' will have to be fitted to epistemological and ontological requirements. And finally, answers to
the question may reasonably be expected to permit a relatively
smooth reading of the entire range of occurrence of 'exists' and its
cognates in natural languages, without disallowing—for demonstrable advantage—technical proposals that depart here and there
from ordinary grammatical intuitions. In this respect, the analysis
of 'exists' is a very paradigm of philosophical practice.

The point of these considerations is simply that only by linking
an analysis of 'exists' to the substantive issues regarding cognition
will it be possible to assess the competence of any particular thesis. It is, for instance, entirely possible to say that whatever we
may refer to exists, in the sense, trivially, that we do refer to *what*
we refer to, that we are talking about what we are talking about.
So, if I refer to the number four, the number four exists—there is
a number such that it is the square of the first prime number
larger than one (but there is no number such that it is the square
of a prime number larger than one and smaller than two). Similarly, I may refer to Othello as the husband of Desdemona in
Shakespeare's play *Othello* (but there is no one who is the brother
of Laertes in Shakespeare's *Hamlet*). The important consideration
is that, in so speaking, I exhaust the sense of 'exists' in terms of
reference and predication: whether numbers or fictions exist in
some specifiable sense other than the sense in which we may make
reference to them does not here arise at all. I cannot, therefore,
merely by the admission of a "domain of values" to which I may
make reference, sort out the difference between the nature of
numbers and the nature of fictions and the nature of perceptual
objects and the like. If, for instance, we should want to say that fic-

tional creatures don't exist—for reasons bearing on our theory of what may be found in the world—we may still wish (preserving the usage just employed) to say that we can *refer* to fictional entities: the same is true of whatever we speak of, impossibilities and contradictions, for instance—which it would be an embarrassment to say exist, in any full-blooded sense at all. Let us, then, say that, where we hold that we may think of, or consider, or admit, or refer to, or speak about, whatever we may (in purely grammatical terms) make predications of, we are referring to what "exists$_1$"— which does not, as such, commit us to holding that what we refer to exists in the actual or real world ("exists$_2$," or "really" or "actually exists"). Hence, there is a strong reason for supposing that some additional distinction regarding existence is needed, beyond the merely syntactical features of sentences that correspond to reference ("that of which we are speaking") and predication ("that which we say of it") or is captured by some minimal semantic element that merely reflects these ('there is' or 'there exists' or 'this . . . is'). We *could,* if we wanted to, hold to the minimal sense given—but only at a certain price; *and,* in so doing, we should have removed the question of existence—of what exists$_2$—from the center of philosophical dispute. For, on the alternative considered, referring to anything trivially entails its existence. But we should not have removed the question of *what we ought to admit exists* (exists$_2$)—either of what we ought to admit we may refer to, or of what among what we refer to, exists—bearing on cognitive claims and the palpable differences between numbers and fictions and perceptual objects and the like. The question of whether 'exists' ('exists$_2$') is a predicate, then, is, in reality, the question of how to relate the analysis of existence to the central issues of philosophy, particularly those concerning ontology and cognition.

In fact, to talk about what we ought to admit we refer to, or about what we ought to admit exists among what we refer to, *comes to the same thing.* For, if, on cognitive grounds, we decide that we cannot be referring to Pegasus (even though, on grammatical grounds, it appears that we often refer to Pegasus), because "there is" nothing that instantiates whatever properties would uniquely single out what we allege we are referring to, then in effect we deny reference where we would deny existence; and if we admit that we may refer to what does not exist, then we should be bound to sort out, among the things we refer to, what exists and what does not. Hence, both accounts oblige us to be able to specify the conditions on which we should admit the existence$_2$ of anything. (We cannot fail to notice, of course, the ease with which locutions conveying the sense of 'exist$_1$' are conflated with locutions conveying the sense of 'exist$_2$.' Although this can be avoided—at the price of considerable circumlocution—we may allow the ambiguity if it is understood that we may refer to, or speak about, what does not exist$_2$; alternatively put, what exists$_1$ need not exist$_2$ and questions of what "actually" or "really" exists are questions concerning what exists$_2$.) Hence, just as there may be constraints on what may be said actually to exist, so there may be constraints on what we may actually refer to; but these need not be the same. We may, for instance, admit that we refer to fictions but not to square circles (on the grounds of the logical impossibility of there being anything [in the sense either of 'exists$_1$' or 'exists$_2$'] to which we could refer). And saying this much entails nothing regarding what actually exists (exists$_2$). Hence, there is no difficulty, if a sentence like 'Santa Claus does not exist' be admitted not to be self-contradictory, to allow as well, as not self-contradictory, 'There is (exists$_1$) an x such that x is Santa Claus and x does not exist (exist$_2$).' Alternatively put, the admission of 'exists$_1$' is itself designed to accommodate a familiar idiom at the same time it exposes the inability of that idiom to capture what is essential to our discourse about actual existence. To speak of what exists$_1$ is simply to speak of the *referents* of our discourse; to speak of what exists$_2$ is to speak of what, among those referents, are also (actual) *existents*.

We have, therefore, a choice before us: we may hold that whatever we may refer to, exists$_2$. On the other hand, we may hold that among the things to which we may refer is a subset of things that exist or are actual; in this sense, referring trivially entails existence$_1$ and referring does not as such entail existence$_2$. Schematically, we may allow or refuse inferences from statements like '*Fa*' to '($\exists$ *x*)*Fx*'—with the semantic equivocation on 'exists' noted; the same is true for inferences from '*Fa*' to '($\exists$ *x*)(*x* = *a*).' The ulterior reasons lie with the plausibility both of saying that we cannot refer to "nothing," to what has no existence at all, and of saying that, though we may, in a grammatical sense, refer to them, fictions, imaginary entities, and the like do not exist.

2. Existence and Quantification

Let us consider, in order to canvass the issue effectively, the logical behavior of the following statements:

a) No tame tigers exist.
a') No tutoring centaurs exist.
b) Some tigers are tame.
b') Some centaurs are tutors.
c) Scott wrote *Waverley*.
c') Bellerophon rode Pegasus.

It is reasonable to take a) in such a way that 'tigers' designates a class of existent$_2$ creatures. Hence, it would normally not capture the sense of a) to paraphrase thus: (*x*) (if *x* is a tiger, then *x* is not tame); one wants to say also that the paraphrase must at least be a conjunction of the universal and the so-called existential generalization, There is (exists$_2$) an *x* such that *x* is a tiger. This is the point, of course, of permitting—as schematized in the traditional Square of Opposition—the inference of existential statements from universal statements. But, since 'centaurs' is normally taken to designate a class of non-existent creatures, it may reasonably be argued that the appropriate paraphrase of a') cannot be a conjunction of the same sort as may be provided for a). For, if the inclusion of a corresponding existential statement conveys that there *exists*$_2$ a centaur, then, *ex hypothesi,* even if a′) were true, its would-be canonical equivalent would be false; and if some conjunction were provided as an equivalent paraphrase, the existential generalization would have to be of the form. There is not [or does not exist$_2$] a *y* such that *y* is a centaur—which is not uniform with the would-be paraphrase for a). Hence, it appears, on the policy suggested, that, although a) and a′) are grammatically quite similar, they must be assigned logically distinct forms in order to preserve the point of their ordinary use. But this is, to some extent, inconvenient or inelegant, since it seems to oblige us to read the English quantifier 'No' in two different ways and in particular to read it in accord with certain antecedent intentional or empirical considerations that cannot be extracted from the mere surface grammar of sentences like a) and a′). Consequently, since if we wish to assert the existence$_2$ of some tigers and deny the existence$_2$ of centaurs other devices are at hand, we may recommend the uniform translation of a) and a′) as universals of the form: for any *x,* if *x* is *F . . .* We should then have construed the English quantifier as functioning univocally and as replaceable by the symbol '(*x*),' and we should have reserved the negative and affirmative force of 'No' and 'All' for other syntactically distinct elements of the canonical translation. We should also then have eliminated the need, at this point, for conceding structural distinctions between sentences like a) and a′) based on considerations of intention or empirical knowledge. But the most important consequence, for our purposes, is simply that the term 'exists' drops out and appears not to be required: the universal generalization, whether in English or in canonical translation, says nothing about existence (existence$_2$) at all. Nevertheless, since there is assumed to be some domain or set of values with respect to which a given universal is true or false, the question of existence$_1$ is embedded in universals (or of existence$_2$, depending on the semantic interpretation of 'exists' and of the notion of a "domain of values"). This provides a reason for disallowing inference from the universal to its corresponding particular and for restricting inferences sketched in the traditional Square to the contradictories alone. But, again, since a) and a′) may be read as signifying that, among the things that exist$_1$ (or exist$_2$)—the domain of reference—there is not to be found . . . , the question of existence$_1$ (or existence$_2$) is embedded in negative existentials (as it is in their corresponding universals). That is, to say '(x) . . .' is to say '$\sim(\exists x)\sim$. . .' Hence, the proposal actually reintroduces the question of existence and still fails to capture the difference between reference to tigers and reference to centaurs.

It would normally be supposed that, in asserting b), one asserts that there exists$_2$ at least one tiger and that that tiger is tame. Here, the English quantifier 'some' is taken to be replaceable by the so-called existential quantifier '$(\exists x)$', whose use is said to convey existence. The trouble is that, preserving uniform translations for grammatically similar sentences, we should have to render a sentence like b′) in the same way as b): thus, $(\exists x)$ (x is a tiger and x is tame); and, $(\exists y)$ (y is a centaur and y is a tutor). Here, we must note that centaurs, after all, do not exist$_2$. And yet, b′) is *true,* for we assume that we are speaking in the context of Greek mythology (ignoring here, for simplicity's sake, questions of tense). We *could* simply take it that the putative paraphrase of b′) is false because it does affirm existence and we might hold that the normal intent of b′) is rendered in such a way as the following: 'Some mythological accounts indicate that some centaurs are tutors.' On this view, the accounts exist (exist$_2$) but centaurs do not; and, although 'centaurs' may be said to occupy an existentially quantified position, the entire sentence is placed in a context of indirect discourse, so that the actual existence of centaurs need not be conceded in conceding the truth of what is said. But although this is a possible maneuver, it can be bought only at the price of replacing given sentences by others that are not remotely equivalent in sense and only at the price of not being able to provide straightforward paraphrases that are uniform for sentences that appear to be grammatically uniform. We could, of course, hold that b′) is true *and* that centaurs do exist but exist in mythology rather than in the real world. That is, we could hold, minimally, that, in existential statements, what is referred to is said to $exist_1$ (uniformly, therefore, for tigers and centaurs) and that centaurs $exist_3$ (in a mythological world) rather than $exist_2$. In that case, either 'exists' and '$(\exists x)$' must both be construed in the sense of '$exists_1$' (which, then, fails to capture the distinction between real and mythological entities), calling for an analysis of what $exists_2$ and of what $exists_3$; or else 'exists' and '$(\exists x)$' will both be construed in the sense of '$exists_2$' (which, then, necessarily makes b') false, though it is ordinarily or at least sometimes read as true); or else either 'exists' and '$(\exists x)$' cannot be thus univocally construed or there are multivocal senses of both (that may be matched) or there are alternative criteria (answering to the actual world, the mythological world, and the like) for the use of 'exists' and '$(\exists x)$' univocally matched in the sense of '$exists_1$.'

One can see that there will be no antecedent limit to the number of relevant worlds, once it is conceded that, although things exist—in the same sense of 'exist'—they nevertheless may populate entirely different worlds (which is, to say the least, to go contrary to one of our original conditions regarding the analysis of 'exists'). Also, the only sense in which the required univocity can be preserved, under the circumstances, is that of '$exists_1$'—which, precisely, raised our original question. Here, we are reminded that the issue of existence is embedded in universal statements (in the sense of '$exists_1$,' '$exists_2$,' or any other semantical interpretation of 'exists') or else, for existential and singular statements, comes to no more than that of reference to the "entities" of some domain or set (that, significantly, may be specified without any linkage to the actual world). We may also denature the force of the existential claim and hold that affirming existence (by way of singular statements and existential generalizations) must be seen as relative to some "domain of discourse": that, for instance, although it is true that some centaurs are tutors, it is true only relative to the domain of mythology and not to the domain of the real world. If this means that 'exists' is merely an ellipsis for 'exists-in-the-real-

world,' 'exists-in-the-world-of-mythology,' and the like, the suggestion has the interesting consequence that it obliges us to equivocate on 'exists.' We could, perhaps, introduce an entire range of
existential quantifiers—'$(\exists x)$,' '$(\exists 'x)$,' '$(\exists ''x)$,' '$(\exists '''x)$,' . . .
—each of which would correspond to the distinct domain of dis-
course in which reference is being made. But this, precisely,
makes it impossible to paraphrase without appealing to prior intentional and empirical (even ontological) information. In any
case, to speak in the alternative ways here suggested is, effectively,
to preclude *nothing* from occupying a referential position or from
serving as a value of a bound variable. This, indeed, has its advantage, just in that it frees the syntax of singular and existential
statements from ulterior cognitive and ontic considerations; but,
having introduced, in various ways, alternative domains of discourse, it also leaves us with the problem of providing criteria by
which to distinguish one from another.

We may put the argument in another way. The question
whether what we are referring to (that, trivially, exists$_1$), exists$_2$, is
an entirely eligible question. *Referring* to something, as in thinking, believing, considering, conjecturing, is intentional in nature
—may be regarded as an intentional act—in the sense in which,
precisely, *what* we are thinking of, that *about* which we are thinking, need not exist (exist$_2$). Consequently, to admit a domain or
set of "entities" to which we may make reference by way of singular and existential statements does not commit us in any way—
unless by an independent convention or constraint—to the existence (in *any* but the trivial sense given) of what we are speaking
about (that is, *that* it is merely what we are speaking about).
Hence, merely to predicate something of something—of something taken to be a member of some range of things—has absolutely nothing to do, as such, with whether what is thus referred
to, exists (exists$_2$). Otherwise, we should never be able to say—
what we want to say—that although Bellerophon rode Pegasus,
neither Bellerophon nor Pegasus ever existed; that though Chiron
tutored Aesculapius, neither Chiron nor Aesculapius existed. We

must be able to preserve reference, whether by singular referring expressions or by general terms, without it being the case that whenever we make reference, what we refer to must exist. Otherwise, what exists—where 'exists' is taken as adequate for all cognitive contexts—can never be specified canonically (by the use of bound variables) unless, ideally, at the end of science or, provisionally and corrigibly, at advanced stages. For instance, proper names occupying what, on syntactical grounds, would normally be a denoting position in a sentence cannot, on syntactical grounds merely, be confirmed as used to refer to anything at all or to anything that exists$_2$. To speak of reparsing names by uniquely satisfied indefinite descriptions presupposes knowing what unique descriptions *whatever is being referred to* satisfies. Consequently, there can be no purely formal basis for replacing proper names purporting to be used referentially, by descriptive expressions: cognitive considerations obtain whether we are referring to what exists$_1$ or to what exists$_2$; proper names can be said to have connotative sense, only (and derivatively) on cognitive assumptions *about* what is being referred to; and where we do not know what is being referred to, or where nothing actually is being referred to, there can be no formal rule for the replacement of a given proper name by any significant descriptive expression at all. In any event, there cannot be a uniform practice for replacing proper names by indefinite descriptions under these different circumstances. Also, even if we admit that whatever is a distinct particular is discernibly distinct, it does not follow that we must be able to provide that property by which whatever is discernibly distinct from everything else can be shown to be such. Hence, to leave uninterpreted whatever property and whatever kind of property we take to single out uniquely any given particular is simply to adopt the principle that whatever is a distinct particular has *some* such property. But this is a concession that may be made (even vacuously) without making reference to anything at all.

Reference, then, is an intentional act, though the "objects" of reference may be treated both extensionally and non-extensionally. And if the act has the same logical properties whether or not we are speaking about what exists$_2$, we cannot convincingly hold that, regarding fictions, we refer to or are speaking about names and descriptions only and, regarding actually existing things, we are speaking about objects by using names and descriptions that designate them. It is sufficient that reference is intentional and may be dyadically construed, so that, although our discourse is "about" these intentional objects and although we may make predications of them—neutrally as far as existence$_2$ is concerned—we cannot be said to be committed, in admitting a "domain of discourse," a "range of values," a "substitution set," a "collection of named objects," or the like, to more than the existence$_1$ of the members of such a domain or set. In fact, all that has been said thus far simply counts against construing quantifiers and their putative equivalents in natural languages as conveying any ontic or existential import at all—except in the trivial sense of 'exists$_1$.' This frees us both to entertain in a fresh way the concept of actual existence and to compare the advantages of alternative interpretations of the quantifiers themselves, without tendentious commitments in advance. Whether the universe is so rich that it may be said to contain unnamed objects or objects not nameable in a finite interval of time or not denumerable or whether, pragmatically, all objects referred to in considering the truth of any quantified statement may be viewed as serially introduced by name by some finite process is neither here nor there; for the question of whether what is thus referred to, exists$_2$ remains unaffected. (It is also true that such alternative interpretations may not yield equivalent results.) But this means, once again, that what we *ought* to admit as values in cognitive contexts depends on the criteria of application of 'existence$_2$.'

3. The Sense and Criteria of 'Exists'

Let us turn to consider the way in which we speak of existent things; for, in effect, this is to fix whatever we wish to capture in some suitable notation.

It is not regularly noticed that, in speaking of what exists (ex-

ists₂), we characteristically shift between remarks about what there
is in this or that restricted sector of the world and about what
there is in the world itself. The shift seems innocent enough, but it
can be made to yield an insight about profoundly different questions concerning what *exists* or what *there is*. If I ask what there is
in this room, I should normally be supposed to have asked what is
to be *found* in the room, what is *located* in the room, what can be
seen, felt, smelled, heard in the room and so on. The answer that
will be given will depend on two distinct considerations. For one
thing, what will be identified will accord with our principles of individuation; perhaps there are two chairs, a lamp, a table, several
magazines, and the like. And for another, the confirmation of
what is said to be present in the room, to be in the room, or to
exist (because it is in the room) will accord with our principles for
validating existential claims; for instance, perhaps the chairs and
the lamp and the like can be seen. Here, certain obvious warnings
are in order. If the principles of individuation are altered, or if
there are alternative such principles that may be consulted, relative to our question, then *what* is said to exist will vary with the
principles selected. If, for example, we do not normally individuate the spatio-temporal parts of chairs and lamps, then in re-
sponding to the question of what there is in the room, it would be
puzzling were someone to reply that there are so many chair-
stages present in the room through a given interval. But it is a
conceivable reply, *if* we may provide for such individuation and if
the principle of such individuation is adapted *to* discourse about
what, for instance, is in this room. On the other hand, if our views
of what can be discriminated by some given mode of sentience or
cognitive capacity can be altered, then, of course, what may be
said to be in the room (or in any suitably selected "sector" of the
world—say, of what may be said to be in the mind) will be variable as well.

We may, to put the matter most briefly, concede a univocal
sense to 'exists' if we distinguish between the sense and criteria of
'exists,' much in the way in which we speak of the use of 'good'

and similar expressions. It is entirely eligible to speak of determining whether this or that exists—say, perceivable objects and
sub-microscopic unobservables—by different means, without in
the least wishing to deny that such entities exist, if they do exist,
in the real world. The formulation is, in fact, redundant, which
suggests usefully that the question of whether something-or-other
exists concerns the specification of suitable criteria or grounds for
determining existence. The "real world," then, is simply the "domain of discourse" within which a certain preferred set of such
criteria is decisive; or, it is the context provided by whatever satisfies such criteria with respect to which further questions about
what else exists may be raised. On this view, it is unnecessary to
generate questions about the relationship between different
"worlds," unless to speak thus is merely a picturesque way of
querying the conceptual connections between alternative sets of
such criteria—applying, say, to the "real world" and to "fiction"
or "mythology" or "possible worlds" or the like. But not only may
such alternative criteria distinguish the real world from the
"world" of fiction (or, say, from the "world" of numbers, if one
wishes to enforce the distinction); they also may serve to distinguish, notably with respect to the real world, between what may
be said to exist in some particular sector of the world and what
may be said to exist *simpliciter*.

Consider that we may refer to *what* we imagine to exist and to
what we imagine to have such and such properties. Here, the
question of existence does not arise, once we have specified the
import of expressions like 'imagine to exist' and the relationship
between identifying imaginary things and identifying real things.
But regarding what there is in this or that part of the world and
what there is (or what there is in the world) is a decidedly more
complex matter. For, it is conceivable that what there is cannot be
specified unless it can be identified as being in this or that sector
of the world. *If* numbers, for example, exist, then although there
may be criteria of some sort for determining what numbers there
are, we could not plausibly provide relevant criteria for determin-

ing where in the world (or when) numbers may be found to be. And if we insist that only what exists in some sector of the world can be said to exist, then numbers, classes, and other abstract entities will be said not to exist at all. It will hardly matter, apart from considerations of ontological taste, since *if* they exist, numbers and classes (possibly, then, pains, thoughts, images) will be identifiable as existent things on the strength of criteria significantly different from those employed in speaking of perceptible things; and if they are denied existence, it will be possible still to refer to them. Apart, then, from the rather special challenge posed by numerical entities and the like, to say that something is real normally is to say that it exists in some sector of the world. If a chair, for instance, is to be found in a certain room, then it is or exists there and, for that reason, is real. But it is also conceivable that, at least provisionally, one may concede that a chair exists because, say, it can be seen or found in a given room and yet insist that *chairs do not exist (or are not real)*. The reason will, perhaps, be of the following sort. Given the macroscopic distinctions provided by our language, it may be confirmed that, indeed, there is a chair in a certain room; but, urging a certain (alleged) ontological economy, one may insist that when we speak of chairs we are actually speaking of what may suitably be (eliminatively) reduced to the properties of sub-atomic particles and that only such particles exist, that only such particles are real. We may, that is, distinguish between what is said to exist in this or that sector of the world (relying on such epistemically relevant sources of information as our senses) and what is said to exist *simpliciter* (relying on certain preferred ontological rules for reinterpreting, say, perceptual information). The seeming paradox, then, may depend on a choice of priorities.

In any case, it is sufficient for our purpose to notice that questions of what there is may differ from questions of what there is (or exists) in a given sector of the world, that sometimes what is said to exist in a given sector may be denied existence or reality *simpliciter* (as when one says, somewhat paradoxically, that pains exist when they are felt but that there are no such things as pains), that sometimes what is said to exist *simpliciter* cannot intelligibly be said to exist in this or that sector of the world (as when one claims that numbers are real entities), and that what may be referred to, need not exist at all. It goes without saying that, on any comprehensive view, we should want a coherent account of the various sorts of asymmetry indicated—which sets constraints on ontological alternatives. But these considerations, important as they are, merely complicate relationships among the criteria by appeal to which we decide whether, in respects given, this or that may be said to exist or said to exist in a certain sector of the world. It is fair to say that in a completely articulated theory of reality, serviced by a language adjusted to discoveries of the sort indicated, any discrepancies between what is said to exist in a given sector and what is said to exist *simpliciter* will have been eliminated. But there is no question that we do not possess any non-controversial criteria for determining existence *simpliciter* (that is, the "real" entities of the world). For instance, "to be is to be perceived" fails to accommodate the continued existence of what is actually (on any consistent account) unperceived, fails to accommodate the existence of perceivers as such, fails to accommodate the existence of what is not open to perception at all. Similarly, "to be is to be the value of a bound variable" fails to accommodate the non-existence of what may be such a value, fails to accommodate the indecisiveness of mere canonical formulae that themselves depend on antecedent rules of relevant and admissible paraphrase, fails to accommodate the fact that we merely register by means of such formulae (if we wish) what we already know regarding what things exist. Alternatively put, we appear not to possess any plausible set of necessary and sufficient conditions for determining what exists *simpliciter:* all such conditions appear to reflect partisan tastes. Particular ontologies remain defeasible in terms of internal coherence and compatibility with such independent conditions as bear on the grammatical flexibility of our language and on the conditions for confirming whatever is admitted

to be part of the body of our knowledge. But that means that alternative and incompatible ontologies (so designated on the provision of a suitable criterion) may, if severally consistent with such
minimal conditions, be justifiably collected like so many postage
stamps. The prospect of a stricter "science" of ontology that dis-
confirms competing ontologies in favor, finally, of what "there
(really) is" awaits the convincing specification of conditions adequate to the task. Where it is lacking, we may concede that if one
ontology may coherently be fitted to some antecedent range of
truths, then alternative ontologies may, with ingenuity, be so fitted
as well. Here, we do not confirm one ontology as against others
—on the evidence—as much as confirm that ontological alternatives are so linked that the viability of any one (whether with regard to one's own language or with regard to some alien native's)
entails the viability of others. Skepticism, therefore, is inappropriate in ontology. In any event, we may helpfully remember that
we lack a distinct cognitive faculty by which to discriminate reality, in the sense in which, by sight, we discriminate colors and
shapes.

4. Existence Construed as a Predicate

But our question remains, Ought existence to be construed as a
predicate? And now, it seems entirely fair to say Yes—but if it is,
it is a very special one. Suppose, to suggest a promising maneuver,
I ask you what a centaur is. You answer that it is a creature of
flesh and blood, with a horse's body and legs, and a man's head
and upper torso and arms. And, you add, it is an imaginary creature. Clearly, you have used the characterizing concepts in a way
that is neutral to whether or not centaurs exist: you have added
that a creature of *that description* is a creature that does not exist,
is merely imagined to exist. It is true that the characterizing concepts used are normally used in speaking of things that do exist,
but the meaning of 'creature of flesh and blood,' 'horse's body and
legs,' and the rest does not entail existence; the meaning of these

concepts is quite distinct from the criteria by which we may determine whether, *indifferently* to whether what we are referring to
exists$_2$ or is imaginary, it is true to say that it is (exists$_1$) a creature of the description given. It may even be claimed that it is a
defining property of centaurs that they are imaginary—which
complicates any would-be attempt to distinguish between essential
or defining traits and the "property" of existence. Nevertheless, if
'exists' designates a property, it designates a relational property of
a peculiar sort. For, consider that it cannot be a relational property like that of being to the right of something or to the left of
something. If something *that exists* is to the right or left of something, then, trivially, it exists occupying that relationship; and if
something imaginary is to the right or left of something, then, trivially again, it is imaginary though it occupies that relationship.
The same is true of non-relational properties, of course.

Let us say, then, that existence is a property of the following
kind, viz., it is the property something (in the sense of 'exists$_1$')
has in being veridically accessible to a certain set of criteria (the
criteria of existence$_2$)—that is, it is the property of satisfying
those criteria. In saying this, I mean that it is a relational property, first of all; but, secondly, I mean that it is a property that
things have only in virtue of a certain condition satisfied by whatever other properties and relationships things may have. If, for instance, a dagger to which we refer has a certain length and, in
having that length, has it in such a way that it has the relationship
of being veridically accessible to the criteria of existence (say, is
perceivable), then the dagger exists and is real; and if it does not,
then it is imaginary or fictional or some such thing. Furthermore,
to say that the relationship in question is one of veridical accessibility to certain criteria, is to say only that the thing in question
(the dagger) exists or is real if and only if it could satisfy those
criteria. If actually to perceive a dagger entails that there is a real
dagger to be perceived, then the thing referred to (the dagger) possesses the relational property of veridical accessibility to the criteria of existence (it satisfies the criteria). We normally consider

whether things exist if we are in a position to assert that they exist; that is, we normally construe the matter in some cognitively determinate way. But this is quite unnecessary, since many things may exist that we know nothing of. Here, then, we see the convergence of epistemological and ontological considerations. If 'exists' is univocal, then whatever exists that we know nothing of, and whatever we may justifiably claim to know exists, do exist— in the same sense of 'exists' and in the same real world. Nevertheless, although the existence of anything does not depend on our knowledge of its existence, *that* it exists *is* nothing more than its accessibility to preferred criteria of existence, that is, its accessibility to perception, inference, and the like. Consequently, the relationship in question concerns the capacity of a thing to be related in a certain way to beings capable of knowledge. (Also, to say this much is to dispose of any worry that the condition given need be construed in a viciously circular way.) This is the point of such familiar formulas as "To be is to be perceived" (which is inadequate) or "Pains exist insofar as they are felt" (which is misleading).

One of the important by-benefits of our formulation is the exposure of the weakness of (even if there is no logical fault in) the Ontological Argument. For, whether that God exists follows from the premise of the conceivability of a being than which there can be none greater depends entirely on whether conceivability itself may convincingly serve as the very criterion of existence, veridical accessibility to which is sufficient to establish God's existence. Even if necessary existence is said to be a perfection, along with omnipotence, omniscience, "omnibenevolence," we should have to admit an equivocation on 'exists,' since to ask whether God or anything else exists (holding univocally to what has been posited as the sense of 'exists') is to ask whether what, *of which this or that may be predicated* (including the perfections), *is* veridically accessible to the criteria of existence. The statement, 'It is possible that it is necessary that God exists' is false (hence, is necessarily false). Existence, therefore, cannot be a perfection of anything—

cannot be a property necessary to anything. It is a second-order relational property, a consequential property, that whatever we designate or refer to may, contingently, possess. Whatever necessarily exists (as possessing a perfection) may exist; but whether there exists anything (exists$_2$) that necessarily exists (now a distinct perfection) depends on veridical accessibility to criteria that, in the nature of the case, cannot be satisfied by the inspection of predicates alone or by the inspection of the *idea* of a necessarily existing being. Alternately put, it is simply not incoherent to ask whether there *is* anything that necessarily exists; or, if God's conceivability entails His existence, the argument is won by fiat alone, thereby rendered *sui generis* and made to rely on an otherwise altogether dubious criterion—that the intelligibility of a certain idea entails the existence$_2$ of that of which it is the idea. So it is the compression of the Ontological Argument—not its power—that stupifies. In context, there is no clear difference between speaking of a *sui generis* argument for establishing God's existence and of the arbitrariness of the criterion on which God's existence alone is established: the epithets merely reflect alternative ontological tastes.

It needs also to be remarked that some philosophical traditions speak of God and *Dingen-an-sich* as of entities that are unknowable in principle. But this is incoherent if what is meant is that God and particular *Dingen-an-sich* do exist; and if what is meant is only that certain entities that we know to exist we know to be not accessible, say, to perceptual discrimination, the concession is clearly not a relevant one.

5. *Ontology and Science*

Obviously, the definition of 'exists' leaves entirely unresolved the ulterior question of what exists and what justifies the preference of these or those criteria for determining what there is or what exists *simpliciter*. But this is the special strength of our proposal, that it permits the pursuit of those matters in a way that is as neutral as possible to alternative ontologies and in a way that is altogether free of the tendentious constraints of well-entrenched notational schemes.

There is only one indispensable constraint on such ontologies, namely, that, as has already been said, we are all in touch with one, common world primarily by way of sentient experience. Obviously, this condition affects the range of eligible ontologies, affects therefore the selection of suitable criteria of existence. Its defense can be undertaken only in terms of disallowing radical skepticism and solipsism and of preserving the publicity of the real world and at least the (public) intelligibility of what is not in every relevant respect publicly accessible—as, discriminations in private experience and distinctions regarding imaginary "worlds." For, any attempt to verify that there is a real world, by way of satisfying the criteria of existence, cannot fail to be questionbegging. To verify that something exists$_2$ entails that there exists$_2$ a public world; but to verify that something exists$_2$ presupposes that there exists$_2$ a public world. Justifying the attempt to verify any relevant claim must be considered in terms of the presupposition of a public world—hence, in terms of the problem of skepticism, not of evidence; but verifying *any* relevant claim draws us on merely to questions of evidence—that preclude skepticism.

Given this minimal condition, we are bound to admit as eligible alternatives whatever theories concede a public world, speaking either of what exists in some sector of that world (empirical science) or of what exists *simpliciter* (ontology). Consequently, to the extent that, in an idealized account, what exists may be restricted to whatever exists in some sector of the world, science and ontology may be regarded as the same inquiry—distinctions being made in terms of relative abstraction and generality only; and to the extent that incompatible, alternative ontologies may be compatibly generated for any true account of what exists in some sector of the world, ontology may be regarded as a distinct, second-order investigation of the findings of science. In either case, the meaning of 'exists' will remain univocal though criteria vary. And, since the admission of a public world is inescapable for both these alternatives, quarrels about what *is* or is *real* will at least implicitly and provisionally concede what we know to *exist in some sector of the world*. Beyond these considerations, what is needed is a reasoned defense of the criteria by which existential claims and claims entailing existential claims are confirmed or disconfirmed.

In any case, the concept of existence as a second-order relational predicate is entirely flexible enough to accommodate whatever comprehensive theories we may invent regarding the nature of the world. For, although existence is a property of things, it is not a property that can be sensed or perceived or discriminated in any way in which the other properties of things may be discriminated; it is, on the contrary, a property that things possess in virtue, precisely, of their being perceptible or sensible or thinkable or inferable (in accord with certain preferred appraisive criteria). An object referred to, whose properties are, say, actually perceived, is an object that actually exists; also, an object whose properties, though not perceived, are nevertheless perceivable, exists—in the same sense of 'exists.' Also, in saying that existence is a second-order (consequential) predicate, no more is meant than what is naïvely conveyed in saying that the question of existence may arise only when we are clear about what we are referring to and what we are prepared to predicate of it from some appropriate (first-order) range. This is the sense in which existence both adds and fails to add something to the concept of a thing. To say that something exists is to say that a thing of a certain description is related in a certain determinate way to the cosmic system we call the real world. From this point of view, nothing can be said merely to exist. The remark must be an ellipsis for saying that things exist in that they can be perceived, sensed, thought, inferred, and the like. Hence, we may say that the bare predicate 'exists' designates a determinable relational property of the sort specified and that our theories of what confirms existence provide us with the determinate forms of existence. But this confirms once again the significant convergence of scientific, epistemological, and ontological interests and the prospect, given competing theories at every level, of competing notions of what it is to exist and of what in fact exists.

A few details remain. It may well be, for instance, that one is tempted to admit the necessity of cognitive criteria of existence but to deny, at the same time, that 'exists' is, or need be construed as, a relational predicate of the sort posited. If the economy could be worked, it would be entirely in accord with the foregoing argument: we should, then, speak of a centaur's existing if our criteria of existence were appropriately satisfied, without speaking of existence as one of its properties. But consider only that 'being perceivable' is normally viewed as designating a property of things *and* that perceivability serves as a criterion for determining whether something of this or that description does exist. That is, being perceivable is, if it is a property, a second-order relational property of just the sort existence is, except that it specifies the kind of criteria on which the property of existence is veridically ascribed; the counterpart predicate, for imaginary things, is 'imagined to be perceivable' or 'imagined to be perceived.' Consequently, there is an important run of usage that supports the thesis. Also, if 'exists' is not captured quantificationally *and if* we wish to assign it a syntactical role in our canon, it appears to be both economical and fitting to construe it as a predicate.

A further, and final, consideration may be helpful. Santa Claus —the Santa Claus we refer to—is an imaginary person. We may say that he is essentially imaginary, in the sense that were any actually existent person alleged to be one and the same person as Santa Claus, the claim would, necessarily, be false. There is, from this point of view, no "possible world" (no possibility with respect to the actual world) in which Santa Claus could actually exist. Correspondingly, Socrates is a person that actually existed. We may say that the person we refer to, in referring to Socrates, is a person that is essentially actual, in the sense that were any imaginary person alleged to be one and the same person as Socrates, the claim would, necessarily, be false—although it is possible that

Socrates cease to exist (actually) and even that Socrates never existed at all (that is, the man who actually did exist). When we refer *to* Santa Claus, we refer to an essentially imaginary creature; and when we refer *to* Socrates, we refer to an essentially actual creature. Socrates does not necessarily exist, but referring to Socrates is referring to a creature who is essentially actual. (That is, to say that Socrates is essentially actual is to say that it is possible that he not exist but it is impossible that he be imaginary [only imagined to exist].) If it turns out that Socrates did not ever exist (that there was no creature who was the actual Socrates), then, of course, some imaginary Socrates cannot be one and the same with the actual Socrates; but this is not to say that a creature we imagine to exist (Socrates) cannot actually exist. I can imagine that there was, in ancient Greece, a certain gadfly philosopher married to the woman Xantippe, and that *that* man was Socrates. (There is, clearly, a possible equivocation on the expression 'imagine to exist'.)

Also, although Socrates is essentially actual, it is not convincing to hold that all of his properties are essential properties: it is surely not essential that Socrates died of hemlock. On the other hand, respecting imaginary creatures, it is quite difficult to distinguish between essential and inessential properties—even where properties ascribed (construed on the model of the actual world) appear to be incompatible with one another (for instance, that Santa Claus has a very long beard and that Santa Claus has a very short beard). The easy way out with imaginary creatures is simply to disallow the contrast and to speak, rather, of Santa Claus's having the property answering to its being the case that some say he has a very long beard and some say he has a very short beard.

It is possible, then, that actual creatures not exist and it is possible that actual creatures not possess the properties they possess (unless these are essential) or possess properties they do not possess (unless these are incompatible with their essential properties). And to talk about these possibilities may be construed as talking about "possible worlds" other than the actual world. But there are, as we have seen, critical constraints on what may be said to exist (in the merely referential sense) in the actual and / or some possible (but not actual) world. Any allegedly possible world in which Socrates is said to exist must be the world in which he actually exists, since Socrates is essentially actual; and any possible world in which Socrates is said merely to be imagined to exist (to be imaginary) is not a world in which *our* Socrates could be referred to at all. That is, there is no possibility that *the actual Socrates* is an imaginary creature. I may, of course, imagine or refer to King Arthur and wonder whether he is actual or only an imaginary creature. Existence, then, as the relational property it is claimed to be, is, necessarily, a contingent property. But, although it is contingent, it is an essential property, in the sense that what is actual cannot be imaginary and what is imaginary, actual (for instance, if Socrates is perceivable, then he cannot be merely imagined to be, but not actually to be, perceivable). If Socrates is actual, then *some* properties of a certain range that may be veridically ascribed to him will be perceivable, as opposed to being merely imagined to be perceivable. I may wonder, being uncertain about the referent of a particular account, whether what is being referred to (in a story-relative way) is actual or imaginary: no referent can be both actual and imaginary though I may be uncertain which it is.

If these arguments have force, then there is a critical respect in which the analysis of 'exists' must be brought into accord with cognitive questions, in particular, with questions regarding how we come to know of the existence and properties of whatever we may refer to. And this, again, is preserved by construing 'exists' as a predicate. Alternatively put, the short argument holds that if reference is intentional, we may refer to what does not (actually) exist; and that if we may do so, there is no way to capture existence quantificationally; and that if there is not, there is no viable alternative to that of construing 'exists' as a predicate.

V

IDENTITY & INDIVIDUATION

We suppose that everything is identical with itself and that whatever is true of something is true of it. The remark seems to be a truism and its denial, self-contradictory. But there are complications both because things are sometimes identified under alternative descriptions or in accord with different idioms and because relationships other than identity are not always easy to distinguish from it. In the first respect, it is difficult to deny that constraints may affect characterizations of what, putatively, is one and the same thing though identified in terms appropriate to different idioms (as for instance in speaking of lightning and patterns of electrical discharges, as one and the same). In the second respect, identity and the corresponding use of 'is' must be distinguished particularly from the concepts of spatio-temporal continuity and composition and their grammatical features. As it happens, these three concepts, characteristically conveyed by distinctive uses of the verb 'to be,' have applications that both intersect with, and are independent of, those associated with one another. For instance, questions of continuity do not concern such identities as that of 7 and 5 + 2 but they do concern such identities as that of Alexander the Great considered as a man leading the Macedonian armies and Alexander the Great considered as the boy Aristotle taught: the spatio-temporal continuity between the man-phase and the boy-phase of Alexander is characteristic of entities of a certain sort that persist through change. On the other hand, spatio-temporal continuities may obtain in spite of the fact that what is identified for given continuities need not be phases of one and the same thing (for instance, as when a chair is fashioned out of a tree). Similarly, things may persist as one and the same though their composition change (as when a tooth is repaired with silver amalgam); and the material out of which something is made may remain the same though something be fashioned out of it other than what it originally was (as in playing with clay).

Puzzles regarding identity run deeper. They may, conceivably, arise merely because of the grammatical features of sentences in which, incidentally, questions of identity are at stake (as for instance in the context of believing that Cicero denounced Cataline while not believing that Tully denounced Cataline, though Cicero and Tully are one and the same man). Or, they may arise, as has been remarked, because what may be predicated of a thing may sometimes be restricted by the description (and the idiom associated with it) in terms of which it is identified: thus, even if human beings were said to be identical with a certain congeries of molecules, ascriptions of intelligence or humor could not meaningfully be made of a collection of molecules. But, in addition to these obvious complexities, problems regarding identity confront us wherever spatio-temporal discontinuities or decomposition obtain (as in dismantling a boat). For there, anomalies characteristically arise and no settled rules for determining what is one and the same are forthcoming: reidentification appears to be informal, often linked to our interests and intentions, and determined rather more by decision than by finding. Normally, when we speak of identity (often termed strict identity) or when we speak of spatio-temporal continuities and discontinuities relative to what is one and the same through change, we require the use of terms designating sorts of things (so-called sortals) with respect to which some particular thing is identified as a thing of that sort and the same thing of that sort, under altered circumstances. It is clear that spatio-temporal continuity does not require that whatever is continuous with something, in the respect intended, need be either of the same sort or the same particular of any given sort; and composition precludes identity though not the possibility that what anything is composed of and that which is composed—in one sense, at least—may be of the same sort.

So-called theoretical identities are of a mixed nature. Sometimes, they are taken to be strict identities, by which is meant that what is thus characterized is one and the same thing of a given sort. The paradigms of strict identity (as in speaking of Cicero and Tully) are thought to behave in such a way that whatever may be truly predicated of what is identified under one designation may be truly predicated of it when identified under any other designation. But some alleged identities of this sort are not easy to mark off, precisely because, for given runs of properties, it is not possible to predicate the same properties of what purportedly is one and the same thing. Here, to vindicate the claim of identity, an explanation is due by means of which to show that the apparent discrepancy is neutral to the issue and rests on extraneous complications. Sometimes, so-called theoretical identities do not, unless vacuously, rest on the use of sortals; thus for instance one may claim that water is identical with (is the same "thing" as) a certain composition of hydrogen and oxygen molecules or that a particular physical body is identical with a particular collection of molecules. Sometimes, so-called theoretical identities are said to hold of events, states, conditions, relations, qualities, and the like; and here, difficulties arise not only with the usual problems regarding justifying claims of identity in the face of not being able to say the same things of whatever are alleged to be one and the same but also with the complexity of referring to events and states and the like as if they were, quite straightfor-

wardly, individual things of given sorts. Finally, we sometimes speak of theoretical identities where, in fact, we mean only to say that, for certain purposes, we are prepared to treat things that are distinct as if they were one and the same; and, of course, wherever what is suitably correlated, for instance causally, that we are tempted to treat in terms of strict identity, even though discrepancies of the kind already mentioned obtain, we may, for good reasons, prefer to construe as theoretical identities of this last sort—that is, as "identities" that are not identities at all.

All of the complications noted regarding strict identities faced with spatio-temporal discontinuity or decomposition quite naturally affect as well the identity of persons and artifacts of every sort—what may be called cultural entities. But these entities exhibit peculiar properties of their own, such that, as with music for instance, one and the same sonata may be identified in any number of different performances: such entities are embodied in appropriate physical ways, are not abstract entities; but the identification of the physical sounds, say, in which they are embodied is not equivalent to the identification of the sonata thus embodied. And, in principle, this peculiarity applies to the identity of persons just as it does to that of artifacts.

1. Identity, Continuity, and Composition

We are most at home, in speaking of the self-identity of things, with such statements as 'Scott is the author of *Waverley*.' Trouble arises because statements seemingly grammatically similar—or at least not obviously dissimilar in ways relevantly bearing on the question of identity—may be offered, that cannot easily be taken to express the same sort of identity or to express identity in the same way as expressed in our statement about Scott: for example, 'The man now commanding the Macedonian armies is the very boy Aristotle taught.' Also, trouble arises because the copula 'is' (or any of its grammatically alternative forms) is used in a considerable variety of senses, without at least obvious grammatical flags attending, that mark such different senses, and without any obvious classificatory principle that promises to collect in a systematic way all such variant senses.

It is true that identity is characteristically affirmed of actually existing things, but that this is not a necessary constraint is obvious if we remind ourselves that Poseidon and Neptune are said to be identical, Don Quixote and the knight of the sorrowful countenance, Hans and Fritz and the Katzenjammer kids. In fact, the interesting feature of our discourse about identity and certain similar relationships is, precisely, that the concepts in question may be characterized in a way that is entirely neutral to that of existence. And this is useful to remember, because the verb 'is' is often used in multiple senses within the same sentence and by means of the same token utterance of the same word. We may then, as we shall see, ignore entirely the use of 'is' conveying existence, in our analysis of identity and similar concepts. Furthermore, apart from an interest in the puzzling features of the very concept of identity, it is important to realize that a number of ulterior questions are intimately linked to the analysis of identity and that their own exploration decisively illuminates the tenability of any would-be accounts of identity. This is nowhere clearer, for instance, than in a close study of the so-called mind-body identity theory.

To proceed then, in the Scott case, 'is' is said to be used in the sense of expressing strict identity; in the Alexander-the-Great case, it is said to be used in the sense of expressing spatio-temporal continuity (with reference to some identity)—whether or not such continuity is, in general, a necessary or sufficient or necessary and sufficient condition for strict identity (a matter that is readily settled if we consider that '$7 + 5 = 12$' expresses a strict identity). What *is* clear, however, is that what appears on the right hand side of the 'is' in both instances is not a mere predicative expression, does not designate what is predicated of what is denoted by the proper name ('Scott') or by the definite description ('the man now commanding the Macedonian armies') on the left hand side of the 'is.' What is apparently true of both statements is that what is identified by the use of the left hand expression and what is identified by the use of the right hand expression, respectively in each statement, *is the same thing.* Granting so much, we are obliged to explicate the concept of being the same thing (or being self-identical) simply because all discourse presupposes, at the very least, speaking about and referring to the distinct things that are to be found in the world and because statements of self-identity are taken to be logical truths. Hence, a reasonable strategy dictates uncovering the variable circumstances in which anomalies obtain regarding what, extensionally considered, would normally have been expected of valid identity claims. For, if 'Everything is identical with itself' is a necessary truth, the normal way in which to demonstrate that things putatively identical are not identical is to show that what may be truly predicated of what one term denotes cannot be truly predicated of what the other term denotes. Nevertheless, the failure to do so may be attributed not to the failure of identity but to the failure of some linguistic substitution thought to bear directly on identity.

If one were to schematize the relationship of identity, as is normally done, one might write the first statement as 'Scott = the author of *Waverley*' and the second statement in a similar way. But this maneuver would not, of itself, explicate the difference between the use of 'is' in the two statements and, in fact, might well be taken to obscure that difference. For, Alexander ("the man now commanding the Macedonian armies") may be the same "thing" as "the very boy Aristotle taught," in a sense compatible with that in which the man is spatio-temporally continuous with the boy but not in the sense in which the man is the same boy or the boy, the same man. On the other hand, Scott *is* the author of *Waverley* in the sense in which he is the *same man as the man* who is the author of *Waverley*. What this shows, at a stroke, is that to hold that A is strictly identical with B—in the sense intended in the Scott-case—presupposes that a certain kind of thing may be identified with respect to which we may individuate instances and by reference to which alone the identity claim is rendered intelligible (*and* that an equivocation on 'man' obtains in shifting from the Scott-case to the Alexander-case). To say that A is identical with B is to say they are instances of some kind of thing and that, in fact, they are one and the same instance of that kind. This is not to say that, *if* one introduced a distinction of a different kind of thing, A and B might prove not to be the same instance of *that* kind of thing even though they must be admitted to be the same instance of *this* kind of thing—which is an incoherent thesis, in the sense proper to strict identity, though not, it is sometimes thought, in the sense proper (and restricted) to mere spatio-temporal continuity. (The *boy* is not the *same man,* nor the man the same boy—which is to say that the boy-phase *of* Alexander is not the man-phase—which exposes the equivocation and undermines the alleged relativity of strict identity). It is to say only that identity, though not merely relative, designates a relationship that cannot be specified without being able to specify as well the kind of thing with respect to which a certain individuating claim is rendered meaningful (that, for instance, Scott is just that particular individual [man] who wrote *Waverley*); and it is to say that a systematic theory of what may be said to enter into strict identities (particulars associated with distinct sortals) must be developed if strict identity is to be preserved and freed from paradox. One must be able to say, for instance, that the phase-sortals 'boy-phase' and 'man-phase' are related to such sortals as 'person' in such a way that to say that the boy Alexander is not the man Alexander is not incompatible with saying that it is one and the same person who *was* that boy and *is* this man: the problem clearly bears on the use of tensed references and life-histories. Also, it is here that the notion of natural kinds emerges, the difficulty with which is—to put the matter indirectly—how to tell which kinds are natural and which are not, given that true statements cannot, as such, discriminate between the two.

A further word about temporal reference will be helpful here. The concepts of past, present, and future function referentially, not predicatively; but the tenses serve both a referential and a predicative function. Expressions like 'later than,' 'earlier than,' and 'at the same time as' are relational predicates designating properties for a certain range of objects. If the number 7 is strictly identical with the number $5 + 2$, neither tensed reference nor the ascription of the relational properties designated appear particularly relevant. Regarding Alexander, however, to say that it *was* Alexander whom Aristotle taught and *is* Alexander who now commands the Macedonian armies conflates both predicative and referential considerations regarding the use of the verb. For, to speak thus is to say that the boy-phase of Alexander preceded the man-phase of Alexander; and again, it is to say, regarding the actual Alexander, that reference to his boyhood must—from the present vantage—be made to the past, whereas reference to his manhood may be made to the present. Also, sentential contexts employing predicates designating temporal relations often exhibit referential opacity (or, perhaps more plausibly, equivocation). Events, however, are not essentially past, present, or future, by nature; only reference to them requires distinguishing, say, between what could now be observed or what could be reported to have been observable at some other time t. The network of time is an essential part of the network of reference. One important consequence of the distinction intended is that it clarifies the sense in which, unless we may appeal to story-relative identification, which may not be decisive (as in speaking of the first grand-daughter born to Tricia Nixon), we cannot make reference to future individuals, *of whom* we may predicate this and that: we can only speak, by way of existential generalizations, of what may, in the future, instantiate a given set of properties. For, we must remember that, regarding any indefinite or definite description, it is logically possible that nothing satisfy a given description and also that, for any indefinite description, it is logically possible that more than one particular instantiate the attribute thus designated. Reference, then, is temporally asymmetrical, but we cannot speak in a comparable way of the relational properties mentioned. Also, if we concede that the network of reference must be global—in the sense in which effective reference presupposes a single, comprehensive system of relationships (even in speaking of plural "possible worlds" a unified network is presupposed)—then talk about the reversal of time for instance, as opposed to the reversal of certain processes temporally identified, is, if past, present, and future are construed in terms of reference, simply incoherent.

To return to identity, the problem grows when one realizes that we say (fashionably, perhaps) that water is H_2O or that a table is just (a certain collection of) sub-atomic particles. Here again, we may be tempted to schematize what is said as, 'Water = H_2O,' but a difficulty arises as to whether we should want to admit that the sign ' = ' as here used expresses strict identity or something else. We may here intend that water is composed of, or constituted of, hydrogen and oxygen molecules; but *if* we wish, in saying that water is H_2O, to express *this* truth (among various possibilities), then the identity sign will have been rendered inapt. For, the statement may be taken properly to predicate something of water, namely, its being composed of hydrogen and oxygen molecules— and then it will have a different logical form altogether. Or, the statement may be taken to affirm that the composition designated by 'H_2O' is the composition of water (or that water is the composition designated by 'H_2O')—which cannot be rendered merely predicatively, though suitable predications can always be substituted. Consider, in the latter case, that one's tooth is repaired by replacing part of the bonelike process with silver amalgam: the tooth remains one and the same tooth through the change; what may be truly predicated of it (that is, of a phase of it) at one time may not be truly predicated of it at another; and its composition or what it consists of may be altered though it remain one and the same. (And what it is composed of may become the composition of something else.) This is not, it should be noted, strictly true of water *if* water is essentially composed of, or consists of, what is designated by 'H₂O'—but this bears more particularly on the concept of essential properties than on the concept of composition or constitution.

To take a case somewhat different from those already introduced, if I say, "My table is (composed of) [though, in a sense, it need not consist of] (pieces of) wood stolen from the Palace of Versailles," it is clear that one need not suppose that the properties of my table may be truly ascribed to those pieces of wood, or the properties of those pieces of wood, to my table. The statement given, then—if it is not construed merely constitutively, as with water's being composed of hydrogen and oxygen molecules, that is, that the properties of water may be reductively explained in terms of the properties of the sub-molecular structure of water—says that the table has been generated from (composed of) those pieces of wood; or, it says that what is identified by the use of the right hand expression is spatio-temporally continuous, through some interval at least, with what is identified by the use of the left hand expression. But the sense in which the one is spatio-temporally continuous with the other is quite different from the sense of the Alexander-case; for, in the Alexander-case, although the boy is not the man and the man is not the boy (in the sense of strict identity), the boy and the man are the same *person* (in the sense of strict identity)—*a fortiori,* the man (boy) is not composed of (or does not consist of) the boy (man) in any sense at all. In the table-case, the table *is* the pieces of wood in the sense in which the wood is the source of the constituent parts or is the constituent material of the table and / or in the sense in which the table has been generated from those pieces of wood; but none of these senses is the sense of strict identity.

To say that A and B are spatio-temporally continuous, in a sense relevant to claims of strict identity, requires that a kind of thing be identified in terms of which the identity alleged may be considered and the *point* of the claim of continuity may be made. But to say only that what is identified by D are the generative components out of which C is composed is to say that C and D are spatio-temporally continuous in the special sense that being composed of D may be predicated of C; it is emphatically not to introduce the notion of a kind of thing with respect to which C and D may be construed as different spatio-temporal phases or slices or parts. The Morning Star, once again, is not composed of the Evening Star; it is the same *planet* as (in the sense of strict identity), and it is spatio-temporally continuous with (in a sense excluding generation), the Evening Star. To say that C is composed of (generated from) D is to say that C and D are different things, though not necessarily different kinds of things (for, when a long pole is composed of short poles assembled together, it turns out that that which is composed and that of which it is composed are things of the same kind).

It should, of course, be said at once that the intuitive notion of strict identity—what may be called the paradigmatic criterion of identity—is quite simply the notion (allegedly drawn from Leibniz's law) that A and B are identical only if whatever may be truly predicated of A may be truly predicated of B and whatever may be truly predicated of B may be truly predicated of A. The trouble is that complexities are bound to arise. For one thing, it seems logically possible that indiscernibly different things may instantiate any formulable set of general predicates (that is, predicates that do not entail singular reference): without a theory of what is essential to identity, the stalemate cannot be blocked. For another, the identity of things cannot be equivalent to the substitutivity of terms (a thesis actually closer to the sense of what is called Leibniz's law), for *terms* designating the same thing (even for the most standard specimens) cannot always be substituted in relevant sentential contexts preserving the truth of any statement thereby expressed: hence, without a theory about which predications are decisive for identity, substitutivity will not satisfy our need. Indeed, the substitutivity thesis is false and the identity thesis (that everything is self-identical) is necessarily true but vacuous.

What the foregoing considerations show is that spatio-temporal continuity *sometimes* relates to strict identity and sometimes does

not; that composition or constitution—whether generative or not
—is never a question of identity; and that constitution (that is not
of the generative sort) is never a question of spatio-temporal continuity. When I say that my table is composed of pieces of wood
stolen from the Palace of Versailles, I emphatically do not want to
say that the one is strictly identical with the other or that there is
any particular thing of any particular kind *of* which it is true that
the table and the pieces of wood are spatio-temporal phases or
slices. In general, to say that C *is* D, in the sense of being generatively composed of D, is to provide an ellipsis for the predication,
of C, of its being-composed-of-D; and to say that C *is* D, in the
sense of being analyzable (non-generatively) as a composition of
certain independent particulars or of some material, is to speak of
a *sui generis* relationship.

2. Theoretical Identity

It is also sometimes said that C and D are identical, where C is
reduced to D, even though the conditions of strict identity do not
appear to obtain (when certain predications cannot be appropriately paired)—or else do obtain, but only on the fiat of positing
their identity first, which at least threatens to trivialize the issue.
Thus, *if,* in this sense, I assert that water and H_2O are identical or
that a certain table is identical with (a certain collection of) sub-
atomic particles or that a certain political state is identical with
(a) certain (collection of) individuals or that a person is identical
with (a certain collection of) psychophysical processes or the like,
then (trivially), applying the principle of self-identity, what is true
of C is true of D and vice versa; but the ulterior and interesting
question of the putative grounds *on which* this very identity is
posited may then be totally ignored or undeveloped. Alternatively,
so-called identities of these sorts are often said to be theoretical
identities, in the straightforward sense, precisely, that the identities intended do not require unqualified predicative equivalences.
Whatever is true of Scott must be true of the author of *Waverley,*

because "they" are, precisely, *the same man*. Understanding the use of the relevant sortal enables us to assess whether any would-be identity obtains, though individuating criteria need not and do not entail criteria for re-identifying particulars of a given kind under all circumstances. Also, although what is *true* of something is (trivially) true of it, what may be *predicated* of it cannot always be predicated of it under the conditions of an altered idiom or altered sentential context. From this point of view, all contingent identities are theoretical identities, in the sense in which we may inquire—of what is designated by different terms—whether "they" are one and the same (knowing that everything is necessarily self-identical) and on what grounds they may be shown to be one and the same (in spite of extensional discrepancies regarding paired predications.) But *what same thing* are the table and a certain collection of sub-atomic particles? Only if a suitable answer can be given, could the claim that they are strictly identical, in the sense given, be intelligible at all. If it cannot be given—if we say that the two are "the same" but are unable to say that they are the same *this or that*—we have noticeably failed to eliminate what could only be an ellipsis for questions of strict identity. This may not be a fault, as we shall see, but it is most assuredly a fault if the sense of 'is' intended is the sense given of strict identity— that is, if theoretical identity is to be construed as strict identity. For, precisely in lacking an appropriate sortal with respect to which relevant (even if selected) equivalences may be tested, we are obliged (or, more congenially, enabled) to proceed in an altogether different way, to set constraints on identity, from that of examining conjoint predications. Here, then, arbitrariness inevitably looms. Theoretical identity, then, may or may not be construed as a form of strict identity. Where it is taken as strict identity, justification is required for any apparent laxity with respect to predicative equivalences; and where it is not taken as strict identity, it simply does not generate any paradoxes respecting identity itself and serves merely as a convenience of a special sort. Also, theoretical identities are sometimes claimed not only for particulars like physical objects and persons but also between such particulars and what they appear to be composed of (sub-atomic particles, for instance), or of properties or states or events or conditions or the like under alternative descriptions, which way of speaking generates difficulties of its own.

To take a case of an exceedingly complex sort (and of a sort distinct in certain ways from the instances already provided), to say that having a sensation is (is identical with) the occurrence of a certain brain process is not to say, or does not entail, that if a given pain is, say, sharp, that the corresponding brain process is sharp (or even that it makes sense to predicate sharpness of the brain process); or, to say that a given neural discharge occurs at a certain point in the brain is not to say that a thought (alleged to be identical with that discharge) occurs at that very point in the brain (unless, once again, trivially—that is, antecedently admitting the identity and inventing a relevant use for the new expression). What is characteristically intended by the claim (at least) is that events or conditions of the one sort are so significantly correlated to events and conditions of the other and that explanations of the one are (asymmetrically) provided by reference to the other, that the two may be treated as one and the same (and that that treatment may be justified by the correlation and explanation that obtain). Where a stronger sense of identity is intended—reductive identity, here—a logically weakened analogue of the criteria of strict identity is employed and must be justified. In answer to the question "C and D are the same *what?*" one may be able to say only that they are the same. To say that they are the same "thing" is vacuous as it stands or, perhaps, is to refer to a determinable sortal at best. If C and D were said to be the same person or physical object, we should have the use of sortals forcing the usual strict identity. And if they were said, rather, to be the same event or action or state or the like, then, though we should have the use of sortals, it would remain problematic what the nature of the indicated particulars is and, therefore, what might be made to serve as suitable conditions of identity (even allowing liberties with respect to predicative equivalences). At any rate, alleged identities of the latter sort cannot be straightforwardly appraised without an independent examination of the logic of referring to events and the like. We may, therefore, leave these complications unresolved for the time being. We shall return to them in another context, of course.

Where, for theoretical identities lacking a common sortal, it is difficult to assign, independently, the same temporal or spatial or other properties to what is said to be identical, it becomes additionally difficult, if not impossible, to formulate a plausible criterion on the strength of which what is said to be theoretically identical cannot, with equal force, be said to be only significantly correlated—even causally correlated. But the fact remains, characteristically for mind-body identity theories, that just the predications that have challenged the advocates of strict identity are the ones that would require the extenuating argument.

Finally, in this regard, wherever reductive identities involve considerations of a non-generative but compositional sort (as in speaking of the identity of water and H_2O), we may discard the view that we are speaking of identities—either strict or theoretical —and hold instead that we are speaking only of composition. Thus, we may say that water is composed of H_2O (perhaps even essentially composed of H_2O) but not, for that reason, identical with H_2O. Correspondingly, persons may be composed of physical bodies though not identical with them. On the other hand, it would be inappropriate to hold that a person's having pain is composed of a brain's (or body's) being in a state of a certain neural discharge: should we wish to press identity here, compositional considerations would not directly bear on our claim. We are left, therefore, with theoretical identities construed as strict identities —for which, we are bound to explain the failure of predicative equivalences; or, with theoretical identities not involving sortals in the manner of strict identities—for which, we are bound to explain the sense in which the relationship in question is one of identity at all.

We may fix in another way the weakness of theoretical (that, reductive) identities lacking determinate sortals. We may say, for instance, that the sub-atomic "parts" of water are not, in the relevant sense, *proper parts* of water. (There are, clearly, alternative
senses of 'proper parts' that do not bear on the issue—for example, a functional sense in which the heart is a proper part of the
human body.) But drops of water are proper parts of water, in the
sense in which the essential attribute of being aqueous is ascribable to a particular drop just as it is to the water of which it is a
part; and molecules of oxygen are not proper parts of water in
that sense, since being aqueous cannot be ascribed to them. Let us
say that molecules of hydrogen and oxygen are *compositional
parts* of water, never proper parts of water; and that drops of
water are proper parts of water, though they may be construed as
compositional parts as well—characteristically, in a generative
sense. An identity affirmed of a certain patch of water and of a
certain set of particular drops of water entails some suitable spatio-temporal continuity, either of generating or dividing the patch
in question, and is established by reference to a suitable sortal.
The Morning Star and the Evening Star are not proper parts of
Venus, simply because Venus is not composed of its *phases* (the
Morning Star is a planet-phase rather than a planet; less elliptically, the Morning Star is a phase-of-a-planet). There is, therefore,
a multiple ambiguity affecting the preposition 'of' among the pertinent cases. 'Of' is used in expressions designating proper parts of
things (as in 'drops of water,' with reference to a patch of water):
there, attributes corresponding to the same sortal apply predicatively to both entitites. 'Of' is also used in expressions designating
phases of things (as in 'the boyhood of Alexander,' with reference
to a certain person): there, distinct sortals are introduced for both
entities (if we may speak loosely of entities), the one logically subordinate to the other in order to provide for identification and
identity claims. Also, 'of' is used in expressions designating compositional parts of things, notably but not necessarily where the
use of the 'of' of expressions designating proper parts is not in-

tended (in 'drops of water,' as before, or in 'the sub-molecular parts of water,' with reference to a patch of water): where attributes corresponding to the same sortal apply predicatively to both entities, a generative sense of composition is often intended, compatibly with strict identity (by way of the continuity of phases); and where the same sortal does not apply, generative composition cannot lead to comparable identities; also, of course, where nongenerative composition is intended, it is still the case that a common sortal is usually lacking.

One of the important by-benefits of the distinctions provided is that we may see at a stroke what is uncompelling about programs advocating the reductive elimination of so-called "common sense" ways of speaking of the things of the world in favor of so-called "scientific" modes of characterization: whatever is attributed to things classified with respect to "common sense" sortals (for instance, blueness, of water) as well as whatever is thus qualified cannot be repudiated as non-existent, non-occurrent, merely apparent, or the like, by reference merely to what can be said regarding entities identified in accord with "scientific" sortals (for instance, sub-atomic particles). The argument is absurdly simple: there is absolutely no reason to suppose that what may be said of things identified with respect to one sortal must or even can be said of things identified with respect to some other. Even if the properties of common sense entities (say, water) could be suitably explained in terms of the properties of its compositional ("scientific") parts (say, the sub-molecular structure of water), it would not follow that the entities and the properties of the entities of the *explanandum* were unreal, non-existent, or the like. On the contrary, to construe sub-molecular structures as compositional *parts* is to provide, at one and the same time, for the relationship of *explanans* to *explanandum* and for the admission as real of that of which the structures are the parts. It is simply a *non sequitur* to move from selected predicative asymmetries regarding what is identified with respect to *distinct* sortals to the conclusion that there are no things of a given sort because of what is true of actual specimens of another sort. There is no compelling reason for saying, for instance, that, although (according to the common sense mode of speech) water is blue, since colors cannot be ascribed to *its* sub-molecular structure, *it* (now, no longer referentially clear) cannot be blue or cannot really be water: the sub-molecular structure *of* water is *not* water, but that hardly shows that drops *of* water are not water or that there is nothing that is a drop of water. There is, thus, a gap in the argument that converts remarks about compositional parts into remarks about theoretical identities (lacking sortals) and converts remarks about such identities into remarks either about strict identities or about eliminative claims (that is, claims in which what is putatively about common sense entities is said to be "really" about "scientific" entities—a thesis sometimes termed "eliminative materialism"). This much at least may be provisionally conceded to essentialism: if what is attributable to something in virtue solely of which it is a thing of a certain sort cannot be attributed to something independently identified by reference to another sortal, what is thus identified cannot be one and the same. Obviously, however, the concession is incomplete, for we should still need a theory of basic sortals in terms of which given runs of predicative asymmetries could be countenanced without denying relevant identities.

We may concede, also, that we have a strong ontological bias in favor of whatever may be individuated or suitably linked to whatever may be individuated. This is not to say that whatever can be individuated are real entities (the Homeric gods, for instance) or that whatever is real is capable of being straightforwardly individuated. But where individuation fails or is distinctly weakly drawn (as perhaps, with events, beliefs, attributes), we are disinclined to construe what is discriminated—where alternative devices are at hand—as entities. But there are complications. For instance, if trees and stones are existing entities, then it would seem that water and coal and air are also real (substances), though— designated by mass nouns—they are not individuated like particulars. We can always introduce, however, partitive (*not* instantiative) devices, as in speaking of "drops of water," "bars of gold," and similar metrically conceived divisions—by which we treat what mass nouns designate as composed of what count nouns designate, where the one are proper parts of the other.

This device does not seem to be as easily available for such would-be abstract entities as attributes. Yet, we do speak of "the wisdom of Socrates," "the yellow of Van Gogh's *Sunflowers*," and the like. Here, the difficulty of admitting universals like wisdom and yellow as entities is palpable. Apparent individuation depends on the individuation of more fundamental entities—persons and paintings—and whether *that* wisdom or *that* yellow can be reidentified in other contexts is as undecidable as it would be if we attended only to the meanings of attributive expressions. Did Solomon, for instance, embody that wisdom that Socrates embodied? And which of Van Gogh's other paintings embody the very yellow of *Sunflowers?* To hold that a given attribute may be ascribed to a set of particulars is neither to decide that there are abstract entities (classes) of which they are members nor to decide that there are abstract entities (attributes) which they partition (much as with the use of mass nouns). The issue rests with the analysis and ontological implications of similarity. The difficulty with both classes and attributes is ontological redundancy—with classes: paradox as well; with attributes: the difficulty of reidentification in addition. *If,* however, we wished to introduce attributes as mass entities, we would have to speak, say, of "paintings of yellow" and "persons of wisdom," meaning—in so speaking—partitive particulars of the attribute itself. But then, the compositional parts could not be taken as proper parts and would themselves be typically designated by other count nouns. These perhaps are the strongest reasons for regarding attributes as ontologically unhelpful.

3. Discontinuities and Strict Identity

It is clear, to return to an earlier issue, that most questions of strict identity—bearing, say, on the identity of physical objects

and persons—are intimately connected with spatio-temporal continuity. It is, of course, possible in principle that what is spatio-
temporally continuous with something, independently identified, is
not to be construed as a spatio-temporal part or phase of that very
thing of which the other is a spatio-temporal part or phase (our
table and the Versailles lumber-case). It is logically quite possible
that a particular of one kind be transformed into a particular of
another kind when certain changes and alterations (not involving
any temporal or spatial or causal discontinuities) have reached a
certain critical point; this is, for example, regularly supposed in
the literature of the supernatural, in speaking of the transformation of men into vampires and werewolves. On the assumption of
this literature, what is the non-vacuous sense in which the spatio-
temporally continuous particulars are merely parts or phases of
one and the same entity? (They may, of course, be said to be
phases of the same *person,* but only on the strength of a new
theory, a theory of new kinds of beings). And, though Lepidoptera
identifies an order in terms of which caterpillars and moths may
be treated as spatio-temporal parts or phases of the same member
of the order, there need not, logically, have been such a classificatory provision. It is also possible (as the fission of amoeba shows)
that what is spatio-temporally continuous may (and, sometimes,
must) be individuated as distinct particulars of the same kind. In
any case, the complications can be decisively formulated.

Imagine, to consider the issues more closely, that there is a boat
B that exists intact at time t and that, at $t,$ there also exists a supply of planks from which we may select replacements for all the
planks of B. Now, a man C replaces the planks of B one by one
from the available supply. One is inclined to say that, although C
replaces one plank at time $t',$ B continues to exist through the interval t-t' or, alternatively, that the boat at t and B' (the boat at t')
are spatio-temporal parts or phases of one and the same boat (B).
From this point of view, one is *inclined* to say that if all the
planks of B are replaced one by one, continuously, B will have
continued to exist through that entire interval—or, if the planks

originally belonging to the boat at t are all replaced by other planks at t', then B may be said to have continued to exist through the interval t-t'—even though none of the original planks of B will remain in what we affirm to be B at the end of the interval.

It is also extremely important to observe here that, even though one speaks of spatio-temporal continuity respecting the replacement of planks, the idiom is a loose one; for there may, actually, be distinct intervals in which one plank is removed and another not yet inserted. This suggests that the notion of spatio-temporal continuity is entirely compatible with spatial discontinuities and temporal discontinuities and has to do more with life-histories, careers, and similar theoretical considerations (possibly even with certain patterns of decomposition) than with unbroken continuities.

Imagine, however, that, independently of C's activity (and perhaps unknown to C), D collects the planks discarded from B (that is, the boat at t) and assembles them into a boat. If we had merely considered the original boat as decomposed into its constituent planks and those planks reassembled as a boat, we would have been *inclined* to say that the new boat (call it B″) was one and the same boat as B (or, alternatively, that the boat at t and B″ were spatio-temporal parts of B). The obvious trouble is that identity is transitive and that no interpretation that preserves both lines of argument is tenable, for B′ (the boat at t') and B″ are, on any view, not identical (or parts of one and the same boat)—there remain two boats, on any view. What this shows is that spatio-temporal continuity is not a sufficient condition of identity and that we have no clear rule for determining *which* instance of such continuity is decisive for deciding identity in cases of the sort just supplied; all we can say is that to prefer one line of argument disqualifies the other, but nothing short of intentional considerations (choosing, for instance, C's point of view or D's or, independent considerations such as the normal voyage patterns of B) can decide which alternative to prefer. Usage and common sense favor both to some extent. Also, it must be noted that even, *at times,* when some object is decomposed (as a watch or bicycle or boat), *it* is said to exist in its decomposed form ("There is my bicycle scattered on the basement floor"); but also (an analogue to the puzzle of selective spatio-temporal continuities), *if* the parts of the bicycle or watch were scattered all over the world, we should then be *disinclined* to speak of the bicycle's or watch's continuing to exist (in scattered form). This merely confirms the inherent informality of strict identities based on spatio-temporal continuities and / or involving decomposition. In fact, to link strict identity with the admission of spatio-temporally distinct phases of one and the same thing is simply to provide a device for outflanking or neutralizing the strenuous requirements of strict identity. Also, it should again be noted, there is no necessary congruence between identity and composition or constitution; for, on the hypothesis, the planks that constituted B might well come to constitute B″, even if B″ were not identical with the boat at *t* (that is, even if B″ were not a spatio-temporal phase of B). Also, if the argument holds for boats (artifacts, admittedly), then it very probably holds for such complex entities as persons (not artifacts, to be sure, but culturally emergent and culturally specified entities nonetheless). The spatio-temporal continuity of (human) *bodies* cannot, on that assumption, be a sufficient condition for fixing the numerical identity of *persons*.

But now, to identify some particular or to reidentify it or to identify one and the same particular in its spatio-temporally distinct phases presupposes that it is a particular of a certain kind and that we have a principle of individuation with respect to that kind, in terms of which to enumerate numerically distinct instances of that kind. So the problem of identity cannot be entirely separated from the problem of individuating members of species or instances of kinds. Yet even here, there is a degree of freedom that may be insisted on, which the following two examples may serve to clarify and which may serve as well to cast some further light on the complexity of the notions of identity already introduced. Imagine, following science-fiction stories, that some master criminal plans to commit a crime on planet A and establish an alibi for the time of the crime on planet B. Contrary to planetary law, he has one of his henchmen use a certain machine to "beam" him secretly to both planets; that is, some kind of fission is made to occur and a duplicate progeny (not altogether unlike what happens with amoeba—or, perhaps, even with clones) is "beamed" to planet A and planet B. It may be granted that the progeny are not (strictly) identical with the progenitor, though they are spatio-temporally continuous with the progenitor (though not with one another). Also, a reverse use of the machine will (as our criminal realizes and intends to exploit) reunite the duplicate progeny into what we should be *inclined* to say was the original progenitor: no mingling of members of different pairs of such duplicates, we may suppose for simplicity's sake, is physically possible. Both members of the progeny appear to preserve the memories of the progenitor and are capable of similar acts; one commits the crime intended on planet A and the other establishes a plausible alibi on planet B. Imagine that the crime and the *method* of arranging the crime and alibi are discovered when one of the progeny is killed (in a quite conventional way). Might it not be reasonable, given legal considerations at the very least, to take the living member of the duplicate progeny as the same person as (as strictly identical with) the original progenitor (that is, as spatio-temporal parts of one and the same person)? or, had they both survived, could it not be said that both are one and the same person as the progenitor (in another sense)? They could not (in the second case) be strictly identical, but they might well be said, in some sense, to be "theoretically identical"; although, if they were, we should have to admit that theoretical identity was not transitive and that an individual might, under certain circumstances, be said also to be in two places at once. This is not to argue that the putative theoretical identity actually holds but only that there is a considerable informality involved in positing such identities; and that the liberality and varying practical reasons for insisting on an identity of this sort may well work havoc with certain seemingly indispensable features of identity (if and only if theoretical identity were construed as a form of strict identity)—for instance, transitivity and the intuitively strong principle that nothing can be in two places at once (though something, like a dismantled bicycle, may be identified as occupying discontinuous space). We are obliged to conclude, here, that the coherence of our notions of identity and continuity must be adjusted and blocked out from time to time—given, at the very least, technological innovations—and not merely taken as a discoverably changeless set of rules.

It is also worth noting that the concept of theoretical identity here advanced is, in an important respect, quite different from the reductive identities considered earlier on. For, here, a relevant sortal is available—that regularly enters into considerations of strict identity—and spatio-temporal continuities (that would otherwise generate incoherence) are open to interpretation along the lines of such theoretical identity. Legal contexts and contexts of habit and conventional expectation are, probably, the most natural setting for such "identities." But it must be said again, what is said to be identical thus is not strictly identical: we merely treat the particulars involved as if, within severe constraints, they were identical (but are not).

The other example intended is this. Imagine, following horror stories, that we individuate things in the usual way until we are struck with the possibility that we are being confronted with a particular of some hitherto unknown species of being. We single out, for example, a certain living man, a certain wolf, a certain bat, a certain cloud, a certain corpse. But we begin to suspect a certain spatio-temporal continuity among the manifestations of each of these *and* a unity of intelligent purpose in the states and behavior of all of these. Arguing, that is, from analogies concerning the use to which spatio-temporal continuity is put in confirming *other* identities, we theorize that the ordered manifestations of these putatively different things are actually spatio-temporal phases of one and the same individual; and having determined this, we cast about for a characterization of the kind of thing (say, vampire) conforming to such individuation. The point is that, al-

though, normally, to identify a given particular entails individuating with respect to a given kind of thing, *sometimes* (given *that*
antecedent practice), we may plausibly argue that we have one and
the same particular and construct an account of the kind that conforms to our judgment. Perhaps it may be said that this is what
happens when unknown specimens (like caterpillars and moths)
are judged, for the first time, to be spatio-temporal phases of the
same particular thing and the order of Lepidoptera is then designated (though, logically, it need not have been) as the kind of
thing corresponding to the identity alleged. Certainly, it is only in
contexts in which what are construed as instances of certain species are reinterpreted as phases of ulterior species, that initial criteria of identity may not depend on antecedent criteria of individuation and may even, serving to identify new particulars, set
constraints on such criteria. Limiting ourselves to the present context, however, the central considerations appear to be these: that
anomalies can always be generated for strict identities when at
least spatio-temporal continuity or decomposition is considered;
that theoretical identities, lacking appropriate sortals (to speak
here of "the same thing" or the like is not to speak of determinate
kinds of things) cannot be viewed as strict identities without suitable explanation; and that theoretical identities that presuppose
sortals of the kind employed in strict identities but that do not require an accounting of predicative asymmetries or anomalies
about incompatible attributes are simply not strict identities at all
but merely enable us to treat distinct particulars as if, for relevant
purposes, they were identical. For the latter kind of case, then, it
is not even required that the alleged identities be transitive or
symmetrical.

The ulterior question, of course, concerns whether there are
necessary restrictions on the identification of whatever would
count as a distinct particular or distinct kind of thing. About this,
we may briefly note the following. If we assume that different
kinds of things have essential properties and if we assume that
particulars have essential properties *qua* this or that particular,

then whatever is identified as a thing of this or that kind cannot be so identified if it lacks an essential property of that kind, and whatever is identified as this particular instance of that kind cannot be so identified if it lacks an essential property of that instance. We may well wonder whether the man we take to be Socrates could be Socrates if he were not snubnosed; or whether Lucy Westenra (in the story *Dracula*) could be the same person though not the same (or, a) woman when transformed into a vampire; or whether Christine Jorgensen could be the same person though not the same (or, a) man when transformed into a woman. What we must see is that, given the informalities in determining identity and the distinction between identity and composition, we can if we wish—short of the ontological discovery of the allegedly essential properties of natural and exclusive kinds—answer all the implied questions in the affirmative. Consider, also, that when we excavate a cavity in a tooth and replace the diseased material with silver amalgam, we do not, in altering the composition of the tooth, necessarily replace the original tooth with another; and should we *gradually* replace *all* of the original material, we should merely be faced with a decision (as already sketched) among eligible alternatives—no matter how plausible it may be, in different contexts, to prefer one alternative to the other. Perhaps, for instance, even a fresco of Leonardo da Vinci's, deteriorating beyond control, is, if repaired as it decays, in the precise manner of the artist, still entitled to be said to be the same fresco though the entire composition of its surface layer be replaced. What the limit of tolerance here may be cannot be foretold.

4. Instantiation and the Identity of Cultural Entities

We may add a final, large complication. If we are prepared to concede that *the same poem* may appear on indefinitely many printed pages, then it is clear that poems cannot be reduced to the physical marks on a page and that reference to such entities as poems complicates the logic of identity. For, what may be affirmed and denied of particular printed instances of the poem (including differences in ink and printing type and even verbal errors or variations) cannot, on such grounds alone, be ascribed to *the* poem and yet the poem may be identified as the same poem through an entire set of such printed instances or inscriptions (that is, the poem is a particular and not a class of instances or inscriptions). If it is said to be an abstract entity (which is implausible), it remains an entity whose identity is necessarily linked to the identity of physical objects (or inscriptions) and whose properties are at least a function of the properties of those physical objects. Identification of a poem may well rest on the use of "prime instances" of the poem (the author's final handwritten version, for instance) but the poem is an entity—given the practice of referring to poems—of a distinctive kind. The printed versions are said to be "instances" of the poem in that they conform to whatever is judged essential to the poem (a certain intelligible structure, for instance) even though they may vary among themselves in all sorts of assignable ways. What may be truly predicated of the putative instances of the poem may not be truly predicated of the poem of which they are said to be instances. The instances are not spatiotemporal phases of one and the same thing, and the relationship between the two cannot be construed merely as compositional or as mere membership in a class. In talking of a poem, we do not suppose we are talking of a set or class of things. The particular set of marks on a page constitutes a distinct object—often called a "copy" of the poem (although 'copy' suggests that resemblance or a thoroughgoing isomorphism is required, which is not true: think of alternative performances of the *same* sonata)—which may be minimally regarded as a bare physical object (the marks on the page) *or* as a copy *of* the poem. The point is that the conditions under which the bare marks are construed *as* a poem are just the conditions under which different sets of marks may be construed as alternative copies of the same poem. Here, the very existence of a certain kind of object depends on the conventions and traditions of a human society. The poem that appears in different copies is self-identical, though the copies are numerically distinct from *one another*. If the distinction is allowed, then seeming anomalies paralleling those concerning phase-sortals and sortals on which the use of phase-sortals essentially depends are bound to arise. A given object, identified in purely physical terms, may, when suitably construed as a more complex object—by reference to certain conventions—be ascribed (emergent) properties not otherwise ascribable (for instance, "meaning," "significance," "symbolic import," "emotional quality," "purposiveness," "design") in virtue of which numerically and physically different objects may be construed as "instances" or "tokens" or "copies" of the same more complex object. They are, then, instances of the same *object,* not merely instances of the same *kind* of object (though they may be this as well); they exhibit, therefore, a *sui generis* form of instantiation, which corresponds to a distinctive use of the verb 'to be' —not to be confused with that of strict identity or with that of predication or composition.

If the claim holds for poems, then it holds for all objects of art, in the largest sense of 'art': hence, for words and other linguistic entities, for machines, for collective entities like churches and states, and the like. Also, the admission of such entities provides a partial clue to the identity of such complex entities as persons. For, although the same music, instantiated in numerically distinct performances, is normally identified by reference to a score, a painting (though not an etching) is normally identified by reference to a unique physical object that, construed in terms of a tradition, is ascribed certain emergent, intentional properties. If the painting may be said to be composed of pigment (both compositionally and generatively), it nevertheless possesses, *qua* painting, properties not reducible to mere physical properties—though it may possess such properties—and, should paintings come to be individuated in the way etchings are, their connection with unique "bodies" would have to be denied. Similarly, a person may be composed of physical materials and yet, in the context of human culture, particular physical bodies may be construed as (may be said to embody) persons, that is, may be construed as entities having properties not (or not obviously) reducible to physical properties; and if, by way of technical or evolutionary novelty, one and the same person may come to be instantiated in different bodies, we should have to treat persons as entities rather like works of art. Cloning, in fact, may be counted as the biological counterpart of what etching is to the art world and may, conceivably, extend to entities having minds and even to persons.

The upshot is that the logic of identity, particularly where spatio-temporal continuity, decomposition, and culturally emergent entities are concerned, is decidedly informal and open to systematic revision in the interest of conceptual coherence and the accommodation of novelty. In particular, looking ahead to further complexities, the relationship between the mind and the body and the analysis of what it is to be a person are inescapably affected by the general differences among the categories canvassed and by the informality with which even the identity of physical bodies and artifacts, under conditions of discontinuity, decomposition, and emergence, is fixed.

Beyond this, it is useful to note again that questions of identity, continuity, composition and constitution are very closely connected with questions of what there is in the world. But the sense of 'is' intended in raising questions of the latter sort is a sense in which 'exists' may fairly be substituted in sentential contexts. And this is a substitution, it is important to stress, that cannot be made for the uses of 'is' obtaining in the range of cases just canvassed.

VI

ACTIONS & EVENTS

Actions are events, but it is difficult to say what the difference is between a mere event and a human action. It is tempting to claim that some interior effort of the will must be present in order that an action (signing a check, for instance) obtain. But involuntary, accidental, unintended acts must be admitted as genuine acts; acts of negligence cannot be accounted for in terms of the will; and if the exercise of volition is itself construed as an interior action of some sort, then, on the thesis, it will need to be similarly supplemented. For these and other such reasons, it is unpromising to analyze actions in terms of the addition to a given physical occurrence of some allegedly decisive interior mental ingredient. On review, it proves to be more useful to construe physical events as actions by redescribing them within the context of human institutions and practices. If actions, then, are a species of event, causal explanations of actions will have to be admitted as entirely in order. It is perhaps possible, in principle, to construe actions as occurrences identified by interpreting the physical events that embody them in accord with relevant social conventions and practices; causal explanations might

146

then be restricted to the entailed physical events and would not be applicable to the supervening actions themselves, for, on the thesis, actions are not the same as those events. Still, the alternative will be unable to accommodate what appear to be familiar causal questions bearing on actions, such for instance as may concern learning and teaching, influence, persuasion, and the like. The admission of causes affecting the performance of actions does not, however, preclude human freedom and choice. Only certain extreme theories—that hold for instance that whatever occurs necessarily occurs, that whatever occurs could not but occur—are incompatible with human freedom; but such theories are not required by the development of the sciences or the nature of physical laws. Freedom does not preclude causality, only the operation of particular kinds of causes, such as compulsion. And choice is not so much an action as a qualification of an action, bearing jointly on the presence or absence of particular causal factors and on the motives, reasons, and the like of the agent involved. Furthermore, the specification of an action can only be the specification of someone's action: a physical event construed as an action is assigned to some agent or person as that agent's action; consequently, persons cannot as such be said to cause the actions they perform, unless what is meant is that their impulses or motives or the like (that is, impulses or motives that are also assigned to them) cause or are part of the cause of their actions.

Because they are identified as such in accord with prevailing or preferred social rules, norms, conventions, or practices, human actions exhibit certain distinctive features. For one thing, determining how many and which acts have been performed when what appears to be a single, continuous physical occurrence obtains is a question that cannot be settled on causal grounds or even on the basis of an agent's own intentions; social conventions—for instance those of the law—are characteristically decisive. For a second, given variable interests and practices, acts are usually able to be redescribed by eliding with their description what may otherwise serve as the description of their *consequences. Constraints on such elision are open to debate and presuppose either extremely formalized behavior (as in chess) or ulterior knowledge regarding the allegedly appropriate norms, objectives, or interests of human nature itself—that, on the thesis, ought not to be obscured. And for a third, action, particularly deliberate and purposive human behavior, invites explanation in terms of reasons, motives, intentions, and the like—which, though not incompatible with causal explanation, cannot be a species of causal explanation itself. The essential reason is that whatever is a cause of a given thing is a cause of it, regardless of the description or designation under which it and what it causes are identified; for, as it happens, a reason that an agent has for an action he performs (unlike a cause) is, properly, a reason for it only under selected descriptions. What may serve as a reason may well serve as a cause (one's greed, for instance); explanations both by reasons and by causes must conform to appropriate constraints (some descriptions, after all, may prove to be extraneous, from the point of view of explanation); but, given the essential difference between reasons and causes, explanations by reasons cannot be construed merely as an adjusted or special sort of causal explanation. Alternatively put, causal explanations presuppose laws and explanation by reasons presupposes rules, social practices, norms. Clearly, the breach of a rule will not, under any circumstances, entail a physical impossibility.*

Just as actions, as actions, are what some agent does, so too, events, as events, are what befall, or occur to, some suitable subject. There are no actions without agents (though we may speak of types of actions) and, normally at least, there are no events that are not undergone by something. The upshot is that, in our usual discourse about events, as in speaking of Caesar's death, we are prepared to predicate dying or death of Caesar. It turns out to be extremely helpful to treat events themselves (including actions) as if they were individual things; for then, we may describe them in whatever convenient way we wish. The chief advantage comes to that, for when we speak of events in the idiom of prop-

*erties ascribed to objects and persons, difficulties arise about ex-
plicitly fixing reference to one and the same event, by way of the
structural features of the sentences we use. This is an important
consideration, but it cannot justify us in denying that reference
to events (as to entities of some sort) is itself a grammatically dependent convenience resting on whatever may be suitably predicated of such entities as physical objects and persons. Of course,
whether we may construe events as the "real" entities of the
world is an eligible (ontological) quarrel, but it does not bear on
the analysis of sentences regarding events in contexts in which it
is also admitted that we refer to physical objects and persons and
in which given events befall such entities. The attempt to ignore
or deny the dependency mentioned leads to anomalies.*

*Reviewing the analysis of action in a somewhat larger context
than before, we may see that certain physical occurrences suitably construed in terms of the patterns of human society and certain physical bodies similarly construed may, respectively, be
identified as, or construed as embodying, actions and persons.
The juxtaposition forces us to consider what relationship holds
between the mind and the body and, since knowledge and belief
as well as other particular mental states are ascribable to persons
or fair surrogates—but not, on any obvious grounds, to mere
physical bodies—we are also obliged to acknowledge the con-
verging importa..ce of the concept of a person for the whole of
our inquiry.*

1. The Nature and Causes of Actions

The classic conceptual question that is asked about human action
is this: What must be added to a man's arm's rising to qualify as a
man's raising his arm? If it is provided, the addition is often construed in terms of the will (or such mental states as motives); and
action, viewed as involving a certain effort of the will, is characteristically and redundantly described as free action. The trouble
is that if the effort of the will that is alleged to obtain is itself an

(interior) action, then it too will require the same addition (a certain effort of the will) and the analysis will be faced with a vicious regress; and if the effort of the will is not construed as an action performed by an agent but rather as an interior cause of some sort —of events inferior to actions but entering into the composition of an action—then difficulties will arise respecting the nature of human freedom, the role of persons in actions, and the analysis of what, precisely, an action is; and, whether as an action or an interior cause, the will would, then, be supposed to affect physiological processes and the like, respecting which there is not the slightest basis for admitting such influence or intention to influence or even awareness of the possibility of influencing. And again, if it is (somehow) construed as a cause of an action (perhaps an action itself) that is itself not caused or at least not caused in the way other natural causes are caused, then the causal continuum of nature will be breached in a seemingly ad hoc way. Also, if either an effort of will or a motive were assumed to be a necessary condition for the occurrence of an action, then inadvertent and unmotivated actions would have to be denied. On the other hand, if it is denied that anything (occurring within the man himself) must be added in order that the event of the arm's rising qualify as the action of the man's raising his arm, then it is usually held that the event (or happening) is the action but is identified thus in a suitable context of discourse—characteristically in the context of the institutionalized rules of social life. From this point of view, explanations of events and explanations of actions are of the same fundamental sort, causal explanations (since, whatever causally explains bodily happenings must, on pain of contradiction, causally explain whatever is identical with such events); and no contracausal distinctions need be admitted in order to identify human freedom as opposed to mere causal determinism.

The trouble here is that there does not appear to be any comprehensive and uniform characterization of an action such that a given event may be identified with a particular action (rather than with some other), that the very individuation of actions does not seem to be entirely congruent with causal explanations, and that some forms of explanation of actions are not reducible to (without being incompatible with) causal explanations. The puzzles for the opposing views may be further enlarged, if we concede that some events may properly be construed as human actions even if they are not freely performed, even if they are performed under duress or compulsion and the like; also, some events may properly be construed as human actions even though their occurrence does not directly involve one's will or motives or intentions or the like. That is, it is entirely possible that action obtain although the usually attendant mental events fail relevantly to occur in the interval—for instance, the onset of thought, emotions, images, beliefs, desires. But to raise these possibilities is merely to suggest the considerable complexity of the concept of an action.

If we think of an action as an event like *signing one's name* or *signalling* or *making a move in a chess game,* we are apt to construe it as an event that is caused by some suitable agent, a person (or, if we think of *hunting* or *stalking* or *eating,* animals, by way of an arguable courtesy). But, in speaking thus, we should have to hold that a person causes an action in a sense to be distinguished from his intentions' or volitions' or efforts' causing that action; for, either these latter are themselves ulterior actions that, once again, *he* produces or else they are, admittedly, causes of what follows—which will then not be what *he* produces (being produced, say, by his intentions) and hence will not be actions at all. On this view, we should have to insist on a distinct kind of causation—agent-causation—instances of which would not be reducible to any enumerated set of causes rendered in terms of such factors as intentions and volitions. The thesis is an extravagance, since, normally, we wish to hold both that some agent produced a certain action *and,* say, that it was a direct causal consequence of his intention, desire, or the like. So if it were possible to signify that an agent produced his own action at the same time that certain causes interior to his own career served to explain the occurrence of his action, it would be possible to obviate the invention of agent-causation. An easy way to accomplish this is simply to construe speaking of an agent's producing an action as predicating the action of him or as assigning him responsibility (or liability) or assigning the operative causes to him (in the sense in which, say, the effective beliefs, desires, motives are *his*): on such a maneuver, it would no longer be necessary to acknowledge agent-causation as a distinct and *sui generis* kind of causation. Furthermore, the specimen characterizations of actions given—signing one's name, signalling—would then prove to be ellipses for *one's* signing his name, *one's* signalling, and the like (or else characterizations of *types* of action, not as such performed, that collect whatever particular actions particular men perform). But, since reference to persons (or other agents) is then essential to the identification of an action as an action, without at all entailing agent-causation, we can eliminate such causation entirely from the explanation of actions (which, of course, is not to eliminate *one* action's causing another action to occur). For, the assignment of an action to some particular agent is already accomplished in characterizing and identifying it as a particular action: if intention and volition served to explain an action in causal terms, it would obviate agent-causation without disallowing the assignment of an action to the agent who produces it. To say that an agent produces a certain action, then, would be to say that an action occurs and that the causes of the occurrence include, relevantly, events interior to the mental life of the agent. On this view, an agent cannot cause his own action, though one of his actions may cause another action on his part (as when throwing a punch causes one to try to maintain his balance). But this restriction does not affect the relevance and admissibility of any mental conditions interior to the life of an agent. Thus, although the concept of a motive presupposes the concept of an action, an agent may have a motive without necessarily acting on it or, *a fortiori,* without necessarily performing the action intended (as when a man refrains from killing his wife though he has a motive, or kills his mother-in-law by mistake, thinking she is his wife). Also, if to admit causes of an action may be entirely compatible with the freedom of the agent involved, then there cannot, in principle, be a class of actions that cannot be caused by the agent's own antecedent actions; for, where what causes an action may be identified independently of, and is only contingently connected with, that action, there cease to be any relevant reasons for precluding the agent's own antecedent actions from serving as possible causes.

Thus, *if* we once admit that actions can be caused, we should have no conceptual grounds for denying that what may serve as the cause of actions include whatever may serve as the causes of events in general (of which actions are a species). If a hailstorm may be part of the cause of my raising my arm to protect myself, then if a fly's buzzing may be part of the cause of my raising my arm to fend it off, then if another's punch may be part of the cause of my raising my arm to defend myself, then my imperilling my balance on a tightrope by placing one foot in front of the other may be part of the cause of my raising my arm to correct the balance. This will be true even if a given action is not actually caused by another action (of the same agent) and regardless of the analyzability of the given action in terms of simpler, component actions and regardless of the spontaneity of, or absence of recipes for, the successful performance of the action in question. In fact, if one's action of moving a stone (M) entails the event (S) of the stone's moving, it will even be possible to speak of M's causing S to occur: this would mean merely that the action itself was not uncaused and that, by suitable redescription, some relevant action or event could be identified, numerically distinct from the event of the stone's moving, that could be said to cause that event and not to entail it—one's exerting a certain force, for instance.

In general, logical and causal necessity must be distinguished: to speak of the cause of A causing A—though necessarily true about a contingent event—is not to speak of necessary causation (whatever that might be made to mean). *If* causes are designated in terms of their effects, they are not less genuinely causes for that (having the intention of doing A may well be a part of the

cause of A); the causes of actions need not invariably be formulated in terms of their effects (the onset of greed with respect to B
may be the cause of doing A); causes are not as such incompatible
with free actions (as in remarking that his conviction and judgment may have caused him to vote the way he did); actions are
not invariably free, though not less genuinely actions for that (for
instance, we say he acted inadvertently, accidentally, unintention-
ally, compulsively, obsessively); and interior volitions matching
every action are fictions—which, therefore, do not bear on the
causal issue at all.

Nevertheless, it is possible, though extremely awkward, to deny
that actions are caused at all, in the sense in which speaking of actions may be construed as interpreting entailed events in accord
with certain conventions and in the sense in which causal considerations may be restricted to the events entailed. On that view, we
should have to deny that actions are a species of events. We
should also find it difficult, if not impossible, to accommodate,
within the idiom of action, discourse about learning, influence,
persuasion, education, compulsion, obsession, accident, inadver-
tence, and the like. And under these conditions, we might well be
obliged to admit inherent difficulties in reidentifying one and the
same action under alternative descriptions. To preserve causal
connections is to preserve some range of extensional discourse regarding actions. But, as we shall see, complications arise even on
this constraint.

Further adjustments are needed, however, because of the mixed
and varied circumstances under which we are prepared to speak of
the acts or actions of men. For example, a man may be cited for
an act of negligence in that he simply fails to perform some other
act required or expected of him in some relatively formalized or
institutionalized setting. Here, there is no distinctive bodily movement (like the arm's rising) that is construed as an act or action; it
is, rather, the absence—where expected—of any movement that
could be construed as the required action or as the related action
of trying to perform that action, that normally justifies us in

speaking of an act of negligence or omission. But if such acts are admitted, then it is a foregone conclusion that no single, comprehensive formula of action will be forthcoming. In fact, if we press such cases, we shall see that it is curious to suppose that the agent performed or caused a certain act of negligence to occur, that it is difficult to assign a time to the act's performance (though the negligence may be assigned temporal coordinates), that identifying the act as an act does not presuppose that the agent's intentions or volitions and the like caused it (without supposing that it was uncaused), and that its individuation does not, characteristically, depend on operative causal or intentional factors at all. Consider only that the event (which will usually be admitted to be a single, continuous event) of a fist describing an arc in space and making forcible contact with another's jaw may, under suitable circumstances, be individuated as distinct acts of assault, resisting arrest, causing a disturbance, interfering with the performance of a policeman's duty, and the like. The important consideration is this, that the physical movement of the fist need not vary in the least respect, when, under different circumstances, it counts as three or five or thirty-five distinct acts; individuation here depends entirely on the state of the law. But this shows very clearly that the individuation of acts often depends decisively on factors other than causal and intentional factors (sometimes without, sometimes with, regard to these).

It is instructive, therefore, to see that the concept of an act or action by no means functions homogeneously with regard to admissible instances. Sometimes, bodily movements (events, happenings, occurrences) are construed as actions—which quite naturally invite causal explanation and assessment in terms of freedom. Sometimes, no particular movements obtain but are rather conventionally expected or required of agents during intervals in which they perform or could perform other actions entailing bodily movements—which, again quite naturally, do not invite causal explanation or assessment in terms of freedom (except in terms of the capacity to act of one's own volition) but do invite appraisal in

terms of normative responsibility and the like. As a first approximation, we may say that to characterize an event of the first sort
as an action is to *describe* someone's behavior and that to identify
an act of the second sort is to *ascribe* a certain import to someone's behavior and that act-ascriptions (by no means confined to
omissions) presuppose a range of act-descriptions.

2. The Identification of Actions

It is, it must be noted, difficult to fix the conditions for correctly
describing someone's behavior as an act or action or even for individuating actions. Two distinct but related problems arise. For
one, it appears—excepting certain conventional constraints to be
considered—that the description of an action and its consequences
(that is, its import, not any independent causal outcome) can always be elided to form a description of a bona fide action that,
characteristically, can be construed as the same action as the original. And for another, it appears to be impossible to formulate a
compelling and comprehensive rule for reidentifying one and the
same action under alternative descriptions and for distinguishing
distinct actions under descriptions not substantially different from
those that single out the same action. The only context in which
such a rule operates is one in which either act-ascriptions obtain or
in which, as in chess, the only actions admitted are those, precisely, that are defined by the constitutive rules of the game or endeavor. Here, then, a host of puzzles arise.

Imagine that, in a chess match, I move my queen from one
square to another. I may, in so doing, place my opponent's king
in jeopardy—in check, in fact. In the context of a game of chess,
the moving of the queen *is* the action of placing the king in check.
It is possible also to hold that the moving of the queen has the
consequence (that is not an action) of placing the king in check.
Here, the elision of act and consequence is effected in such a way
that 1) the act under the original description may be identified with
the act under the elided description; 2) the constitutive purpose of

the game justifies the identification; 3) events (such as hesitantly moving one's fingers to move a piece, without actually touching any piece) that, apart from the chess game, may be construed as actions are not admitted as actions at all (chess moves), that is, as actions constitutive of the game; 4) elisions of act and consequence that fail to preserve or obscure the point and purpose of the game and of particular moves (such as moving a piece with the consequence of distracting the attention of some spectator) are disallowed, in redescribing actions performed in playing a game of chess. Consequently, in chess, strictly construed, we may admit only certain events as actions and we may elide (the description of) act and consequence within certain limits only; and restrictions of both sorts are governed by the constitutive rules of the game. It is also, of course, possible to say that the act of moving the queen entails, under the circumstances, the distinct (but not separable) act of placing the king in check. Clearly, only a convention can, in such cases, decide between speaking of the act and its consequence, the reidentification of one and the same act under alternative descriptions, and the entailment of one act by another.

But consider that life is not a game. If I move my hands up and down on a pump handle, with the consequence—since, unbeknown to me, the well water is poisoned—that the house water is poisoned, with the consequence that the inhabitants of the house are poisoned, can elisions or entailments comparable to those admissible in chess be introduced as admissible redescriptions of my action? The trouble is that to answer either affirmatively or negatively presupposes that there are rules for the "game of life," reference to which will decide admissible descriptions of actions and admissible elisions and entailments—that is, rules for individuating the constitutive acts of the "game of life." But such rules, precisely, are what we lack and cannot, in principle, supply once and for all. It is of course entirely possible that someone may, in accordance with one convention or another, reidentify one and the same act under alternative descriptions or distinguish entailing and entailed acts; and, provided that his usage is relatively explicit and consistent, he may be understood. But if a quarrel arises as to whether there really is here one act or two or an act and its consequence, we could not possibly resolve the matter save by stipulating or adopting a convention—which would then change the force of the initial quarrel. Alternatively put, the conventions for individuating actions are by no means as settled as those for individuating physical objects; nor are the reasons for introducing such conventions, of a uniform kind or as intimately associated with the provision of a coherent and comprehensive theory of the external world. But this confirms what we have already glimpsed, that the individuation of actions does not necessarily depend on causal or intentional considerations (that is, considerations of personal intention).

The admission has deeper consequences.

If there were fixed goals or purposes or norms or rules of life, then the rules for individuating and reidentifying actions and for the elision of act and consequence could be readily specified, in a way that would parallel our practice with respect to chess. Now, institutionalized practices and conventions approximate the condition but not decisively. For, chess is nothing but a conventional game and the trouble with the conventions of society is, precisely, that they are regularly challenged and altered and often conflict in a variety of ways. Chess *is* the game defined by a certain set of rules, which rules call (in this sense) for no justification; but the conventions that obtain in any society are just what critics and defenders regularly seek to justify in terms of some non-conventional norms or rules of life. To the extent that we operate within a conventional system, we shall, more or less, be able to identify and reidentify the same and different actions under alternative descriptions (as in the cases of pumping water and striking an officer) and we shall be able, also, to set limits to the elision of act and consequence (as, for instance, in refusing to allow a redescription of a murder and its fortunate consequence in terms merely of gaining the consequence). The only question that arises, therefore, concerns whether there are discoverable norms or normative rules that set constraints on the identification of actions and on the elision of act and consequence—norms or rules that cannot be reduced merely to the prevailing ideology or preferred values or the historical accidents of a given society. Clearly, the question comes to this: Does man have a natural or essential function *qua* man? For, if he does not, then the individuation and elision of acts are, in principle, a conventional matter, however naturally they may appear to conform with the interests of a given society. And if he does, then, given such norms and rules, questions about elision and individuation can, rather as in chess, be decisively resolved.

The entire matter may be put conditionally here, for it is more important to grasp what would be presupposed in articulating the rules for individuating and eliding acts than in actually doing so: we manage, within limits, to provide for some range of reidentification and distinction among acts and actions and for the admission and rejection of elisions among acts and consequences; but these depend, minimally, on a policy of act-ascriptions (as in criminal law, in contractual relations, and in formal sports) or on highly formalized activities in which admissible acts are constitutively defined by the rules of those activities (as in chess) or on the basis of formulable interests (e.g., prudential interests) assumed to prevail in a given context of discourse. Where the conventions are themselves under fire, or where the act-descriptions provided are thought not to be merely conventional (as when redescriptions of actions that would obscure or elide some act's classification as murder is disputed), the theoretical justification required for disallowing any and all alternative conventions for individuating and identifying actions (supposing, of course, that there is some interest in advancing such conventions) must rest on a cognitivist claim regarding the normative values appropriate to human life, that is, that such values are in some fair sense open to discovery. To the extent that such a justification is either difficult or impossible to provide, the individuation and elision of actions are entirely conventional matters answering to certain relatively regular interests of diverse societies. Clearly, this has enormous consequences for the objectivity of history and of political and moral activity. For, if cognitivism with respect to normative values is incapable of being defended, then the implicitly normative import of our conventional description of human actions betrays our partisan commitment to one set of values or another: to appreciate this, one has only to think, for instance, of contrasting bourgeois and Marxist descriptions of transactions involving property. Consequently, historical descriptions are objective (in default of moral cognitivism and the like) only relative to some given convention; seen from the outside—either from the critic's point of view or from the view of the field anthropologist—they are themselves the expression of ideological alternatives and inescapably partisan. Were it not for the fact that the individuation and identification of physical objects do not entail *such* normative preferences (rest on more fundamental considerations), the admission would work havoc upon any attempt to construct a coherent picture of the world. But what we may say, here, is that the theory of human action concerns a relatively superficial (however important) stratum of the world. That is, whatever the ultimate, ontological connections between human actions and the physical world (clearly linked to intelligibility and cognition), the description of actions as objectively discernible within a wider range of objects and events itself presupposes the describability of conceptually simpler and more fundamental things; for instance, physical movements, described in non-intentional or non-teleological terms, are themselves entailed by, but do not entail, such significant human actions as signing a check or moving a pawn or signalling a turn. And, more generally, actions presuppose entities that may exist at particular times without performing any actions at those times, but the occurrence of actions without agents is impossible.

Again, although established conventions provide for objective characterizations of actions relative to the governing rules and interests of such conventions, one may always ask what any man *as a man* has done, has actually done. And, in the sense in which, in-quiring thus, we are not bound by the recognized roles, offices, relationships, institutions of a given convention, we can describe what men fulfilling their roles and offices are *really* doing, by reference only to an ulterior theory of normative human values (for man *qua* man), in terms of which to differentiate what men *appear* to be doing (including what they believe they are doing) and what they are really doing. But if, as already suggested, such theories cannot be cognitively validated, then there is no exclusively correct way of describing human actions and all such descriptions are inherently partisan and conventional in nature.

3. Explanations by Causes and by Reasons

These considerations illuminate a further feature of our discourse about actions. For, if the classification of actions answers most directly to certain socialized interests having to do with normative appraisal (with what is forbidden, permitted, blameworthy, functional, neutral, negligible, and the like), then it is not likely that the explanation of actions should always—though it may—take the form of a causal explanation. And, *if* the usual reidentifications of action under alternative descriptions be allowed, then it is logically impossible that familiar explanations of actions—in terms of intentions, reasons, purposes, and the like—may be subsumed as a subset of causal explanations. But this is not to say either that actions cannot be provided with causal explanations or that reasons and intentions that enter into non-causal explanations of actions cannot also enter into causal explanations of the same actions. Thus, concede that one and the same action may be described as: a) flicking a light switch; b) turning on the light; c) illuminating the room; d) alerting a prowler. Let us suppose that the agent does what is described under a) with the intention of accomplishing what is described under c), but does not have the intention corresponding to d). If, *ex hypothesi,* we may elide the act-description and the consequence-description to provide a redescription of the act in question—that is, admitting description c)—then the act as described under a) may be said to be explained by redescribing it under description c). The question is whether the explanation is, and must be, a species of causal explanation. Admittedly, having the intention of illuminating the room is, here, a causal factor leading to the action of flicking the light switch and, as such, the explanation of the action is cast as a causal explanation. But if the explanation of an action by reference to the intention with which it was performed or the purpose it was to serve or the reason for performing it, is (and cannot but be) a causal explanation, then reference to the intention or reason or the like (that plays a causal role) must be relevant to the explanation of the action *under whatever description it is identified*. Surely, *if* the intention had by the agent enters into a causal explanation of his action because it is the cause or part of the cause of his action, it will do so, regardless of the description under which it is identified. The intention of illuminating the room, for instance, does enter into a causal explanation of the action of alerting the prowler. It does not, however, enter into an explanation by reasons (by way of reference to reasons, intentions, purposes, and the like) of the action *under that description;* for, *ex hypothesi,* the agent does not have the corresponding intention and having the one intention does not entail having the other. In this sense, explanation by reasons is description-relative in a way in which causal explanations are not (because causes are not); *a fortiori,* explanation by reasons cannot be a species of causal explanation, although reasons and intentions may function as causes of actions performed.

It is important to be clear about what has been demonstrated here, which is not altogether easy to state unequivocally. *If* explanation by reasons is a *species* of the genus of explanations distinguished as causal explanations, then whatever is essential to the genus will appear in the species. But it is essential to the genus that explanations (of the causal variety) are not description-relative, *in the sense* that a causal explanation is an explanation that holds of some appropriate item identified under whatever description we may provide—which is not to say that a causal explanation can be offered for everything that can be individuated, that there are no constraints on the nature (consequently, on the describability) of whatever is subject to causal explanation, or that causal explanations, *qua* explanations, are not subject to suitable logical constraints. But if, on the hypothesis, what serves as a reason explaining an action is a cause or part of the cause or the cause of that action, then *whatever differentia* distinguishes reasons from mere causes, that very item—as a reason—must be relevant to the explanation by reasons of the given action under any description. Explanation by reasons cannot be a species of explanation by causes if a given reason is not, wherever (*per* genus) relevant as a cause of some action, *relevant also* as a reason or part of the reason or the reason of that action (under alternative descriptions). It is perfectly possible to say that if an agent acts on a reason he *has*—where, if he has a reason, his having it causes him to act thus—explanations by reasons (of this restricted sort) entail causal explanations (and do so trivially); but this is merely to say—what is important enough and has been disputed—that what may serve as a reason may also serve as a cause. But it would be a mistake to hold that an entailment of this sort is itself tantamount to a demonstration that explanation by reasons is a species of explanation by causes (unless such an entailment was merely so christened). And, if explanations by reasons may be provided for actions, where the explaining reasons need not be *had* by the agent (where, say, a man signals, without intending to signal at all), which are (on any reasonable view) of the same logical sort as the explanation by reasons of an action for which the agent *has* reasons (where he intends to signal, for instance), then we see even more forcefully both why it is unnecessary to construe explanation by reasons as a species of explanation by causes *and* why it is utterly inconclusive to attempt to force the subsumption merely by showing that explaining a given action by reasons —*where the reason supplied is a reason had, in the causally relevant sense*—entails explaining that action by causes. The possibility of one and the same thing's serving as both a reason and a cause (by way of being a reason *had,* in the causal sense) has nothing whatsoever to do with distinguishing the logical features of explanations by reasons and explanations by causes.

Alternatively put, we may say that causal contexts are extensional, in the straightforward sense that whatever serves as a cause does so under any description or designation provided. But contexts of causal *explanation* need not be extensional, in the sense that what serves as a cause *and* conforms to a certain model of linking sentences in a perspicuous explanation of the causal sort requires that *what* serves as a cause be specified under certain descriptions or designations only. Consequently, the provision of causal explanations presupposes causal linkages among what can be extensionally identified. But *what* serves as a reason, *qua* reason, can be specified only in a non-extensional context; and rationalization, like causal explanation, is similarly non-extensional. For, if an intention or reason or the like suitably rationalizes an action, the action so rationalized cannot, preserving truth, be identified under any and all alternative descriptions or designations. Thus, if intending to illuminate the room rationalizes the action of turning on the light, it does not rationalize that action under the description of alerting a prowler. But then, clearly, rationalization cannot be a species of causal explanation, for it presupposes that *reasons* are specified only in non-extensional contexts, whereas causal explanation presupposes that *causes* are specified always in extensional contexts. Thus, we say that we may confirm singular causal statements even when we are unable to provide a statement of the covering laws under which a suitable causal explanation may be provided. If we take statements of the schematic form, '*a* because *b*,' to be confined to causal contexts (but not to obtain in contexts of causal explanation), we could link, say, *events* causally under the rubric. But then, we should not be obliged to treat '*a* because *b*' as non-truth-functional, simply because there would then be no relevant connectives linking *sentences* to consider. And if we take '*a* because *b*' as in the context of causal explanations, then '*a*' and '*b*,' construed as sentences about what is identified under the first schema, are themselves specified in a non-extensional context where, furthermore, 'because' cannot be treated truth-functionally. Thus, if it is true that the President of France's making a speech caused a world crisis, then it is true that De Gaulle's making a speech caused a world crisis, and it is true that the longest-nosed Frenchman's making a speech caused a world crisis; but it does not follow from this that if De Gaulle's making a speech (that is, the *statement* that De Gaulle made a speech) causally explains the occurrence of the crisis, then the longest-nosed Frenchman's making a speech causally explains the occurrence of the crisis. To preserve explanatory power is to do more than to preserve truth. But on these grounds, we need not deny either that causal contexts are extensional or that extensional contexts are truth-functional.

The difference between the two species of explanation is critical. Causal explanation presupposes that a lawlike connection holds between cause and effect, even where it is not yet possible to formulate the relevant law; but explanation by reasons presupposes, rather, a background of institutionalized rules and norms of behavior, the breach of which is not physically impossible but which invites appraisal of some relevant sort. The one sort of explanation is not subsumable under the other, and that we concern ourselves with explanations of both sorts vis-à-vis actions tends to confirm the mixed nature of the concept of action itself. In general, the rules intended have normative import relative to some alleged interest, and actions falling under such rules may be appraised as correct or incorrect or as forbidden or required or permitted or as serviceable or as functional or not or as neutral or negligible to the interests given or the like. Sometimes, as in chess, the rules are relatively fixed and explicit and complete. But, with respect to the relatively informal life of a society, what often pass as rules are projected regularities—open-ended rules, if that is not construed as a contradiction—informed by some purpose, in terms of which to understand the point of repeating a given action (even by way of qualitatively different movements) or of performing alternative actions serving the same end. And, of course, it is always possible that some quite arbitrary action be performed, lacking any fully institutionalized use (simply raising one's arm, for instance, for no ulterior reason), whose admission as an action rests upon construing a given event as suitably analogous to the paradigms of action that are admitted. The informality cannot be eliminated.

4. Freedom and Choice

Having grasped this distinction, we may return to the question of causality and freedom. For, human freedom, the ability of an agent to perform an action of his own volition, need not be contra-causal at all, hence not incompatible with any form of defensible determinism insofar as it is merely a causal theory. Some forms of determinism will be incompatible with human freedom, in the sense that whatever *causal* factors are required for freedom may be inoperative on *some* determinist thesis. Thus, for instance, if an agent's putative intentions or reasons or purposes never play a causal role or a sufficiently decisive causal role in the production of an action, then human freedom will have to be denied. And if human freedom presupposes real possibilities—that is, that an agent can effectively choose between alternatives that he considers —then a determinism that denies real possibility, that holds that whatever occurs is physically necessary, is incompatible with human freedom. But there is no evidence to support such a determinism and our causal explanations do not require it. In fact, physical laws are taken to be operative only given that certain initial conditions hold, and whether these could not have been otherwise is characteristically undecidable even if we could supply an additional, antecedent lawlike conditional that itself presupposes other relevant initial conditions; under these circumstances, lawlike connections are formulated with an implied and incompletely specifiable *ceteris paribus* clause. Hence it is that lawlike or nomic universals are read as or yield subjunctive conditionals and, in the form in which we presently understand them, are entirely neutral to the concept of human freedom—though not, necessarily, to the range of actual freedom.

Still, human freedom does presuppose that certain selected forces do not obtain or do not play a decisive causal role in the production of actions. For instance, if a man does what he does under drugs, hypnosis, compulsion, and the like, then he has not acted freely. This is not to say that he has not performed an action. The line between a mere happening and an action is difficult to draw—and is at best informal—but it is not sufficient (on the arguments already advanced) to discount an event as an action merely because the agent has not acted freely. For instance, a compulsive murderer may, as such, commit acts of murder and a man may play a game of chess under hypnosis. So, freedom is a qualification of the way in which an action is performed—characteristically, an appraisive qualification bearing on responsibility and liability and the like—that obtains when certain causal influences are lacking and certain causal influences are present (those in particular that bear on deliberation, choosing, formulating purposes, intentions, reasons, and the like). It is, therefore, a concept characteristically employed in qualifying actions for which certain causal explanations are not appropriate (where others are appropriate) *and* for which explanations by reasons are always appropriate. But, in any case, it is entirely coherent to speak of free actions where causes operate on *agents* (as in education), and it is coherent to speak of *actions* that are not free where suitable causes also affect agents (as in following a post-hypnotic suggestion). Again, actions are qualified not only as free but as voluntary, involuntary, deliberate, intentional, inadvertent, and the like; and these qualifications are regularly not confined to causal considerations, reflect rather the governing institutionalized interests —not by any means restricted to questions of guilt and blame—in terms of which certain descriptions and redescriptions of a given action are sustained. Thus, for instance, a young boy who has neglected his school work all year turns in an impressive project at the end of the year: since it was unexpected (without raising a question of fault or blame), one wonders whether it was done voluntarily, of his own volition. Again, a man who has repudiated a friend of long standing, because of some imagined insult, is persuaded by his wife to make up; her insistence causes him to decide (impulsively) to do so, though it is against his inclination. In a sense, he has acted involuntarily. What we see from these and endless other such cases is that qualifications of these sorts cannot meaningfully be applied to all actions, that apparently complementary qualifications (the voluntary and involuntary, for instance) are not actually complementary and obtain on decidedly informal and variable grounds, and that the governing considerations for their ascription are primarily those relating to personal and institutionalized interests and normative values.

In general, it may be said that distinctions respecting volition, choice, and freedom—the use of nominalized expressions is, frankly, characteristically misleading—are invariably adverbial. To choose, for instance, is not to perform an act as such but to perform an act "choosingly," that is, in a way that involves deliberation regarding alternatives relative to some objective and a state of mind disposed to that alternative believed and judged to be best or better under the circumstances. If free acts were acts that are chosen and choice were itself a free act, we should be driven to a vicious regress. Again, the qualifications here considered are all somewhat idealized in accord with the norms and practices of a given society: ascriptions of volition, choice, and freedom typically rest on the briefest, even incipient, forms of thought, reflection, decision, argument, formulation of purposes. There are no straightforwardly necessary or sufficient conditions (unless trivialized) regarding determinate psychological states that govern the ascription of choice and the like; what are used are institutionalized rules informed by the interests of a society bearing on responsibility, praise and blame, accomplishment. But this is to say that to speak of choice is more like rendering a verdict regarding one's action than providing a description of interior mental states. Also, even if we cannot speak of actual choice where no congruent action actually obtains, there is a difference between the capacity to judge which of two alternatives is the better relative to some objective and the capacity to act in accord with that judgment; and there is a difference between so judging on rational grounds and rationally acting on that judgment. If, for example, the drug addict is rationally capable of judging what is best for him, he need not, for that very reason, also be capable of acting (or choosing to act) in accord with his judgment: he may show a weakness of will (*akrasia*) where he shows a strength of judgment. Again, though he may judge one alternative to be better than another, *ceteris paribus,* a man need not choose that alternative, since his *ceteris paribus* considerations may override the judgment. A man may be a rational akrasiac and, also, may reasonably not act in accord with a judgment servicing given wants or desires. In the one case, though his reasoning be impeccable, other of his psychological powers may be impaired (unless we claim, unconvincingly, that an agent invariably knows what his abilities are). And in the other, though his argument be decisive, the bearing of his reasoning on the reasonableness of his attendant behavior is contingent on the bearing of the *ceteris paribus* consideration. For reasons of this sort, the so-called practical syllogism reduces to the theoretical syllogism. For, we cannot (distinguishing judgment and volition) do more than construe the beliefs and desires of an agent as entailing or embodying certain premises; and we cannot (unless trivially) suppose that, given the premises of a practical syllogism (in terms of his beliefs and desires and the like), a man is bound to act or to intend to act or to be committed or disposed to act (the counterpart "conclusion") in accord with the premises: to be committed to acting, *ceteris paribus,* may effectively be to be not committed at all; and the akrasiac need not have made an error in reasoning at all. The logical relations within so-called practical arguments are identical with those of theoretical arguments, and the relationship between reasoning and action is not that of argument at all. (All of this is typically obscured by assigning so-called practical reasoning to the ideally rational man and concluding, say, that the akrasiac is not rational.)

It is also useful to distinguish actions from what may, technically, be called deeds, that is, from what an agent "does." For, although it is true that when an agent performs an action, the action is something that he does, not everything that he does— following linguistic usage—is properly construed as an action. For instance, an agent may bleed or die or sleep or suffer, but these are normally not things that he does by way of performing actions (there is, for instance, no relevant sense in which he does what he does in accord with a custom or practice or rule—a man does not actually sleep, though he may go to bed in order to sleep, in accord with a rule). Here, it seems we admit that the agent does these things because of their obvious importance to the prudential concerns of men, which therefore may bear decisively on matters of responsibility and liability and the like; although, we do not hold that men doing these things are responsible or liable for them as such. And it is, perhaps, from such a range as this that what we call acts of negligence and omission (not merely deeds, though not necessarily deliberate or intentional) have been elevated, precisely because responsibility and liability are assigned. But the distinction suggests further the connection between actions and events. Actions, clearly, form a subset of deeds and deeds, of events. And all the problems regarding the individuation and elision of actions may arise in the context of events (that are not actions or that, though they be actions, are construed merely as events). Events and deeds that are not actions, of course, call only for causal explanation; and actions are open both to causal explanation and to explanation by reasons, where the latter is not reducible to or able to be subsumed under the former. Events that are deeds correspond to verbal formulations in which agent-pronouns may be followed by event-verbs: thus, 'He died,' 'He is bleeding.' And actions (that are deeds) correspond to such verbal formulations in which what the event-verbs designate are governed in the manner described by institutionalized rules and the like: thus, 'He murdered,' 'He promised,' 'He shifted gears.'

5. The Description of Events

The problems concerning events in general—beyond the special problems already indicated respecting actions, that is, the problems of individuation, reidentification under alternative descriptions, elision (and, in fact, therefore, problems about the ontological status of actions)—tend to collect around two considerations. For one, the very concept of an event is unclear; and for another, we require a theory of events that countenances familiar entailments among sets of sentences purportedly about the same event. Our usual way of speaking of events is to assign them, as an essential property, temporality (or spatio-temporality). Thus, to speak of the death of Caesar as of an event is to speak of something that occurred at a certain time (or during a certain time) or of something that has a certain spatio-temporal attribute. Clearly, the individuation of events requires a theory of time and space; but the prospect of defining time and space independently of events (and objects) or of events independently of time and space seems impossible. In practice, therefore, we proceed by way of spatio-temporal conventions: the birth of Plato preceded the birth of Aristotle by reference to other events that are taken to fix the direction and measurement of time; but on what grounds to identify the temporality-fixing or spatio-temporality-fixing events, with respect to which the temporal location or spatio-temporal location of other events may be decided, raises questions about the ultimate coherence of our global view of the world, including, prominently, the development of physics. The issue requires a theory of referential relations, not a determinate and fixed first referent. Again, are we to say that two events may have precisely the same spatio-temporal attributes—for instance, a transparent liquid cube's changing color and temperature simultaneously; or may a single event involve a complex change—for instance, the event of the avalanche's burying the village? Both ways of speaking are tolerated. It is, in fact, just the stability of our procedures for individuating physical objects by the use of count nouns that we suppose we should have to match if we were to introduce events, actions, states, and the like as full-fledged particulars, that inclines us to demur.

Furthermore, on the strength of such considerations, we are bound to ask ourselves whether 'the death of Caesar' and 'the death of Caesar in the Forum' and 'the death of Caesar in 44 B.C.' identify distinct events or one and the same event. (A counterpart question, regarding actions, obviously suggests itself here.) For, if temporality or spatio-temporality is an essential attribute of events, then if 'the death of Caesar' identifies an event it does so (elliptically, so to say) by means at least of such an attribute. In that case, 'Caesar died in the Forum in 44 B.C.' entails 'Caesar died' because, on the thesis given, 'Caesar died' must be an ellipsis for 'Caesar died [somewhere at some time]'; otherwise, 'the death of Caesar' does not designate an event. (Whether events may be identified temporally only or must be identified spatio-temporally is, of course, another complication, a complication that depends at least on the relationship we admit to hold between the mind and the body.) But, apart from questions of the essential attributes of events, there is no limit to the possible qualification of events—corresponding to the possible qualification of things (the one usually expressed adverbially; the other, adjectivally). Here is the principal reason for construing events as particulars or as values of bound variables, of which we may predicate what we please and of whatever complexity we please.

Thus, 'Sebastian strolled through the streets of Bologna at 2' may be added to by way of an endless variety of modifications without obliging us to deny that one and the same event is being referred to; and the statement entails, in a straightforward way, 'Sebastian strolled through Bologna' (which Sebastian may have done many times), 'Sebastian strolled at 2' (which he may have done in many places), and 'Sebastian strolled' (which, though, if true, he must have done somewhere at some time, may be only one way in which he was wont to walk). These considerations also suggest that the essential temporality or spatio-temporality of events (which we have provisionally conceded) is, however reasonable, a rather incomplete claim. For, it is not at all clear that other qualifications would not be as essential, without our being able to specify the entire range of such allegedly essential attributes. Thus, for instance, it is entirely reasonable to hold that if he strolled, Sebastian must have strolled in some way; that is, the event that is Sebastian's strolling must not only have spatio-temporal attributes but also a qualification as to manner of execution. But then, we should have absolutely no basis for distinguishing satisfactorily between essential and non-essential attributes of particular events. The most plausible proposal, therefore, which is in itself by no means conceptually adequate, is that events (and actions and deeds) may be admitted as particulars, of which we may make the usual predications; but what it is to be an event—and whether events exist or whether there are such entities as events—remains a matter of very considerable puzzlement.

It appears, then, that actions must be the actions of some agent and that agents must be antecedently and independently identifiable. Characteristically at least, events too befall particulars of identifiable sorts. Caesar's death occurs to Caesar; Sebastian's strolling is performed by Sebastian; and the shore's erosion is undergone by the shore. There are, however, some alternative possibilities. A clap of thunder appears to be an event that nothing undergoes in a precisely comparable way, although the event of its being caused is normally amenable to a parallel reading. The question suggests itself, then, whether, in principle, events could replace physical objects as basic particulars, that is, as particulars on the independent identification of which the identification of all particulars of every other kind may be made to depend; alternatively, the question arises whether the distinction between material objects and events can always or ever be maintained. For, it may be possible to construe perceived physical objects as complex events befalling ulterior theoretical entities or as event-slices of such entities (perhaps themselves events). We ought not dismiss out of hand the possibility of such alternative ontologies. Be that as it may, to the extent that events are assignable, in the manner illustrated, to particulars of other sorts, an anomaly arises regarding events that are themselves construed as instances of a kind of particular. For if, for example, Caesar's death is an event and 'Caesar died' is construed as a statement employing the dyadic predicate 'died' linking the individual Caesar and the particular event Caesar's death, we shall be bound to speak of a relationship between two distinct particulars, Caesar and Caesar's death. But, as has already been emphasized in connection with actions, a stroll is not an event unless construed elliptically as *someone's strolling*.

The anomaly, then, is simply this: the alleged relationship *between* particulars (as in construing 'died' dyadically) appears to be a mysterious expropriation of whatever is *internal* to the complex event itself, that *then* serves as one of a relevant pair of particulars (that is, Caesar's-death); what the apostrophe identifies within the event is counterpoised by an unanalyzable relationship between a particular that, as such, is not an event and an event that is indissolubly what occurs to that same particular. Possession will not do for the required relationship. For, if Caesar possesses Caesar's death in the manner in which a boy may possess a ball, then Caesar need not possess Caesar's death when Caesar exists (which is admissible) *and* Caesar's death may exist though not possessed by Caesar (which is not admissible); and if Caesar possessed Caesar's death in the manner in which a ball possesses a certain color (that is, predicatively), then *events are not particulars at all* and the expressions that appear to designate them must be (elliptical) predicate-expressions. On this view, however complex the predicate-expression 'died' may be alleged to be (and we must remember here the possibility of adding indefinitely many adverbial qualifications for event-verbs), death is predicated of Caesar and is not itself a relationship between two particulars, Caesar and Caesar's death; for the point of admitting the alleged (and redundant) relationship is exhausted (non-anomalously) by analyzing the event of Caesar's death itself in terms of predicating death of Cae-

sar. Furthermore—and by no means negligibly—the verbs characterizing the kind of event involved invariably change their sense
when indissoluble events are putatively analyzed in terms of relations between particulars answering to what is internal to the original event. Thus, on the thesis advanced, given the event of Caesar's death, Caesar is supposed *to die the death* and the death is
supposed *to be died by* Caesar. But, to say the least, this calls for
semantic clarification and cannot be expected to rely on the meaning of 'died' in 'Caesar died' (unless it is unnecessary): the new expression 'died' merely sounds the same as our 'died,' but it is utterly different.

Nevertheless, the proposal to construe events as particulars
admittedly facilitates the entailments we find natural (for instance,
the entailment between the proposition that Sebastian strolled
through the streets of Bologna at 2 and the proposition that Sebastian strolled through the streets of Bologna); and, though construing predicates governing event-predications as variably polyadic
places us at a distinct disadvantage regarding the syntax of statements involving such entailments (since the extensions of predicates of different polyadicity are either different or not clearly
commensurate), the alternative proposal itself has a deep and
seemingly irreparable fault. Also, the very entailments that are to
be admitted among statements about events employing predicates
of different degrees of polyadicity are themselves ulteriorly controlled by assumptions of reference and reidentification. But since
to individuate events as things of a certain kind supposes that an
adequate theory may be formulated concerning the properties of
things of that kind, the informality of shifting among variably polyadic predicates is, in principle, benign enough. Again, since it is
conceivable that, in order to preserve the structure of the entailments desired, the adverbial qualification of predicative expressions may yet be suitably regimented, it is not in the least clear
that we need begin with an enlarged ontology. In any case, treating events as the *subjects* of predication is not equivalent to treating them as *entities:* grammar is not equivalent to ontology.

Hence, on the thesis that perspicuous syntactical proposals are less fundamental than the analysis of the things of the world and the attributes and relations they may be said to have, we may—though we conveniently treat events and deeds and actions as particulars—find ourselves obliged to admit that events are, in general, what befall or occur to or through particulars—best rendered predicatively. Whether the thesis holds in all ontological contexts depends on the success with which, as has been suggested, events could function as basic particulars.

Also, any argument against construing events as independent particulars appears to run parallel, for instance, to what may be said against construing pains, thoughts, emotions, and similar mental conditions as independent particulars: to admit the one would appear to be to lose a seemingly strong reason for denying such status to the other. Despite their distinctive differences, then, actions, deeds, events, pains, thoughts, dreams, and the like may be said to be *subaltern* particulars, in that their admission as particulars is essentially the dependent result of construing suitable but contingent predications regarding such particulars as persons and material objects as replaceable by reference to new and indissoluble substantives. That is, the entailments we wish to countenance—as that 'Sebastian strolled through the streets of Bologna' entails 'Sebastian strolled'—may be provided for by linking in a story-relative way the subaltern particular, the stroll or Sebastian's stroll, to what is predicated of Sebastian: that he strolled. Any power that we have to qualify events in as many ways as we wish is then provided for, and we free ourselves from the awkward invention of puzzling relationships between the particulars to which events befall and such befallings now construed as independent events. Also, to construe events as subaltern particulars is to show only a certain conceptual asymmetry between speaking of events (of the sort given) and of persons and bodies. It is emphatically not to show that persons and physical objects are basic to every viable ontology, that events (of some other sort—microtheoretical events, perhaps) could not serve as the basic entities of an adequate ontology, or that persons and bodies, say, could exist without their being in particular states or without particular events befalling them. In short, the grammatical advantages may be secured without being construed in terms of ontic commitment. But, without an independent criterion for individuating and reidentifying events and actions (which, at present, is not forthcoming and which, on the argument, may not even be needed), we can do no better than provide criteria for story-relative identity. This we can do already, and this cannot be bettered by the invention in question.

6. Actions and Persons

A final word about actions is in order. Actions, as has been said, are a species of deeds and deeds, a species of events. But if we construe actions as entailing physical movements, there is no bare physical movement that, added to any set of bare physical movements, would transform events not yet properly counted as actions, into actions; and there is no bare physical movement that, subtracted from any acknowledged actions, would oblige us to convert such actions into events that could not then be construed as actions (however suitably redescribed). There is, then, no prospect of reducing actions to physical movements. The admission, however, is not in itself incompatible with some version of materialism. For, the condition under which events are construed as actions is just that (i) the event is a deed; and (ii) the deed is judged eligible for explanation by reasons, or the deed is judged eligible for causal explanation in which whatever normally serves explanation by reasons serves as a cause or part of the cause of the event in question consistently with certain qualifying norms. For example, the onset of greed may cause me to stumble, but my stumbling need not, therefore, count as an action. The reason is simply that the respect in which greed causes me to stumble may not justify grading (or describing) the event as an action (though it be a deed). If an explanation by reasons is admissible and if what is thus explained is the occurrence of a deed, then the deed is an action; and if a causal explanation of a deed is provided (which is invariably admissible), then the explanation must (if the deed is to be an action) include factors that, on independent grounds, serve to qualify the deed as an action. Consequently, even though we may distinguish between act-descriptions and act-ascriptions, actions are identified only by reference to prevailing practices, institutions, interests, norms, and the like. Actions, then, are events involving persons (or fair surrogates) suitably interpreted in terms of some institutional network (or fair analogue); correspondingly, the causes of actions must include factors that cannot suitably be characterized without reference to that same institutional network. So, not only is explanation by reasons not a species of causal explanation but the causal explanation of *actions* is not, so far forth, reducible to causal explanation in purely physical terms and is, indeed, itself conceptually dependent on the model of explanation by reasons.

Actions are performed by agents, and agents are persons, human beings, gods, Martians, or, by extension, higher mammals that bear a sufficiently close likeness to men—in appearance, behavior non-intentionally construed, and physical nature—to support the epithet. It is sometimes thought that *if* causal accounts of putative actions are admitted, human agency reduces to physical causation. If this were so, then agency would indeed reduce to mere causation. But it need not be so construed; for ascriptions of agency depend on criteria by which to construe particulars otherwise identified as mere physical bodies as creatures capable of being agents, that is, as persons or the like. In this sense, the logical distinction of the language of action depends on the fate of the mind-body relationship and on the analysis of persons; and to characterize some particular as an agent is, in effect, to tender it a certain degree of respect or to acknowledge that it has a certain range of skills and abilities, characteristically those of a rule-following and sentient creature and of whatever that entails. Hence, even if act-ascriptions presuppose act-descriptions *within* the context of the behavior of agents, to construe physical movement *as* human action and the like (to move from mere causation to agency) entails an appraisal or construction or interpretation of such movements in accord with the norms of rule-following behavior.

The upshot, then, is this: actions, though a subset of events, are, when construed as particulars, no more than subaltern particulars. Their specification presupposes persons (or suitable surrogates) to which alone actions may be ascribed. Interestingly enough, the admission of knowledge and belief, of sentience and non-sentient experience, and the like also presupposes persons or creatures having minds of some suitable complexity. There is, therefore, a distinct parallel between our discourse about action and about mental states, and the coherence of all such discourse is itself conditional upon that of the concept of a person. We have gained, therefore, the distinct advantage of uncovering a systematic convergence among a range of concepts of the most fundamental importance.

VII

LANGUAGE & TRUTH

To give the meaning of linguistic expressions, even of non-linguistic occurrences, is to speak a language. Nevertheless, both in learning one's own native language and learning a putatively alien language, it is indisputable that we are able to master given languages and the meaning of particular linguistic expressions from the disadvantaged position of having no (or no relevant) linguistic mastery at all. The disadvantage of the infant is ubiquitous and the more striking of the two limitations, and his normal accomplishment argues that there is no basis for a radical skepticism regarding mutual understanding within a common language or between speakers of distinct, even alien, languages. Speech behavior, like action in general, is identified by construing the bare physical events of making noises, marks, movements in accord with institutionalized practices and rulelike regularities —by means of which given strings of noises and the like are assigned significance or meaningfulness and, indeed, particular meanings. From this point of view, it is impossible to suppose that, say, confronting the speaker of an alien language, we may straightforwardly correlate occasions on which the speaker utters sentences with occasions on which determinate and relevant stimuli may be marked in the environment, while, at the same time, we fail to match his terms as well. To speak of the native's sentences and of the relevance of what he says for whatever we mark off as a perceivable stimulus, in accord with our own language and habits of mind, is already to have imposed a comprehensive linguistic hypothesis on his behavior. Words and sentences, also so-called speech acts and any other allegedly significant units of linguistic behavior, are systematically so interrelated that, in singling out what we take to be the native speaker's sentences on a given occasion of utterance, we have inevitably begun to theorize about his grammar and vocabulary as well. Skepticism regarding the mastery of an alien language supposes, mistakenly, that language is somehow a two-storey system, that we can mark off sentences without correspondingly being able to mark off terms. But the claim is incoherent. Even if differences in the possible parsing of given sentences cannot be correlated with differences of a behavioral kind, the admission of such differences entails the admissibility of non-behavioral grounds on which they may be marked off. Also, if it is claimed that we cannot confirm one (admittedly viable) ontology over others, with respect to a given language, the charge may be granted without skeptical import, since it is in the nature of ontological disputes that this be so and since if one ontology is viable with respect to a given language (including our own) then alternative ontologies must be as well. In a word, such a finding precludes skepticism rather than confirms it.

Also, natural languages are distinguished by their informality, both in the sense that liberties may be taken with whatever idealized linguistic rules we may provide and in the sense that improvisation beyond the range of antecedently formulated rules is always eligible—both falling properly within the boundaries of linguistic competence and intelligibility. But this means at least that a causal theory of meaning must be inadequate and that the explanation of the meaning of any utterances will be given in terms akin to explanation by reasons rather than explanation by causes; it means also that improvisation regarding would-be linguistic rules may be required in explaining the meaning of any given expression. In fact, the condition on which the analysis of intelligible discourse itself depends is the assumption that we share a public world both prelinguistically and linguistically. And it is just this assumption that sustains the admission of what may be called a perceptual core, that is, common sensory discriminations (that cannot and need not be formulated once and for all) with respect to which, critical linguistic distinctions that cannot be sustained on purely formal or intralinguistic grounds may yet appear reasonable—for instance, those bearing on the so-called analytic/synthetic distinction. In a word, in order to support the intelligibility of discourse in any way at all, some set of observation sentences (said to be synthetic) must be admitted— harking back to our public world—and, with respect to such as these, sentences said to be necessarily true because of their meaning (so-called analytic sentences) may be marked off as well. No other solution seems possible. Similarly, the continuing intelligibility of an evolving language can only be explicated in terms of some perceptual core, in the sense just given.

In the spirit of sharing a public world, the most important linguistic utterances are those that concern claims of truth. But the nature of truth is itself somewhat problematic. It is not unreasonable to hold that statements are true if and only if what they assert conforms with the facts about the world. The trouble is that facts cannot be identified independently of true statements: facts are, tautologously expressed, whatever about the world correspond to true statements. The upshot is that the criteria for ascribing truth to a given statement cannot be made to depend on some alleged discernment of the correspondence mentioned: truth is timeless and ascriptions of truth (and, therefore, the correction of apparent errors) are acts performed at particular times under particular circumstances. Also, facts are not the things of the world but only what, regarding the things of the world, corre-spond to true statements; they are not linguistic entities but only what, heuristically provided, subtend what true statements state. Hence, any attempt to fix purely semantic or linguistic conditions on which given statements in a natural language would be true would be obliged to address itself to the difficulty of formalizing, in accord with preferred models of sentence structure, the appar-ent structure of important runs of sentences, particularly those that bear on belief and similar (so-called propositional) attitudes. Also, to speak of the conditions on which given statements are true inevitably presupposes their relevance, that is, that they con-form to the meaning of such statements. Hence, there must be a difference between giving the meaning and giving the conditions for the truth of particular statements.

There is no uniform way of providing the meanings of words and expressions, both because linguistic expressions are of signifi-cantly different sorts and because instruction may be effective in a variety of ways. Essentially, to give the meaning of an expres-sion is to identify the rulelike ways in which it behaves in the context of using sentences to perform whatever characteristic acts we do thus perform. More narrowly construed, to give the mean-ing of an expression is to give, where relevant and possible, an-other expression that may properly replace it in the context of a certain run of sentences (said to be the connotative meaning) or to give, where relevant and possible, a sense of the objects or re-ferents that the expression designates (said to be the denotative meaning). Often, however, we can do no more than give a sense of the rules governing the use of the expression; and here, we sometimes say we are giving the meaning of a concept or explain-ing a concept—the concept that answers to the rulelike use of the expression in question. But then, returning to our initial theme, since to give meanings is to use language, linguistic behav-ior itself cannot be reduced to more elementary processes.

1. Learning a Language

What the nature of language is is in many respects the most baffling of questions. If things may, in some sense, have meaning independently of language—as when one says that rain clouds mean rain or that those spots mean measles—the attribution of meaning presupposes language. But, in the most distinctive and characteristic sense in which we speak of them, meanings attach to pieces of language. Yet, although language is surely the most remarkable and distinguishing achievement of man, the most intimately human and ubiquitous of his skills, it is hard to say what a language and what meaning are. Our habit of speech inclines us to speak of meanings as of things, for we appear to individuate meanings, to identify one and the same and different meanings for different expressions and the like; but what it is to be a meaning remains unanswered and seems an awkward question. Also, it is difficult to say how to determine whether an apparent piece of language to which meaning would normally seem to attach, actually has meaning (or is meaningful); or to say how to determine or how to present the meaning of any suitable piece of language that admittedly is meaningful.

Two initial, boundary conditions seem useful to establish: one inhering in the very nature of language learning; the other, an empirical possibility, evidently rather rare on earth but surely occurrent. The first condition is that men are born without a knowledge of the tongue that, as we say, is their native language. This means that, whatever the conceptual difficulties, it must be possible to learn a language without having mastery of any; and yet, all accounts of instruction in the meaning of linguistic expressions themselves presuppose some measure of competence in a language, either the very one in which given expressions are unfamiliar or another into which given expressions may be translated. The second condition is that, on occasion (or hypothetically), language users may come into contact with an utterly unfamiliar lan-

guage (Martian, for instance) and may, by observing the behavior
and apparently concomitant circumstances of use, satisfactorily
learn to speak this alien language. Here, substantial constraints on
speculation suggest themselves. For, if we do not, *ex hypothesi,*
initially know the language in question, then *if* learning the meaning of expressions in a language initially requires either paraphrasing (within a common language) or translation (from one to
another), then it would be impossible ever to learn a hitherto utterly unknown language. But surely this sort of learning must have
obtained many times in the past among adventurous peoples moving rapidly and far beyond their own borders; and, in principle, it
might well happen in outer space. *And,* since the first condition is
even more strenuous than the second regarding comparable
objectives—learning an unknown language—the unfailing fulfillment of the first renders the prospect of fulfilling the second quite
realistic.

If the learning of an alien language were admitted to be at all
possible, then it would be unconvincing, at any arbitrarily selected
moment in such learning, to intrude the threat of radical skepticism. That is, if we can imagine learning an utterly alien language
up to a point, we can have no justifiable basis for claiming that we
could not learn the rest of the language beyond that point or learn
it in a way that would, in principle, put all skeptical doubts regarding alien grammar and alien semantics to rest. The only possible basis for such a charge would require that language as such be
essentially a two-storey affair and that the second storey of a language could, demonstrably, be learned only by learning what be-
longed to the first storey *and* that alternative but non-equivalent
hypotheses regarding the semantics of the second storey could always be fitted to the total range of putative language behavior but
could not, in principle, be differentially confirmed or disconfirmed. For example, one might suppose that *sentences* could
meaningfully be marked out in terms of sensory stimuli and verbal
behavior apparently occasioned by such stimuli, but that *terms* introduced to parse such sentences could be specified only subse-

quently and in accord with variably semantic hypotheses about the internal grammar of the language—without any incongruity respecting the totality of verbal behavior.

The difficulty here is complex. If skepticism regarding the second storey were extended to cover the first, then we should have to deny that alien languages (including one's own, as in infancy) could ever be learned. If it were specified for a given language, so that *its* first and second storeys could be mapped and the relevant range of alternative hypotheses for the second storey provided, then the thesis would be self-defeating to that extent at least, for we should, *ex hypothesi,* already understand a considerable range of the semantical features of such a second storey. Finally, if some residual skepticism could not, in principle, be overcome here, then it could not be overcome in any language and we should all be in the position—even speaking what purported to be a common language—of fruitlessly trying to learn the inevitably alien language spoken by another speaking the same tongue. But this is to make an insoluble mystery of the very condition on which it makes sense at all to speak of a theory of language. Again, *if* a skepticism regarding alternative semantic hypotheses—that is, regarding the parsing of a total given language—were justified on the grounds of there being no distinctions with respect to linguistic behavior by reference to which we could confirm or disconfirm such alternative hypotheses, we should ask ourselves whether it would even be coherent to maintain that the alleged alternatives were indeed semantically distinct or how, on the assumption, anyone could, in principle, come to know that they were distinct. To know that given expressions have, on the basis of alternative parsings, different meanings entails knowing the meaning of the expressions thus parsed. But if the differences cannot be satisfactorily correlated with behavioral responses to putative stimuli in the environment—where to speak of *dispositions* to respond or of dispositions to respond appropriately is merely questionbegging —we could not consistently admit only behavioral criteria of sameness and difference of meaning. Meanings cannot be primarily a property of behavior if behavior cannot, in principle, justify our distinguishing, say, alternative translations of native expressions or alternative ways of individuating what native expressions purportedly designate. The implied skepticism is self-defeating in just the way in which skepticism in general is. We shall return to the issue.

The conditions, then, are instructive. We cannot expect infants learning a language to explain (linguistically) how, on the way to their virgin achievement, they are accomplishing this; and when they have already achieved it, it is, in a sense, too late—for we ourselves can speculate (however puzzled we are) back to these origins as well as they. In any case, it does not matter for our purpose; for, since children learn a language from an initial stage of no linguistic mastery of any kind, they cannot be *taught by means of language* the mastery of any language. So it is important to note that to give the meaning of any linguistic expression is to use language and that to teach anyone an alien language is to appeal at least to whatever linguistic competence he already possesses. Whatever interest there may be in the very genesis of language, speculation regarding it must be parasitic on a grasp of the nature of the mastery of language; and an adequate theory of meaning can be formulated only for expressions that, as identified, fall within the context of someone's linguistic competence. A corollary, bearing on an issue already raised, is that no language can be identified as radically unlike the language of the field observer; for, to identify some pattern of behavior as linguistic behavior is to be able to specify features that justify its counting as such; and to specify expressions of an alien language, whose determinate meanings are radically incapable of being expressed in the observer language is self-defeating. To say this is not to say that different languages may not be strikingly different in their conceptual orientation or that the vocabulary and constructions possible and favored in different languages do not substantially affect the kind of ease and difficulty with which different peoples may pursue given lines of conceptual inquiry. Also, granting that, in principle, any natural language may incorporate the linguistic facilities of any other, it becomes unclear what the sense is in which the conceptual capacity of different languages may be said to be wider or narrower—in some sense to be distinguished from that merely of social habit and psychological propensity. In fact, the very idea of individuating *all* natural language into exclusively demarcated, alternative systems of expression goes against the historical evidence. Here, then, skepticism reduces to mere empirical puzzlement: Can the noises or scratches we discriminate be construed as linguistically significant? And, if so, what then is their significance?

Two further considerations are in order here. First, the mapping of an alien language does not characteristically depend, and need not in principle depend, solely on apparent linguistic behavior. For instance, even though we lack any knowledge of the language of the builders of Stonehenge, *if* the theory about its construction as an observatory and about the detailed sightings of periodic eclipses and of the rising of the sun and the like is substantially correct (that is, a theory about the nonlinguistic but intentional work of the people of Stonehenge), then we know a great deal about the entities, properties, relationships, and the like that they must have provided for in their language. Secondly, even though we understand what we ourselves say about the putative entities we admit in our discourse, we are entirely capable of puzzling ourselves about what entities there really are—consistently *with* our intelligible usage. Consequently, to concede that there may well be indefinitely many alternative ontologies that may be fitted to the totality of a language in use does not entail any skepticism about the substantives admitted in an alien language. For, on the contrary thesis, we should not only fail to understand the language of alien speakers but should also fail to understand, each with respect to himself, what it is he is talking about! To admit entities like those putatively admitted in *our* language *is* to provide for the ontological puzzle noted (if it is a puzzle); any language that exhibits a comparable indeterminacy (there being no clear rules for deciding the ontological question) is a language that substantially resembles our own. It may be useful to add here as well that, in studying an alien people, the very demarcation of linguistic behavior obviously depends upon a justified partition *within* a larger range of significant behavior that is not narrowly or exclusively linguistic.

2. The Analysis of Natural Languages

Generally speaking, if language is viewed as a specialized and distinctively human instrument servicing survival and the satisfaction of particular interests, then it is reasonable to think of the use of language as the performance of linguistic acts or actions; and, as there are indefinitely many different kinds of acts—even non-linguistic acts—and as there are indefinitely many ways of construing utterances as alternatively describable acts or actions, the characterization and classification of linguistic acts will be bound to seek some conventionally plausible system of a scope and flexibility sufficient to comprehend all possibilities. Here, then, theory, borrowing from a grasp of the prudential and conventional interests of human agents, recommends a way of schematizing the occurrent utterances of the speakers of a language in terms of certain idealized types—for instance, as the act of asserting that something is so or the act of commanding another to do something or the like. Alternative classifications are entirely possible and preferences will be justified in terms of systematic simplicity and economy and range and the like. The key to such proposals, however, is that they must to some extent idealize the model acts they enumerate. The reasons are crucial.

For one thing, natural patterns of speech show a strong tendency favoring incomplete utterances and a reliance on what may be said to be implicit, in the use of such utterances, for those who have a relative mastery of an idiom. Speech, for instance, does not invariably proceed by forming complete sentences, even were it possible to say what a sentence is; and if the performance of distinct linguistic acts were alleged to be marked minimally by the formation and use of complete sentences, we should more often than not be at a loss (contrary to the obviously smooth functioning of linguistic communication) to grasp what particular linguistic act someone had performed. So actual speech should very likely be construed, in all its irregularity, informality, incompleteness, in terms of relatively idealized models and patterns that skilled speakers may be acknowledged to know and to which (on the linguistic evidence available) it is reasonable to assimilate those somewhat "imperfect" specimens. (And this, of course, suggests the implausibility of supposing that we proceed, in the analysis of an utterly alien language, by sorting out recognizably complete sentences matched to whatever may be alleged to be the stimulus-occasions on which they are used as they are.) Whatever criteria may be specified for well-formed sentences within a formalized language, we cannot expect that such criteria will serve as well to mark out, in a natural language, occasioned utterances *as* sentences or as sentences used to perform this or that linguistic act or as sentences so used with this or that ulterior intention. Sentences, words, linguistic acts are coordinate concepts in terms of which to construe concatenations of marks, sounds, movements, and the like as the very use of language.

A second consideration is this. Every living language appears to provide for linguistic improvisation and invention. No finitely enumerable set of sentences or words or phrases or inflections or linguistic acts can be taken to form a *fixed* set for which and for which only any hypothetical, idealized model purporting to identify some pattern of language may be expected and required to fit. Changes in a language include, in time, both the gradual elimination of hitherto standard expressions and standard uses of expressions and the invention of new elements of any of the sorts standardly identified (or of comparable but novel sorts) that function with at least equal authority in the language and that gradually require alterations in idealized models proposed to fit sets of such elements. The result is that the models superimposed on linguistic systems are inescapably normative and not merely descriptive *and* that such models may themselves be deposed or superceded or adjusted, with the evolution of a language, for theoretically cogent reasons. (This is implied, by the way, in speaking of linguistic *dispositions*.) In fact, there is no causal model for the analysis of language that may be said to be straightforwardly confirmed on scientific grounds. The essential reason is implied in what has already been said; for there are and can be no natural laws governing linguistic behavior, in the sense in which what is linguistically deviant may still be linguistically occurrent and in the sense in which revisions of the admissible and inadmissible do not presuppose any changes in causal laws.

If speech is informal, irregular, incomplete, implicit, inventive, then specimens of speech cannot, *ex hypothesi,* behave in fixed, lawlike ways. If the use of language may reasonably be construed in terms of the performance of acts and actions, then, given the larger analysis of actions, it cannot be said to be suitably explicated in terms of inexorable laws but only of rules approximated, in the sense of relative conformity to idealized models and norms. Alternatively, if language is viewed diachronically, then if specimens of linguistic usage obtaining at time t' are reasonably standard at that time but would appear deviant at time t—that is, in terms of rules or norms or models of usage formulated for an interval leading up to time t—then it is impossible to explicate the nature of linguistic regularities in terms of causal laws (whatever laws they may obey) but only in terms of rules—that, *ex hypothesi,* cannot be the same at t and at t'. And if language is viewed synchronically, the question still arises about correct and incorrect usage among statistically available specimens that may be explained in causally comparable ways. The upshot is that the putative rules of language are no more than proximate normative projections open to revision at least for the reason that evolutionary innovation is as characteristic a property of any natural language as relative regularity regarding any determinate element. Put another way, causal laws respecting linguistic behavior—and human actions in general—can be no stronger then statistical "laws," in the sense, precisely, that human beings *habituated in accord with certain rules or institutions* will predictably behave in accord with such "laws" until, what is not physically impossible, they alter established habits and invent new ones. This, at bottom, is the crucial difference between the physical sciences and the so-called behavioral, social, and historical sciences. For, whatever causal regularities may be sorted out in the latter disciplines are regularities concerning rulelike or rule-governed phenomena, that is, phenomena that cannot be characterized except in terms of intentionality, although the physical movements and events in terms of which linguistic and similar behavior is manifested may, of course, be specified and, in principle, explained, *once given,* in terms of physical laws. In any case, questions of physical impossibility do not relevantly arise in the context of meaning and linguistic usage.

To speak, therefore, of the rule-governed or rulelike nature of language is to speak only of projected norms (and, conceivably, alternatively fitting projections) in terms of which the putatively regularized intentions of linguistic improvisation may be assigned, both of those that fall short, for reasons of economy or reliance on implication and the like, of any stated rules and of those that cannot be captured by antecedently formulable rules, for reasons of deviance and departure from given regularities. One sees this, for instance, even in the evolution of the acceptable pronunciation of a given expression: no given rule could conceivably provide—except by way of assimilating intentions (which is, precisely, to extend the rule, to explicate how "to go on" in accord with the rule through innovations)—for all admissible patterns of physical sounds produced. We have only to consider the possible effect of substantial immigration or even of atmospheric and physiological changes affecting a given population. But if the claim is admitted here, it will be seen to affect all generalizations and rules bearing on all elements of language—words, phrases, sentences, speech acts, or any other allegedly significant units of linguistic phenomena and behavior. And if it is admitted, then the theory of significant linguistic regularities is inescapably informed by normative preferences, institutionalized presuppositions, prevailing beliefs, and the like and cannot be confirmed merely on the basis of statistical evidence or of evidence somehow confined to verbal regularities; systematic reasons for alternative preferences will have to be consulted, including that of the difficulty of distinguishing sharply between linguistic and non-linguistic behavior.

Important consequences follow. For, it is regularly claimed that language is a rule-governed activity, rather like chess. It cannot, however, be such, for the obvious reason that the moves or actions or activity of playing chess are defined constitutively by the fixed and finitely enumerable rules of chess; the "rules" of language are neither fixed nor finitely enumerable, simply because the activity of speech tolerates innovation with respect both to truncating any idealized models of rule-governed speech and with respect to indefinitely enlarging and altering meanings, vocabulary, constructions, uses of expressions, and the like. Also, of course, there is no complete set of rules that has ever been formulated for a natural language; there is, therefore, no clear sense in which native speakers perform linguistically by intending to adhere to such rules. So it is misleading to say that one who speaks a language intends what he utters to be understood by means of (another's) grasping the rules of the language governing such utterances or by means of (another's) grasping *that* one intends what he utters to be so grasped. For, there are no fixed, enumerable rules that could relevantly be thus appealed to, that determine all significant combinations of the constitutive elements of speech. It is, of course, true that a complex natural language is relatively conservative and that rulelike regularities can be posited for very large samples of speech. Hence, we may say that a speaker intends his utterances to exhibit such (determin*able*) regularities or intends that another grasp his meaning by grasping his intention to be guided by such regularities (but the claim now appears vacuous and unclarifying); and we may say that only insofar as one is, at least implicitly,

guided by such regularities, one may be said (trivially) to understand the meaning of a given utterance. Alternatively, *for* creatures capable of using language thus, one may, *in* speaking in the
normal way, ulteriorly intend to say this or that in addition and to
be understood to do so by another (equally qualified) by reference
to the rules of language. The implied model, then, cannot apply to
more than a dependent fraction of linguistic use. Consequently,
linguistic communication supposes not merely that speakers are
governed by rules ordering the body of language already deposited
but also that they are guided by the *example* of such rules, so that
their utterances will support rulelike projections of an analogous
sort.

Language users are not merely rule-following animals but rule-
improvising animals. Hence, a causal theory of meaning (in at
least the sense of a thesis that holds that explaining the meaning
of linguistic acts entails construing such explanation as a species
of causal explanation) is untenable—for reasons similar to those
that forestall construing explanation of actions by way of reasons
as a species of causal explanation. To explain the meaning of a
linguistic expression or the meaning of a linguistic act (that one
grasps) is to give an explanation by reasons and not by causes,
without of course denying that causal factors may and must operate. If the intentions a speaker has for performing a linguistic act
are like intentions for performing non-linguistic acts, then the conceptual difficulties of subsuming explanations of actions in terms
of reasons under the genus, causal explanations, will necessarily
apply to linguistic acts as well.

To understand what it is some speaker has said is not to have
been caused to understand it by the speaker's intention to be understood by reference (by the hearer) to the appropriate linguistic
rules that govern given utterances in given contexts and/or by the
speaker's intention to have the hearer understand his intention to
be understood by reference (by the hearer) to the appropriate linguistic rules governing given utterances in given contexts. For, to
understand this intention is (trivially) tantamount to the hearer's

understanding what the speaker has said, by reference to whatever linguistic rules govern given utterances in given contexts. Either speakers' intentions are the vacuous internal equivalents, for the *acts* of speech, of the linguistic rules by reference to which the products of speech (linguistic utterances) are seized as meaningful and assigned meaning or else they are aspects of ulterior psychological states whose content may be linguistically conveyed. In either case, though native speakers are introduced to their tongues in causally significant ways, grasping or explaining the meaning of what one says to another cannot, as such, be informatively construed in causal terms, for grasping and explaining meanings is nothing more than construing and redescribing physical utterances (making sounds or marks or the like), in context, in accord with linguistic rules. To hold, then, that speakers intend to cause a certain effect in their hearers is nothing but a "causalized" version of the fact that competent speakers of a language understand one another by reference to appropriate linguistic rules.

Under these circumstances, language is most reasonably viewed as an institutionalized activity whose norms and rules do not define what is physically impossible or even what is linguistically impossible. Successful communication clearly depends on the effective expectation that speakers will conform relatively closely to conventional norms and rules; departures are tolerable—within the boundaries of intelligibility—to the extent that analogous rules may be improvised for such departures, consistently with some recognizable measure of adherence to the established rules. The improvisations of speakers may well be matched by the improvisations of hearers. Also, the rules themselves are variously projected, by those who have mastery of the language, from a canvassing of observable regularities within that language. This means, then, that it is not so much that would-be rules are tested with respect to the regularities holding among the elements of language as that what is made to count as the elements of a language are, precisely, whatever lend themselves to the most stable rulelike formulations—particularly, those that facilitate the learning of language and the explanation of the meaning of given utterances. It is not so much that language is composed of words and phrases and sentences of this or that construction, thus or so employed, as that we factor what we call language into certain semantical, syntactical, or pragmatical elements, or the like, that promise best to support the stablest run of rules having the widest and most systematic scope. This is why the analytic "parts" of language must be viewed as elements marked by a single, comprehensive theory. Observing an alien language, for instance, one cannot assume that native speakers are recognizably using *sentences* that may be marked off and matched with observable stimuli, leaving us merely to speculate about alternative semantical mappings of the entire language, in terms of words and phrases that fit the alleged sentence units and the occasions of their alleged use. This, to follow a possibility already broached, leads inevitably to a two-storey theory of language and to skepticism respecting the learning of alien languages and even respecting intralinguistic communication. Words (or terms) and sentences are correlative distinctions—as also indeed are speech acts, that is, the use of sentences composed of words to perform distinct kinds of acts (answering to the institutionalized interests and practices of men). We have only to think, pursuing the two-storey model suggested, that to suppose that a native speaker's verbal behavior is pertinently connected with *this* or *that* stimulus—however circumspectly specified, as far as ontology or grammar goes—and that the speaker assents (in uttering his unanalyzed sentences) to whatever the stimulatory occasion provides is, effectively, to have theorized to some extent about the native's vocabulary. Skepticism, here, concerns accuracy about particular details, not the very prospect of providing a detailed parsing. And if we can *formulate* alternative parsings that are globally compatible with the totality of bare verbal behavior, then we have ourselves provided criteria in addition to behavioral criteria by the use of which we may supply further grammatical details; or, to the extent that we cannot, though differences in meaning may be specified, we will have shown the language in question to have the same kind of indeterminacy that our own language has. But to press the last possibility is not to say we have failed in our effort to determine the grammar or ontology of an alien language; it is rather to have succeeded in formulating the boundaries of the inherent indeterminacy of such a language. For, as we have already seen, ontic commitment is conceptually connected with individuation. But counting perceivable things, which is the most basic form of individuation, cannot but be manifested in behaviorally distinctive ways, as in effective work like building, harvesting, marketing, and the like, or in the products of such labor. This will not eliminate indeterminacies within limits set by intelligent behavior, but it must eliminate any radical indeterminacy of meaning or reference regarding our own and alien ontologies. (Also, to pretend to replace *perceivable* stimuli with pre-cognitive afferent stimuli is merely to appear to avoid questions of ontic commitment and to make an utter mystery of verbal assent and dissent on given stimulatory occasions.)

3. Conditions of Intelligibility

The clue provided by the perspective advanced is that to think of sentences as composed of words is to think of the meanings of words as assignable only in the context of regular interrelationships among words in sets of sentences; and that to think of speech acts as distinct, purposive acts performed by using sentences is to think of sentences as strings of words normally so collected in order to enable certain well-established institutionalized acts to be successfully performed. One cannot, therefore, offer a theory of words (let us say, terms marking out alternative ontologies) as somehow distinct from, and yet consistent with, antecedently and independently identifiable sentences and the occasions of their use; and one cannot offer a theory of language in terms of such formal units as words and sentences without attention to the intentional activities men engage in in using such counters in the regularized ways they do; *and* one cannot offer a theory of speech acts marking the use of sentences and their constituent words and phrases, organized in this or that syntactically distinctive way, without attention both to the institutionalized intentions and objectives of a given society and to the general epistemic conditions (perceptual and the like) by means of which reference to a common world is rendered possible—in terms of which actual objectives and their corresponding acts may be successfully undertaken (and even stimulus-occasions fixed and demarcated). An adequate theory of language, then, is linked, at its lower limit, to problems of reference and perceptual coherence and, in its mid-region, to the institutionalized practices of a society (whether performed non-linguistically or by means of language) and, at its upper limit, to possible languages or linguistic distinctions formulable within the conceptual scope of a given language but perhaps not actually occurrent in a designated sample.

Mention of the lower limit of language draws attention to an essential condition for language learning *ab initio,* both intralinguistic and interlinguistic intelligibility, and the limits of semantic evolution and variability. For one thing, the public nature of a language is itself intelligible only on the assumption of a common world perceptually discriminated in relatively common ways, even prelinguistically. And for another, the analysis of any language, however ingenious and variable, cannot—on pain of incoherence—fail to provide for some "perceptual core," in terms of which the possibilities of public communication and of learning both one's own and other languages may be sustained. Otherwise, we fall back to linguistic solipsism and utterly private languages.

It is only on such grounds as these that, for instance, the vexed question of the analytic/synethetic distinction can be at all resolved. Consider, to press the issue, that the sentence 'Water is H_2O' may (on alternative analyses of a comprehensive sample of English) be justifiably taken to be either analytic or synthetic. To construe it as analytic is to place it at a relatively high level of theoretical abstraction vis-à-vis *other* observation sentences that, necessarily then, are synthetic. To construe it as synthetic, on the other hand, is, precisely, to place it relatively close to the "perceptual core" grounding the referential function of language, with respect to which other sentences (otherwise conceivably synthetic) may be construed as analytic.

Now, there is no fixed "perceptual core" that can be formulated as by a set of protocol or basic sentences. To assume that there is is to fail to appreciate the ease with which the analytic/synthetic boundary can be shifted within any language and to fail also to appreciate the theory-laden nature of all verbal distinctions, including those bearing on sentience—the dependence, that is, of the sense of any isolated sentences on the total system that is the language. This is not to say that one cannot understand a single sentence unless he understands all possible sentences in a given language; it is to say only that any and all categorical distinctions are recognizable only within a network of such distinctions. There are no atomic sentences or atomic distinctions that can be grasped as such. On the other hand, although there is no formulably fixed "perceptual core," such a core is, as has been said, presupposed by the very linguistic enterprises we share. The upshot is that, relative to any systematic account of the meaning of words and sentences—as, for instance, by way of employing the analytic/synthetic distinction—*some* set of observation sentences must be capable of being posited and must, as such, be synthetic.

Any sentence, then, that is assigned synthetic standing, on some analysis of the categories embedded in a language, may, by an alternative strategy, by construed as analytic. Nevertheless, there is a limit to the conceptual alternatives possible, namely, that all such alternatives remain suitably linked with our public discrimination of a public world. Hence, there is no way to formulate a fixed, purely intralinguistic criterion for distinguishing the analytic and the synthetic for sentences taken distributively. The solution can only be provided by attending to the referential and denotative functions of the total system of language and, in particular, to what it is that success with regard to these functions presupposes. For, *if* a language functions referentially and denotatively—which is to say, concerns at the very least an objective world distinct from language itself—it must be possible to determine similarity and dissimilarity of meaning with regard to what is denoted and referred to, and there must be some range of synthetic statements that may be formulated and recognized by those who use the language thus. The very intelligibility of language demands these concessions and even the fiction of a two-storeyed language presupposes them.

This is not to say that sentences clarifying, for instance, the meaning of a word are either demonstrably analytic *or* synthetic. *That* specification may well be provided only at a certain advanced level of theorizing about language. I may facilitate your grasp of the sense of some expression not only by providing synonyms or cognate expressions but also by providing—by way of different theories—lists of properties characteristically or normally or essentially or necessarily associated with whatever falls within the extension of the term or even logically or theoretically amorphous collections of facts regarding whatever falls within that extension, believing that such procedures may provide you at least with an effective clue to whatever semantic rules may be plausibly fitted to the use of the expression in question. Teaching the meaning of an expression, then, need not, to be effective, entail teaching the determinate semantic rules assumed to govern its use; and normally—though not necessarily—the necessary and sufficient conditions for the use of any expression will not be formulable at the moment of instruction. Thus, even if it is held that language is rule-governed for any specified interval of use, it cannot convincingly (certainly cannot demonstrably) be held that the teaching of any natural language proceeds by way of the teaching (*a fortiori,* by way of the learning) of some determinate set of rules: it may only be by the barest and most informal approximation to such a set that it proceeds.

There is, then, in addition to relatively clearcut instances of synthetic and analytic statements, a very large range of statements, for a given system of language at a given stage, differing in different ways among themselves, that cannot straightforwardly be judged to be either analytic or synthetic. It is the very informality with which we learn languages—failing, for instance, to be taught *all* the conditions governing the meaning of a given expression—as well as the conceptual connections holding between the sentences we use and the total language evolving in its distinctive way, that forces us to concede such indeterminacy. We cannot, therefore, always segregate changes in meaning and constancy in meaning by reference to the semantical rules governing given expressions, simply because *no one is ever provided with a complete set of such rules* and because it makes no clear sense to suppose that there is such a set to be discovered. Language requires the distinction between what is analytically and synthetically true—which is tantamount to saying that understanding a language entails understanding when expressions are similar or different in meaning—but it does not require that the distinction obtain determinately for all statements formulated in the language. Furthermore, it should be noted that although sentences taken to be synthetic may, by suitable shifts in our theories, come to be taken as analytic, it does not follow that all putatively analytic sentences may, correspondingly, be reinterpreted as synthetic. In particular, it is not clear in what sense logical truths, for instance 'It is not the case that p and not p', can be anything but necessarily true. This is, of course, to say absolutely nothing about psychological states bearing on knowledge and belief. But it is to say that there are inexorable constraints—both in terms of the admission of a public world and in terms of logical possibility and impossibility—upon our alleged *ability* to imagine altering our conceptual system so as to shift the boundary between the analytic and the synthetic.

A related finding suggests itself, with respect to the upper or outer limit of language. Thus, imagine that, in an interval t-t', a language evolves, so that sentences that have been prominently used to make synthetic perceptual statements come to be viewed as analytic and that the meaning of key terms in such sentences is correspondingly altered. How extreme can such an evolution be? The limit is essentially the same already marked out. For, if the language at t' is to remain intelligible to speakers at t (or vice versa), then, regardless of the transformations of the language, there must remain a "perceptual core" common to both—and marked by observation sentences formulable by both—by virtue of the use of which either set of speakers can grasp the altered sense of seemingly familiar sentences just as they may grasp the emergent sense of new linguistic inventions. Thus, the learning of fashionable new slang by an older generation requires, in microcosm, the very continuity of a perceptual core that is entailed in the continued intelligibility—for speakers differently placed through a span of time—of an evolving language.

Finally, in this connection, it is entirely conceivable that theoretical investigations be entertained that leave observational distinctions relatively unaffected. This occurs, for instance, when one speculates about the comparative power of alternative scientific theories to explain the data given. This is, of course, not to say that perceptual terms are not "theory-laden": they are, in the sense in which they enter into systematic conceptual connections with other terms. But it is to say that the distinction—the altogether different distinction—between *explanans* and *explanandum* entails that it be possible to formulate theories about phenomena, identified by means of observation sentences, such that the meanings of observational terms remain, relevantly, unaltered. But if this be true of science, it must be true, *a fortiori,* of metaphysical speculation vis-à-vis the data of the various factual disciplines. If, for instance, sunflowers are yellow, can we or can we not say that physical objects and properties are real entities? The question shows that, in an important sense, metaphysical speculation constitutes a second-order discipline—presupposes, that is, an *explanandum* relatively neutrally identifiable, *about which* practitioners of the discipline may dispute. And this must be so, in spite of the fact that, with the evolution of language, both the theoretical innovations of science and of metaphysics may come to infect and alter the meanings of the principal terms by means of which our language functions denotatively and referentially.

Also, all such distinctions as the metaphysical can be made only by the denizens of the world of language. Starting with what is reasonably clear grammatically—that we may predicate this or that of such and such a subject and that not only may we refer to such subjects but also may identify some range of them by way of perceptual and other distinctions among what may be found in the world—language users may propose alternative ontologies to fit the grammatical patterns of reference and denotation, particularly as these are used to yield extra-linguistic truths. The important consideration is this: metaphysics is a linguistically reflexive enterprise; we may ask what there is, what is real, but only in the context of reviewing the linguistic strategies by which we make true assertions of any kind. Reference is a linguistic feat and denotation, an indissoluble relationship between language and the world. There is no privileged vantage outside of language from which to scan the correspondence between the grammatical referents of our language and the actual entities of the world. Every alleged correspondence is a correspondence formulated and expressed in language. Not only is this true, but it is also true that the distinction between subject and predicate, which appears so essential to any ontological thesis, is restricted to the formal grammar of a language. Even if the alleged asymmetries between discourse about subjects and about predicates are sustained—for instance, that negative properties but not negative individuals can be accommodated without anomaly—no relevant restrictions whatsoever follow on *what* may be admitted to fill the place of individual variables. For example, if 'The balloon is red' entails admitting balloons as entities, then admitting (with adjustments in our idiom) 'Redness is instantiated by this balloon' or 'Red is the color of the balloon' (or perhaps, 'Redness is ballooned here' or 'Redness occurs here balloonly'), universals like colors may be admitted as entities as well. Whatever the formal relations between subject and predicate in grammatically well-formed sentences may be, we should need independent ontological criteria in order to determine, in some canonically preferred sense, which categories of things may or may not occupy the subject or predicate position. But this is to say that ontology cannot be effectively pursued (or, say, that the realist-nominalist controversy cannot be resolved) by syntactical or formal semantical means alone. The distinction between subject and predicate does not correspond at all with the distinction, say, between particular and universal. It is, of course, possible to discover contingent truths about the world. But truth is linguistically engaged, in the sense that we name whatever it is that we speak about and specify linguistically whatever it is that we attribute to it. Yet, so speaking, we may wish to invent some canonical grammar that will perspicuously exhibit the metaphysical proposals we impose on the language in which we formulate our truths. Given the informalities already noted, the "discovery" of *the* deep structure of a language or *the* ontology embedded in it is simply the rhetorical expression of alternatively preferred systems of rules.

4. Truth and Facts

To see the sense in which metaphysics is linguistically reflexive and quite unlike science—in the respect, precisely, in which it lacks independent referential and denotative facilities (if they were available, science would be metaphysics)—and to see the sense in which empirical science itself is linguistically engaged, is to see that, in one sense, the concept of truth cannot be satisfactorily explicated in terms of correspondence between what is said to be so and what is so and that, in another sense, the concept of truth is one of correspondence. We may, for instance, say that what is contingently true is true of this, the actual world. But the alleged correspondence *cannot* coherently be said to hold between what is claimed or stated in some statement and what may be discriminated in some way that is not linguistically freighted. Such a correspondence theory requires the embarrassing admission of the significant but inexpressible—pervasively through all truth claims. If it is to be viable at all, correspondence must hold between what is claimed or stated or said *in* using language and what is claimed or said *about* what is referred to. Facts, from this point of view, are the tautological accusatives of true truth claims. To speak of correspondence between true statements—considered distributively —and facts, therefore, is redundant but not insignificant, since so speaking registers the referential function of acts of assertion. Alternatively put, the correspondence theory of truth is simply an account of truth that brings our use of language, particularly the making of statements, into accord with the (realist) theory that we have cognitive access to the external world. Hence, even the characterization of necessary truth in terms of given statements being true in all possible worlds is nothing but a figurative device for preserving epistemic realism; it is certainly not designed to introduce novel referential puzzles for so-called transworld identification.

Facts, then, are not linguistic entities—are not merely what true statements state (which would provide not only an tautological accusative but one that would render the remark utterly vacuous)—but what about the things of the world true statements stating what they state may be said to refer to and correspond to: they cannot be identified except as that which answers to true statements, but statements are true because the facts are what they are. Statements may be viewed, on their semantic side, as affirming that something is the case: in this sense, what is stated *in* a statement is its own internal accusative (characteristically termed "propositions"). But statements may also be viewed, on their epistemic side, as corresponding, when true, to what is the case, to what obtains in the relevant domain of reference: in this sense, what answers to what is stated *by* making a true statement is the tautological—but not linguistically internal—accusative of that statement (characteristically termed "facts"). The things of the world—which are not facts—existing and occurring as they do and having the properties that they do, vindicate, on discovery, our treating true statements as true. *That* they exist, occur, and have the properties they do is what true statements state and are about, jointly in the semantic and epistemic senses distinguished —which is precisely what the concept of correspondence captures. Also, since facts correspond to true statements (that is, to what is said in making a statement), we must admit as facts whatever corresponds to true negative statements, true subjunctive conditionals, true statements about the future, true statements about fictions, necessarily true statements, general existential statements, and the like. Statements are (referentially) about whatever entities we choose to speak about; and whatever is true about these (whatever is said) corresponds to the facts about these (whatever is the case). So facts cannot be specified except by formulating true statements and, ranging as they do isomorphically with true statements, they cannot be identified as physical objects or as physical objects having certain properties or as events or as states of affairs or the like. They may enter into *explanations* of causal or other sorts but they cannot, as such, have any causal force themselves. They are, from this point of view, only intentionally or heuristically identified entities, identified only as what about the world tautologically corresponds to what true statements state. Derivatively, they are specified by specifying the truth conditions that true statements satisfy.

There are, also, of course, no negative facts to which false statements correspond: false statements are false (on the thesis given) in that they fail to correspond to *any* facts; and (true statements of) disconfirming facts, on some suitable theory of evidence, establish that they do not so correspond. Truth and falsity are ascribable to statements (to what is said in making a statement), on the basis of evidence, in precisely parallel ways; but they are not semantically equipotent alternatives, since 'true' signifies a correspondence between what a statement states *and the relevant facts,* and 'false' signifies that whatever facts there are, what a false statement states does not correspond with any of them and is incompatible with some truth regarding them (hence, with the set of all facts). Falsity, so to say, is putative truth failed.

We may adjust our distinctions here a little more clearly. In making a statement, a man performs an act: he does so by producing certain noises or marks that, by reference to suitable linguistic conventions, explains our grasp of what he said. What he said is embodied in the physical utterance, though it is not that utterance or any allegedly abstract meaning or non-material proposition. What is said is (intentionally) marked as an entity (what we may call a "proposition") that must be physically embodied in (but not identified with) some physical utterance or other and some sentence or other (for instance, written or spoken; or, expressed in equivalent French and English sentences). Propositions thus construed need not, but may, be taken as merely heuristic entities. But if they are not taken heuristically, they are emphatically not mental entities, but embodied in sentences which are themselves embodied in physical marks. They may be construed as cultural entities (a distinction to which we shall return) and they facilitate our talk about synonymy and equivalence in truth value both intra- and interlinguistically. Facts, to which such propositions correspond, are entirely heuristic entities—not the things of the world but that about them to which what is said, when true, corresponds. (It is, perhaps, also useful to remember that we may, if we wish, introduce an analogous sense of 'proposition' for beliefs and thoughts and the like, where such states and episodes do not entail the actual use of or even the capacity to use language—though their "content" is best conveyed linguistically.) Furthermore, correspondence can play no epistemic role in the assignment of truth values. Truth may be characterized in terms of correspondence; but the assignment of truth cannot be, must relate instead to norms of evidential coherence (that is, not to norms of coherence but to evidential norms that preserve coherence)—where, trivially, each confirming statement may also be construed as entailing some correspondence.

The problem regarding truth is, precisely, what is wanted in an analysis. If it is the meaning of 'true,' then the correspondence view seems promising, since it preserves—ironically, by its epistemic vacuity—both the referential sense in which statements are about what obtains in the world and the sense in which statements that are true are timelessly true. But since correspondence cannot, by its nature, supply cognitive criteria of truth, the theory is thought to be deficient. On the other hand, if what is wanted are criteria of truth, criteria for the ascription of truth, then it is impossible to free the analysis of truth from the analysis of knowledge or to escape construing truth in terms of verification and the like; but since ascriptions of knowledge or endorsements of verification presuppose the concept of truth and since such ascriptions are relatively informal and relativized to variable norms of cognitive expectation and are provided only in tensed contexts, to specify criteria for ascribing truth cannot be to give the sense of 'true.' Also, if coherence reduces to mere internal consistency, then the coherence theory of truth is absurd; and if it is made to depend on the appropriate cognitive norms (preserving consistency), then the theory clearly presupposes an ulterior theory of truth—and that theory cannot be a coherence theory. Again, the correspondence theory does not presuppose a speaker or a speaker making truth claims, only sentences that could be used by a speaker on a given occasion to make a truth claim. But this, of course, explicates the sense in which a speaker may say what is true and the sense in which a proposition may be true though not asserted.

We may, then, usefully distinguish the analysis of the concept of truth from that of the epistemic conditions on which ascriptions of truth are appropriately made and from that of the analysis of the predicate-expression 'is-true.' Correspondence is the epistemically vacuous relationship that answers to our admission that we use language to speak about the world (determinately *there*, in some non-linguistically relevant sense): it is, in fact, nothing more or less than the linguistic corollary of the minimal metaphysical presupposition of knowledge, that there is an external world and that we are in touch with it by means of sentience and the use of other cognitive sources. In this sense, neither "propositions" (what may be said to be stated in making statements) nor "facts" (what may be said to correspond to what is stated in true statements) need or even *can* be independently compared. They are, in *this* context, purely heuristic devices for conveying the point that, for particular statements, other (confirming and disconfirming) statements will be taken to have a certain epistemic import. Verification and similar achievements are the effective means by which particular truth claims are vindicated; they provide, then, determinate specifications of correspondence (by detailing the facts or true propositions), but only in the sense that correspondence itself, repudiating skepticism, is presupposed. Finally, the predicate 'is-true' may— in the spirit of a program at least—be semantically explicated as metalinguistically employed in sentences corresponding to the true sentences of some language. The sentence 'The sentence "snow is white" is true if and only if snow is white' captures our intuition here. The program would require that the sentences of the object language be suitably (canonically) described metalinguistically; but it signifies as well that the condition on which the true sentences of the language may be sorted out from the false ones *cannot* be provided by such a merely metalinguistic rule. Alternatively put, what may be called an adequacy condition—namely, the condition that all viable theories of truth agree (as by presupposition) as to which statements are true and false—will be rendered trivial if it provides no more than this (though it will not be unimportant, since there may well be theories that fail even in this respect). If, for example, the adequacy condition holds that an equivalence of the following sort obtains: ' "*p*" is true if and only if *p*'—where '*p*' is merely the name of *p*—then nothing about the structure of *p* will have been specified in specifying its name, that directly bears on any particular theory of truth. Also, natural languages do not appear to provide any comprehensive (or at least any obviously comprehensive) way in which what is stated may be structurally identified by any metalinguistic descriptions of the sentences so used. But then, serious global consequences follow. For instance, the intriguing thesis that the deep grammatical structure of natural languages must, ultimately, coincide with that of the structure mapped for sentences that behave entirely in accord

with the requirements of extensionality and truth-functionality remains entirely uncertain. What is of the greatest importance here
is that we take note of the direct conceptual connections among
certain grand semantical programs, that finally rest on the need to
resolve essentially the same difficulties.

In practice, then (returning to our question), when a statement
is considered epistemically, we turn to the confirming or disconfirming facts to decide its truth; and a statement thus confirmed or
disconfirmed may, properly, be said to correspond to, or fail to
correspond to, the facts. If, in assessing the truth of statements, we
address ourselves to determinate facts, then in remarking that true
statements are true in that they correspond to the facts, we are
saying only that what true statements determinately state correspond to the (relevantly) determinable facts. Only a theory of verifying statements as such, not a theory of the meaning of truth, can
provide us with determinate criteria for locating the facts by
which the truth of given statements can be decided. So statements
of the determinate facts to which true statements correspond are,
inevitably, redundant; but statements of determinate facts (that is,
true statements themselves redundantly elaborated) that confirm
the truth of given statements justify our saying that statements, insofar as they are true, correspond with the (determinable) facts.
The facts that confirm statements are not, determinately so identified, independently identifiable as the facts to which true statements correspond; and to identify them determinately (that is, to
speak thus) is to identify them in terms of some theory of evidence and not of correspondence.

5. Meanings and Concepts

Granting that there is no exit from language even in the enterprises of science and metaphysics—although a body of truths, as
having reference to the world, presupposes a correspondence between language and the world—it is no surprise that the explanation of the meanings of words should be given and only given lin-

guistically. The ways of explanation are multifarious and need not, for instance, even exclude pointing and the like, for ostension (which clarifies, in context, the meaning of some expression) is a linguistic act though it itself employs no words; otherwise, we should be forced here to some ineffable picturing.

Words, then, are counters, noises, or scratches, or the like, that may be connected in certain orderly ways to form sentences to be used in the performance of speech acts. They obey, in the relaxed sense already indicated, rules, and their meaning is specified by means of such rules. In fact, speaking heuristically, concepts are the internal accusatives of words or expressions in the sense in which words or expressions mean what they mean—*qua* rule-governed entities. As a rule-governed entity, 'table' denotes (means) tables but it also means (what is meant or intended by the concept) TABLE. Actual tables are physical objects, capable of being perceived and the like; but TABLE is a concept, the (purely intentional or heuristic) shadow-object that the word 'table' used in some standard way "means." Some words, it is useful to notice, syncategorematic words like the connectives 'and,' 'either . . . or,' have no denotation at all but have a meaning. We may, therefore, usefully speak of the concept of the connective (AND), which is simply an alternative way of speaking of the meaning or connotation of the word 'and' used as a connective. We specify the sense of the word by specifying in any of a number of available ways the rulelike regularities that govern its use; and doing so, we may redundantly speak of having clarified the concept of the connective. Also, of course, introducing concepts allows us to distinguish between having terms in a given vocabulary and having concepts for which one has no terms that belong in the vocabulary given (sorted and organized on some formulable principle). For instance, it is quite possible to have the concept of a certain shade of blue without having, in one's vocabulary, a distinct name or identifying expression for that particular shade. The issue, therefore, resolves itself nicely if we distinguish between terms and concepts used synchronically and diachronically. Concepts, then, may be construed as heuristically identified entities either linguistically confined or confined to the mental (if we wish to speak of the intelligent behavior, or concepts, of non-language-using animals), that tautologously correspond to the use of given linguistic expressions.

Under happy circumstances, one may provide a synonym or a (more or less) paraphrastic equivalent for a given expression. Thus, if I say that 'square' means 'equilateral rectangle' or (more precisely) that 'square' means what 'equilateral rectangle' means, I have explained the meaning of the expression in question by indicating that it is—for the contexts of use supposed—rule-governed in a way that is similar to the way in which the explaining expression is governed. But if one cannot provide a synonym or neat paraphrastic equivalent because perhaps there is none, one would be utterly unable to explain the meaning of such an expression unless there were a serviceable sense of doing so that did not rely on providing such equivalents. The solution is simple and obvious: in such cases, one explains the meaning of an expression by clarifying the rules governing the use of the expression—which is to say, by explicating the rule-governed concept that the expression so used "means." 'Table' means tables (denotatively); 'square' means 'equilateral rectangle' (connotatively); and 'and' means A TRUTH-FUNCTIONAL CONNECTIVE SIGNIFYING CONJUNCTION. There is, admittedly, an awkwardness in speaking of verbal expressions meaning concepts. Adjustment here depends on a sense of nicety, for concepts (like meanings) are, in any case, heuristic constructions introduced to clarify the meaning of expressions (that is, their being meaningful). But we have already caught, in passing, the equal awkwardness of saying that 'square' means 'equilateral rectangle'; it means, *in certain contexts of use,* whatever 'equilateral rectangle' means. By parity of expression, we may say that 'and' means whatever is meant by the concept A TRUTH-FUNCTIONAL CONNECTIVE SIGNIFYING CONJUNCTION. The latter is conveniently specified by an account of truth tables, but the important thing is that concepts cannot *replace* the expressions whose meaning they

supply, whereas expressions that are said to have the same meaning in given contexts of use may replace one another in those contexts of use (though we sometimes—redundantly—say that the
concept of a square is the same concept as the concept of an equilateral rectangle).

This is also why the meaning of a statement cannot be given by
a statement of its truth conditions: expressions designating epistemically non-trivial truth-conditions cannot be substituted para-
phrastically in the original statement; that is, the expressions
matched cannot be said to have a similar use (or, be similarly
rule-governed). Also, the meanings of expressions cannot replace
expressions in given sentences, preserving sense; only expressions
having the same meaning can do this. But we speak (loosely) of
giving the meaning of expressions by giving synonyms or paraphrastic equivalents, which can relevantly replace the original expressions: giving these expressions—which have the same
meaning—we speak of giving the meaning of the expressions in
question. To talk about meanings and concepts is simply to talk,
by way of alternative idioms, of the rules governing the use of
words and sentences and similar linguistic entities.

There is, then, no single, comprehensive procedure for specifying the meaning of an expression. To say that an expression has
meaning is to say that certain counters are rule-governed in a specifiable way; and to say what the meaning is is to specify either
what the rules for its use are or that they are similar to what they
are for some equivalent expression. But in any of the ways of explicating meanings indicated, one cannot identify something more
fundamental than the elements of language itself (meanings or
concepts, perhaps) that, *per impossibile,* verbal formulations collect or grasp or reveal. To speak of meanings is to speak of no
more than of rulelike regularities governing words, sentences,
speech acts, and similar elements of language. The result, returning to an initial theme, is that, although, quite remarkably, children learn their native tongues without prior linguistic mastery, no
one can explain the elements of a language without presupposing

some measure of linguistic competence on the part of his auditor. If we say that adults teach infants to speak, we must be clear that they do not do so by introducing the rules of the language but only, presupposing certain focussed and ordered (prelinguistic) sensitivities on the part of infants, by affecting them in causally efficacious ways. It is quite reasonable, however (and, indeed, it seems irresistible), to hold—given the social behavior of lower animals—that the initial teaching of language depends essentially on the human infant's capacity to learn (and to be taught in non-linguistic ways) the non-linguistic rules and conventions of his society as well. There is a point, then, at which the babbling of the growing infant exhibits a sufficient regularity and articulation and responsiveness to selected stimuli that such babbling may be construed as incipient linguistic behavior, that is, that the categories of language use may be imposed fittingly on such behavior. But whatever the continuity of prelinguistic and linguistic behavior in the physical development of the child, the framework of linguistic categories is *sui generis* and not reducible to that of any more elementary processes. And, in fact, it is just the emergence of suitable rule-governed behavior on the part of creatures suitably endowed physically that justifies our speaking of human persons. In this sense, just as the use of language is a cultural accomplishment not reducible to mere physical movement, so too, persons are entities identifiable only in the context of a culture.

To speak of a language, therefore, is to impose a certain relevant network of rules or rulelike regularities on a given physical system. Sentences, as structurally linked strings of words, are marked out as particulars—specified in accord with a grammatical theory, distinct but not separable from selected (even alternative) physical marks, sounds, or the like—taken as basic to meaningful discourse. Used by human beings, they are employed in characteristic ways in performing essential kinds of speech acts (assertion, command, interrogation). Statements, then, may be construed as subaltern particulars corresponding to the use or possible use of sentences to affirm that something is the case—hence, as that to which truth values may be assigned. And propositions may be construed as heuristic entities corresponding to what may be affirmed in using sentences to make statements—hence, as that in virtue of which different sentences used on some occasion or different statements using the same or different sentences on some occasion may be said to be used to make the same assertion. Similar heuristic entities—meanings and concepts, for instance—may be introduced to mark referentially the matching features of other speech acts or even of words and phrases abstracted from particular sentences.

VIII

MIND & BODY

The central question regarding the mind and the body is just that of how they are related. No sooner do we attempt to answer it then we are obliged to notice how heterogeneous and mixed are the phenomena we classify as mental in contrast with what we classify as physical. It is not even clear that the mental and the physical are exclusive of one another, since mental phenomena appear for instance to involve the use of energy and to exhibit causal properties. Both because minds (in particular, the human mind) are relatively late evolutionary developments and because of the impressive power and coherence of the physical sciences, we cannot but be attracted to alternative forms of the thesis that the world is essentially material in nature. Nevertheless, merely to say so is not to explain the relationship between mind and body; also, there are enormous difficulties facing the various versions of the thesis. Again, since science itself is the achievement of the human mind, and knowledge, what is possessed by persons or creatures having minds, the prospects of the thesis (so-called materialism) depend on a detailed consideration of the features of what we call minds and persons. In any case, it

216

*is difficult to justify ascribing such mental conditions as thoughts
or emotions or reasons or hallucinations to mere physical bodies
or, indeed, to a congeries of sub-atomic particles. Also, it is difficult
to deny that mental states include, prominently, sentient and sentient-like states (for instance, perceptions, sensations, hallucinations, dreams, images, and the like) as well as states of non-sentient or not exclusively sentient awareness and experience (for
instance, thoughts, moods, emotions, wishes, and the like) that
cannot be construed merely as forms of behavior or behavioral
dispositions. A behavioral reading of such states—as, that to
perceive something is to be disposed to believe (to have a perceptual belief) that something is the case—would greatly
strengthen a materialist account, perhaps also those versions of
that account that hold that mental states are identical with physical states. But if the behavioral reading is rejected, difficulties
arise for identity claims: the thesis that mental states can be analyzed adequately in terms of purely behavioral dispositions (so-
called behaviorism) or that behavior itself can be analyzed in
terms of purely physical dispositions proves to be untenable. In
this respect, also, although machines may be said to simulate or
even exhibit the behavior of creatures that have minds, there is no
sense in which we may speak of machines simulating or having
sentient states and the like if we mean by this, states that cannot
be completely analyzed in behavioral terms. And should we be
prepared to ascribe sentient states to machines themselves, we
should correspondingly have to consider an extension of the
mind-body problem. Here, the difficulties dramatize the problem
of ascribing mental properties to suitably selected kinds of
particulars—for instance, to persons as opposed to bodies.*

*The so-called identity theory—roughly, that whatever is
designated by mental terms is actually physical—takes any
number of different forms. On the most extreme version, the
meaning of sentences purporting to be about mental states and
the like can be supplied in entirely physical terms. More moder-
ately, the theory holds either that persons (or sentient creatures)*

are identical with physical bodies or that persons (or sentient creatures) and all their properties are identical with physical bodies and their properties (so-called physicalism) or that mental states are identical with physical states (which raises problems about construing states and other apparent attributes as entities). Bearing in mind the distinction between identity and composition, it is possible to construct a form of materialism (among other alternatives) that is not committed to the identity thesis, that captures the sense both that the world is material in nature and that properties not reducible to mere physical properties and entities not reducible to mere physical entities must be admitted: all that is needed is the concession that such entities as persons are physically embodied (hence, composed of physical materials) though not identical with the bodies in which they are embodied (hence, open to ascriptions of mental properties). In any case, the fact that the range of things to which we may ascribe mental and physical traits differs systematically and the fact that there is no obvious rule by which to explain away such discrepancies consistently with the identity thesis oblige us to consider either that claims of identity are, under the circumstances, not to be taken in their strictest sense or that, in accord with materialist preferences, the identity thesis itself must be rejected.

The mental, as was said, is decidedly heterogeneous in nature. Nevertheless, it is often held that intentionality is the mark of the mental, by which is meant that mental states are directed upon a suitable object, that mental states are not adequately described without mentioning certain objects appropriate and internal to such states—for instance, that one cannot simply be in a state of fear, that fear must be directed, say, upon goblins; or that one cannot simply be in a state of belief, that one must believe, say, that today is Tuesday. The grammatical locutions appropriate in such contexts vary considerably, though it is useful, in formulating sentences that convey such intentional states, to express the relevant objects, wherever possible, in terms of entities like bodies and persons and their attributes or in terms of propositions. Such states and the locutions corresponding to them are intentional in the additional respect that the objects referred to need not (though they may) actually exist and the propositions entailed need not (though they may) actually be true. Hence, one may hunt for unicorns and believe that goblins roam the woods. The difficulty is that the intentional idiom may be applied to what lacks a mind—as when we construe a physical system as maintaining equilibrium, or the processes of a living plant as homeostatically attuned, or a painting as representing Francis I, or a corporation as pursuing its financial interests. In this sense, intentionality cannot be a sufficient condition of the mental; and if we admit that sensations as of pain are mental occurrences, then, denying that they have an intentional character (as distinct from any avoidance behavior that may be contingently associated with such sensations), intentionality cannot be a necessary condition either. Some adjustments are possible here—for instance by qualifying that form of intentionality that is appropriate to minds as ineliminable by paraphrase in nonintentional ways; but in itself, the condition will not resolve the difference between creatures with minds and artifacts or such fictional entities as corporations and nations, and it will not overcome the important exception to its serving as a necessary condition. What is necessary and sufficient for the mental requires, more compellingly, some form of sentience. Thereupon, we may grade creatures having minds in terms of the complexity of intentional states and abilities and the like. Persons, from this point of view, may be said to be creatures that have minds and that have a capacity for language.

Also, persons, like artifacts (for instance, works of art, machines, words and sentences themselves) and such fictional entities as corporations, that depend on persons, are culturally emergent entities. That is, such entities cannot be identified except within a cultural context and are thus identified by reference to the rules, conventions, practices, traditions, institutions of a society. In this sense, the intentional may itself be construed as the rulelike or rule-governed; and persons, (who behave in rulelike ways, as in speaking a language) and other cultural objects must, though embodied, be distinct from the physical objects in which they are embodied. In this way, also, the appropriate linkage between attributes and entities can be sustained at the same time that the account remains compatible with a form of (what may be termed compositional) materialism. That is, we need not, if we wish, admit abstract entities here or non-material substances. But since persons, like works of art, are identified in terms of appropriate mental and intentional traits (in embodied systems), the criteria for their identification and individuation may be quite diverse. In fact, reincarnation, multiple and serial embodiment, and the like are all entirely intelligible, without admitting any form of disembodied existence. And the difficulties encountered in reducing persons to bodies, as in pursuing the identity theory, confirm the sense in which both persons and bodies are relatively fundamental to our account of the basic entities of the world.

1. The Ascription of Mental and Physical Properties

The most casual discourse, particularly regarding men, relies on a distinction between the mental and the physical. But there is no entirely satisfactory account of the relationship between the mind and the body. The principal reason for this, without a doubt, is that the extension of 'physical' is relatively clear—except, precisely, where the relationship is in question—and that of 'mental,' notoriously unclear. And this condition, in turn, is probably due to the enormously impressive unity and power of the physical sciences themselves and to the quite amorphous range of distinctions signalled by the use of 'mind,' 'mental,' and cognate terms. To say this is not to suppose that a conceptual analysis of the physical is secure. Far from it; but the boundaries and salient features of the physical world are reasonably clearly sketched, and our puzzlement there has to do chiefly with the luxury of seeking to formulate a sufficiently comprehensive theory of the physical that will match the gathering unity of the sciences themselves. The "domain" of the mental, by contrast, has often seemed to be a collection of "danglers," in the sense that whatever is allegedly designated there is not easily linked with the lawlike regularities of a seemingly closed physical world—though if mental phenomena, *though* lawlike, may still be danglers, nothing short of a materialistic reduction or elimination will meet the complaint. The embarrassment is obvious, for the very formulation of a competent physical science is, no matter how tightly we may wish to speak, the work of the human mind; and so, dangler or not, we need to sort out the conceptual connection between mind and body.

The will-o-the-wisp is the essentially mental. The touchstones at least of what is physical are spatial extension and the condition of being subject to causal laws or to laws governing the distribution and transformation of energy. Of course, the proper analysis of causality is itself open to quarrel; and there are puzzles of individuation and predication regarding elementary particles that strain our global theses about the physical. Also, it is by no means obvious that so-called mental or psychological phenomena are not subject to causal laws—at least some ranges of phenomena readily dubbed mental or psychological—and this suggests that the mental and the physical may not at all constitute exclusive domains or, that the mental may not be a homogeneous domain. In fact, one of the perennial quarrels relevantly raised concerns whether or not the mental is indeed the physical, whether mental phenomena are reducible without remainder to physical phenomena. Much hangs on this; or, at the very least, much regarding the mental may be clarified by pursuing its prospects.

Two initial considerations may be mentioned to guide our inquiry. For one thing, mind is an evolutionary late arrival—certainly the human mind is, that is, the paradigm of what a mind is and the source of relevant attributions beyond, beneath, and apart from the human. The admission of a physical world without human observers (or even without non-human observers or even without living creatures at all) argues that, in some sense, the world has a determinate order that—though surely discoverable by them—obtains independently of men. Such an order cannot be formulated except by men and this suggests the possible incoherence of asking whether there are (and what are the) natural kinds or essential distinctions present in nature. What human beings discover by means of their science and cognitive capacities is what we attribute to nature, even for pre-observational intervals; the question of the properties and nature of the real world cannot be raised except within the human ken. There is no non-linguistic way to specify the order of nature, but to specify any order in nature is to do more than to explicate our language. We cannot exit from language, but we can distinguish, on suitable theoretical grounds, between what we say about language and what we say about the world: this means that ontology (for instance, questions about the adequacy of idealism or dualism or materialism) is no more ineligible than science, considered only in the light of our essential dependence on language. That dependence precludes the picturing of the real world in terms of prelinguistically defended distinctions, not because either science or ontology is impossible but because incoherent assumptions cannot be made to support either. But the actual achievement of our science, both in terms of our grasp of the genesis of the world and of the explanatory power of the principal causal accounts, conspires to persuade us that materialism may provide an adequate and economical description of whatever is real. And yet, precisely because whatever structure is truly attributable to nature is attributable only by men—including whatever the thesis of materialism is said to comprehend—the success of that doctrine depends, obviously, on the validity of a materialist reading of the concepts of mind and person. It is, however, by no means obvious how to support such a doctrine, apart from and in addition to the entirely trivial claim that a monistic ontology is more parsimonious than a dualistic one, and it is not even obvious what is minimally required by a materialist theory of mind. The so-called mind-body identity theory—that mental states

are, contingently, physical states—is simply one of the strongest
of the debatable materialist alternatives. It is plainly false that the
very meaning of terms designating mental phenomena (in accord
with actual usage) can be explicated in a physicalist idiom. Statements affirming mind-body identities are not, in any obvious
sense, analytic or necessarily true; and it would be scandalous to
claim that an idiom as ubiquitous as that by which mental phenomena are identified and described was out-and-out nonsense.

Dualism, then, arises as a natural option because knowledge of
physical reality can be assigned only to creatures that, in some
sense, have minds. In fact, metaphysical dualists and identity theorists (who are, of course, monists) are agreed in treating minds
and bodies as entities; they disagree only about whether they are
the same or different entities. The scandal of dualism (that is, a
dualism of entities as opposed to a dualism of attributes) lies with
the utter mystery of causal interactions between radically different
kinds of entities and of their conceptual relationship vis-à-vis persons and sentient creatures. But to give up treating minds and
mental processes and the like as entities, in subscribing to materialism, is not in the least to say what the conceptual relationship is
between the mental and the physical. As a materialist, one may be
a behaviorist, a central-state materialist (not necessarily an identity theorist), an identity theorist, an eliminative materialist, or
what I should call a compositional materialist. The relative power
of such alternatives needs to be examined.

A second consideration is this. The domain of the mental appears to be composed of decidedly heterogeneous items—which
affects the prospects both of characterizing the essentially mental
and of providing a uniform materialistic analysis of any kind, of
all that is fairly comprehended within the domain. Unless some
form of the identity thesis is true, it looks extraordinarily difficult
to justify the ascription to bodies of such mental conditions as
thoughts, beliefs, memories, doubts, experiences, emotions, moods,
attitudes, feelings, sensations, attention, awareness, consciousness,
dreams, delusions, hallucinations, images, inclinations, desires,

wishes, motives, intentions, reasons, purposes, goals, projects, strategies, deliberations, interests, plans, calculations, arguments, preferences, and the like. If we require a substantive designating particulars of some distinctive sort, of which these conditions may be predicated, it is characteristic to speak of persons or of minds or of such individuals as are thought to be persons or to be agents of some sort sufficiently like human persons (the higher animals for instance or Martians or gods) to which some selection of the conditions mentioned may be ascribed.

The identity thesis itself may, it should be noticed, be pursued along three somewhat distinct lines of development. Along one, it may be claimed that mental states ascribed to persons are identical with certain physical states that may be ascribed to persons or sentient creatures; on another, it may be claimed that persons (having certain mental attributes) are nothing but physical bodies (having certain physical attributes). The first version, if materialistic, is incompletely formulated; the second, often called physicalism, is a form of reductive materialism. Furthermore, if we speak (along either line) of mental events or mental states as of particulars, rather than predicatively of some particular body's or of some particular person's having a certain state or of a certain event's befalling it (or him), we may be inclined to liberalize the conditions on which the identity thesis may be vindicated—for instance, by admitting (much as in speaking of the identity of lightning and electrical sequences) of semantic constraints affecting cross-category identities. But, apart from detailed difficulties confronting identity theories, it is essential to bear in mind that events and states, construed as indissoluble particulars (of which we may make suitable predications) are, necessarily, subaltern particulars —that is, particulars introduced as (grammatically) dependent replacements for what (by way of variably polyadic predicates) may otherwise be ascribed to bodies and persons. The upshot is that arguments purporting to strengthen the identity thesis and couched *only* in terms of subaltern particulars are inherently defective. For, since they themselves are introduced to capture, in a grammatically convenient way, whatever may defensibly be said *of* bodies and persons, their being treated as indissoluble particulars may well obscure whatever conceptual difficulties would otherwise arise. A third way of speaking of identity—that, properly, is not an identity thesis at all—is to construe talk about persons, minds, mental states, and mental acts as an imperfect or picturesque way of speaking about physical bodies and their properties. Here, no identity is intended, in the obvious sense that a certain mode of speech is to be eliminated in favor of another said to be more perspicuously directed to that to which the first was also, though obscurely, directed. The thesis has sometimes been termed eliminative materialism. We shall return to these issues below.

It is interesting that we often speak of persons (and of the higher animals) as having minds (as well as, selectively, having sensations, feelings, emotions, beliefs, purposes); this suggests, usefully, that to speak of the mind is to speak of determinable mental states of which the states and conditions enumerated are determinate forms. Hence, the identity thesis may fairly be canvassed in that form in which mental conditions of the sort enumerated are construed as predicables—which leaves the ulterior quarrel about ontology as open as possible. If sensations, for instance, are brain processes (significant adjustments may be needed here, if we are to hold to the comparison of predicables), then, indeed, the prospects of the identity thesis are promising. But whatever arguments may be mustered must themselves, to be at all convincing, accommodate several conditions. Thus, the heterogeneity of the items construed as mental leads us to suppose that the alleged identities must be defended for all—or at least for the most important and controversial—of the mental conditions mentioned; for, it is entirely possible that desire, say, may be construed reductively or materialistically and yet sensations may not. Again, although if the identity thesis were valid, mental conditions (as reducible to physical conditions) could be predicated of bare physical objects, the problem is, precisely, to defend such predication; it cannot be justified, for instance, by a mere appeal to onto-

logical parsimony, for such parsimony as we may achieve must—
if it is relevant at all—be provided compatibly with whatever we
are forced to admit is true of the world. To say that sensations are
brain processes, for instance, *because* materialism is, antecedently,
the most plausible and economical ontology is not only irrelevant
and unconvincing, it is to fail to understand the meaning of parsimony itself and the alternatives open to materialism.

We have already noticed a useful adjustment regarding 'mind'
and 'mental' and cognate terms. They designate determinable but
not determinate states and conditions: whatever may have an emotion or a thought or the like has a mind or is that of which mental
conditions may be predicated. The same is true, broadly speaking,
of terms like 'conscious.' There is a sense in which certain mental
states may be unconscious, but such states are attributable to creatures parasitically—either in the sense that the concept of unconscious rage, for instance, depends on the concept of conscious
rage, or in the sense that the creature to which unconscious rage
may be ascribed must, in some other respect, be conscious. Again,
a creature in a rage is conscious, though it need not be conscious
of its being in a rage. So we speak of being conscious in at least
two distinct senses—one, that in which a creature may be cognitively aware of its state (or of anything else); another, that in
which a creature is, at the moment, capable of cognitive awareness
of something, regardless of whether it is aware of this or that determinate and cognizable something. Alternatively put, we speak
of consciousness in the sense in which we speak of the *physical*
capacity of an organism that enables it to be cognizant or aware of
what it may be aware of; and we speak of consciousness also in
the sense in which we speak of an organism's being *cognizant* or
aware of whatever it is aware of—whether entailed in its behavior
(linguistic or non-linguistic behavior) or imputable in the absence
of relevant behavior. The second sense may be elaborated in intentional terms, as we shall see; and the first provides for an account, in purely nonintentional terms, of how consciousness in the
second sense is physically embodied. The ascription of conscious-

ness, therefore, depends on theoretical considerations—namely, on whether the movements of a physical system of a given complexity justify and in what way justify speaking of verbal reporting and the like or of intelligent behavior of a non-verbal sort: the admission of such characterizations entails the admission of consciousness in the second sense, which may then be articulated as sensation, thought, emotion, and the like and ascribed to suitable entities. But the argument for this general line of reasoning has yet to be supplied.

We also, as has been remarked, hypostatize (at least as far as grammar is concerned) minds and persons and determinate mental states (sensations and images, for instance) just as we do, in other contexts, events and actions, dreams and hallucinations. The reason, is that, in order to convey perspicuously the many distinctions we wish to make, our grammar needs to tolerate alternative schemata. Thus, for instance, we may wish to predicate horror *of* a certain determinate sensation without wishing to characterize the sensation as a sensation *of* horror. Were it not for this suppleness, problems would arise regarding the handling of polyadic predicates and of expressions designating the intentional objects of mental conditions. Dreams, for example, must be of something, in the sense in which intentional objects may be assigned to a dream ("I dreamt of Jeannie with the light brown hair")—where such objects may or may not exist—or in the sense in which dreams are related to, or have, a propositional content ("I dreamt that Jeannie had light brown hair"): we may predicate properties of the dream *qua* dream ("It was a boring dream"); we may even predicate properties of the intentional object or propositional content of the dream; and we may of course construe the idiom in terms of indissoluble predicates rather like belief-predicates (predicating dreaming-of-Jeannie-with-the-light-brown-hair or dreaming-that-Jeannie-had-light-brown-hair of me). But none of these grammatical maneuvers need be said to decide, as such, ulterior ontological issues.

The concept of a person, however, proves more resistant to

similar grammatical maneuvers; persons, therefore, seem more difficult to eliminate as basic entities in whatever ontological theories we may favor. That is, the range of particulars to which, properly, mental conditions are ascribed are persons (or other individuals [creatures] that, as "having minds," are sufficiently like persons to justify such ascriptions). But there is a threat of circularity here; for, *if* mental states were identical with physical states and if the latter could properly be predicated of mere physical objects (eliminating persons altogether), then the ontic ineliminability of persons (or of their creature surrogates) could be effectively denied. It is, then, the very difficulties confronting the identity theory that manifest themselves as the putative ineliminability of persons as entities.

Clearly, a corresponding problem confronts physical objects: for, if physical objects are analyzed entirely in terms of physical predicables, the question arises regarding *what* it is to which such conditions may be attributed. Physical properties are predicable of physical objects (or, to avoid begging any questions here, possibly of certain other complex particulars [persons] of which mental conditions are also predicable); and mental conditions are predicable only of persons or minds or creatures having minds or the like (unless the identity thesis [in particular, the physicalist thesis] is true—in which case, trivially, mental conditions are predicable of bodies). But, in any case, the predication of both mental and physical properties presupposes a sufficiently complex range of particulars (physical objects and persons) to support, precisely, that which we call predication. Properties are attributed to propertied particulars. If one theorized that physical and / or mental properties were, in some sense, "ascribed" to bare, propertyless particulars, then that "ascription" would be unfamiliar or at least utterly unlike the ascription of properties to (admittedly) propertied particulars and the allegedly bare particulars would be more than difficult to identify (for insoluble puzzles would arise about the individuation of such particulars, about making reference to them, and about assigning them—consistently with the hypothesis—a "nature"). We can speak of the occurrence of a property only in the sense in which we can speak of particulars that instantiate (the occurrence of) a property; were not such particulars themselves capable of individuation and identification, there would be no sense in speaking of the occurrence or of instances of a given property. But bare particulars, *ex hypothesi,* cannot provide for the actual ascription of given properties to particular things. These considerations suggest—against both the identity thesis and eliminative materialism—the point of admitting physical objects and persons as relatively ineliminable basic particulars, though they are by no means decisive. Also, it is entirely unclear how to demonstrate that attributes designated by paired expressions as apparently different in meaning as physical and mental predicates are, even if they had the same extension, the same attributes. (It is, it may be added, intriguing to speculate that the puzzling features of the would-be modal theorem, ' $\Diamond (\exists x)fx \supset (\exists x) \Diamond fx$ ' [for instance, 'If it is possible that there is a flag with a blue background and three red stripes, then there is a flag such that it is possible that it has a blue background and three red stripes'], depend on the problem of bare particulars. For, the antecedent of the conditional requires only that it itself not be self-contradictory, but the consequent requires that, for a given domain, there *is* a member regarding *which* it is possible that a certain attribute obtain. There are, therefore, greater constraints on the consequent than on the antecedent—read thus; hence, it may be rejected. The reason seems to be that since predication is made of propertied particulars, the limits that may be set on the membership of any domain will set limits on what may be predicated of them, but where possibility is allowed to range over sentences or propositions, we are in effect invited to posit a domain capturing just such a predication. In the one context, so to say, we may consider any and all possible worlds; and in the other, we are committed to a particular world.)

Attempts have also been made to attribute primary (and, sometimes, secondary) qualities to the theoretical entities of sub-atomic physics. But not only is the force of such efforts debatable, it is also conceptually unclear in what sense mental conditions of the sort already enumerated could be at all predicated of such entities; for, of course, the point of the exercise is to vindicate some comprehensive form of materialism. What, for instance, could be meant by attributing the having of a thought to some congeries of sub-atomic particles? The difficulties once again are of a parallel nature: the mental conditions we treat as predicables call for particulars of some distinct and distinctly relevant sort, entities or integers or wholes of a certain marked unity; the same is true of physical properties that, say, are normally available to perceptual discrimination. What, for instance, is the relationship between the spatial spread of a perceivable table and whatever spatial properties are ascribed to the system of sub-atomic particles that (on alternative views) the former is the appearance of or, in some sense, reducible to? Unless questions of this sort can be satisfactorily met, it is hopeless to expect to unseat persons or physical bodies as entities basic to systematic discourse; for, that practice depends crucially on our linguistic devices for making reference and for making predications of what we may refer to, and those devices are normally and satisfactorily employed in connection with physical objects and persons.

2. Behavior and Machines

As I have remarked, the range of mental (or psychological) conditions available for ascription is strikingly heterogeneous. Some distinctions seem clearly behavioral. But it seems incredible to suppose that all mental concepts can be satisfactorily construed in behavioral terms. Images and sensations, for instance, however causally related to behavior, seem to be fairly characterized in terms of the onset or persistence of a mental state or interior episode of some determinate sort, not inherently a disposition to behave in any way whatsoever—which, behavior might precede or succeed. For instance, clasping my foot and hopping around with

a pained expression on my face—or the disposition so to behave
—normally said to be caused by my pain (my being in pain) and
normally serving as a criterion of my being in pain—cannot, on
any plausible view, *be* (be identical with) my pain. So it is quite
unlikely that behaviorism (so-called logical behaviorism) could
provide a comprehensive analysis of all of our mental concepts or
even of what would normally be included among the most central.
But also, it is impossible to give a purely physicalist description of
behavior in terms, say, of afferent and efferent impulses—in the
sense in which, even under experimental conditions, alternative
patterns of physical movement are normally construed as the same
or similar behavior by reference not to covering physical laws but
to intentional, purposive factors that do not themselves readily
yield to reductive (physicalist) elimination. There appears, in fact,
to be no promising way to formulate necessary and sufficient conditions governing the physical embodiment of given behavior—
even for species suitably embodied in particular ways. For instance, there are no necessary or sufficient or necessary and
sufficient physical movements associated with expecting company
or playing chess or requesting the butter. Alternatively put, behaviorism is an inadequate theory regarding the explanation and analysis of behavior, because behavior itself is intelligible only on the
admission of central (formal or functional or intentional) states
(however embodied and without regard to introspectibility), in accord with which, particular bodily movements are construed, organized, *as* behavior. The rat that moves through the maze *finds* its
pellet only in the sense in which *seeking food* is a state or disposition properly ascribable to it; and the native *assents* on some stimulatory occasion only in the sense that certain determinate *facts
linguistically discriminable by him are in question.* Not all mental
phenomena, then, may be construed as behavior or behavioral dispositions (sensations, for instance); and since ascriptions of behavior presuppose formal, rule-governed states, behaviorism itself is
invalid.

Noting the inherent flaw of behaviorism yields another benefit as well. We must distinguish carefully between physically describable afferent and efferent impulses involving the brain and significant stimuli and intelligent responses involving an organism. To construe brain patterns as having a certain "content" or "significance"—to construe them teleologically or intentionally, in the relevant sense—is to ascribe such content *derivatively,* in view of how we may characterize the *actions of the organism* itself. Behavior cannot be characterized except in terms of desires, needs, interests, objectives, sentience, knowledge, and the like—hence, cannot be characterized except in terms of habits, practices, institutions, rules. But to say this is to supply the fatal weakness of so-called central-state materialism. Mental attributes cannot be straightforwardly discovered, in purely physical terms, to qualify individual neural processes; and *what* mental attributes—say, conveying this or that thought or mood or the like—to *assign* to given neural processes obviously depends on what thought or mood or the like may properly *first* be ascribed to some sentient organism or person. The conceptual dependence is clear: the behavior of the whole organism may be analyzed and correlated with detailed bodily sub-structures; the sub-structures cannot otherwise be assigned any particular content at all. Hence, the teleological characterization of brain states cannot serve as a model for a materialist characterization of persons or sentient organisms, for the antecedent admission of such organisms and their attributes is a necessary condition for invoking the model itself. To put the point in a maxim: the brain *uses* information only if the organism *uses* information.

An earlier contrast mentioned (bearing on the occurrence of sensations and images and the like) also affects the much-debated issue of distinguishing between men and machines. The question arises whether machines can simulate whatever mental conditions are attributable to men; and, on its being admitted that they can —for enumerated conditions—the more strenuous question will be pressed, whether the mental conditions marked may be directly attributed to machines themselves. Clearly, the issue identifies another would-be reductive maneuver; for if mental conditions attributable to men were attributable to machines *and* if all machines were, putatively, mere physical systems, then it would seem that men must be such systems as well. But the argument is a *non sequitur* and there are abundant difficulties facing the thesis. For one thing, no matter what machines (as we presently understand them) may be able to simulate (adding sums, for instance, or digging a hole or scanning the horizon for the enemy), there is no clear (and relevant) sense in which (embodied) machines can be said to simulate the having of images and sensations *as distinct from* simulating behavior characteristically associated, in certain contexts of desire and purpose and the like, with particular images and sensations; *and* there are no machines that actually have sensations and images. Here, then, we see something of the strategic importance of resisting a behavioral reading of the various modes of sentience. *If* perceiving colors, for instance, were nothing but the disposition to believe or behave in ways determinably appropriate in given contexts, then the prospect of extending the use of mental predicates directly to machines would be greatly enhanced together with those of a (provisionally) comprehensive behaviorism. But there seems to be no plausible way of construing mere sentience behaviorally, even if the cognitive beliefs implicit in perception, sensation, and the awareness of images and the like may be plausibly construed in terms of behavioral dispositions. A second consideration is this: even if particular mental states are ascribable to machines as well as to men—directly and not merely by way of simulation (or by way of the programmer's intentions) —we cannot, for that reason, say that men are merely numerically identical with machines (of some sort) or mere physical bodies. We can only say (trivially) that men and machines are qualitatively similar in whatever respects the conditions given (whether mental or physical, by the way) may be ascribed to both; such predications can, in themselves, tell us nothing about the nature of the particulars (men and machines) that *have* the conditions in question—for essentially the reason already noted in challenging

the notion of bare particulars, namely, that that of which we normally make predications has some determinate nature, in virtue of
which the predications made are themselves admissible. The ascribability of a property entails only that the range of particulars
comprising its extension are, *whatever their nature,* of such a nature that such ascription is conceptually admissible. But this is, as
it stands, all but vacuous. And *if* all the mental attributes of men
were attributable to machines, we should have to determine
whether, after all, machines were merely physical objects or not;
that is, the mind-body problem would then have to be extended to
machines.

Here, we begin to touch on the most profound puzzles concerning the nature of the mental. But even before we press further, we
may regard as confirmed the heterogeneity at least of what is signified by 'mental.' Some mental concepts are behavioral, some
functional, some not open to behavioral interpretation (as for example covering instances of sentience—the latter themselves being
of a great variety); some cover determinate forms of consciousness, some do not (as covering unconscious states); some cover intentional states (as for instance thoughts and emotions), some do
not, or at least not in the same respect (for instance bodily sensations that are not "directed upon an object"), even if cognition of
them or behavior relevant to them be characterizable only in intentional terms (allowing, of course, for multivocal senses of 'intentional').

3. Intentionality and the Mental

The intentional may be counted among the more promising candidates for the distinction of being the essential feature of the
mental. But, to say the least, the thesis is problematic, given the
variety of senses in which we speak of the intentional; and, to anticipate our findings, it is—as characteristically formulated—
actually false.

There is, of course, a good deal of controversy regarding the putative intentionality of such (intransitive) sensations as pains, aches, tickles, tingles, thrills, and the like. For one thing, there is the supposedly difficult case of a pain in an amputated leg; but the apparent intentionality signified by the expression (which encourages us to assimilate it to discourse about hallucinations and delusions) may be dismissed, if it is seen that 'in an amputated leg' serves to describe a quality of the pain felt (and not a putative physical location) in a way rather similar to the use of 'smell of onions' in order to characterize an actual odor, perhaps even known not to be produced by onions at all. Another consideration is this. One speaks of pain (and of the related array of sensations) as of that which one wants to avoid (or savor or sustain or the like); but this is simply to attempt a behavioral reading of what it is to be in a certain state of sentience, however normal it may be *(not* necessary: think of the masochist or of someone indifferent to muted but discriminable sensations) for certain behavioral patterns to be linked to the occurrence of such sensations. If we say that these sensations must be construed in intentional terms (which is not necessary, certainly not illuminating), it will be for a reason that is both important and *sui generis,* namely, that they exist if and only if they are felt; for textures are not construed intentionally, though they are felt (they exist independently of being felt and cannot be felt unless they exist); and emotions may exist though they are not felt or cognized and, whether felt or not, they must be *of* something, whether the referent exists or not, in the sense in which the full characterization of an emotion requires an intentional object as internal to the emotion itself (as for instance a fear of God or a dread of I-know-not-what—the latter either being directly intentional or construed as strongly resembling emotions that are directly intentional). Also, of course, to say that pains and emotions exist is to treat pains and emotions as subaltern particulars; that is, 'feeling pain' and 'having an emotion' must, viewed within a materialist account not in accord with the identity theory, function as monadic predicates.

The intentional itself is by no means a single or simple or

straightforward concept. On one reading at least, the mental does not always involve the intentional (for instance, pains have no intentional objects, are not directed to some propositional content, are not necessarily linked to attitudes that are themselves intentional); on others, though it may be admitted to involve the intentional, the question remains, precisely, which version of the intentional is meant (for instance, is it merely the sense in which pains exist only for creatures who are capable of feeling, of being aware of, pain?). Again, if awareness of pain is intentional, it does not follow that pain is intentional—in the sense in which, for instance, both belief and awareness of belief are intentional. On the other hand, if the intentional (some usual version of the intentional) is not plainly a necessary condition of the mental, it is not obvious that it is a sufficient condition either; for it seems entirely possible to construe purely physical or non-mental systems in intentional terms. Perhaps the least ambiguous and most striking case is that of homeostasis among plants (as not having minds) or of the equilibrating pressure patterns of the earth. But to offer such instances is at once to suggest a significant difference in alternative uses of intentional concepts and a clue to the nature of mind and persons.

Consider that the purely physiological processes of a living organism may be satisfactorily explained in causal (and nonintentional terms): the ingestion of particular substances is causally linked to changes in the blood, digestive juices, and the like—and so on for all particular biochemical processes noted. Someone theorizes that *that* pattern may be construed homeostatically—to maximize, say, a certain metabolic potential relative to the physical state of a given living system. The advantage of the theory lies not merely in focussing a certain body of science on the central interests of reflecting human beings (who wish to survive) but also in facilitating certain discoveries about other *causal* sequences within the organism that, analogously, fit the homeostatic model. The critical point to notice here is that a given causal sequence (or a given phenomenon that may be identified without appealing to intentional concepts—an increase in blood sugar for instance) *is subsequently interpreted in intentional terms* (as exhibiting a certain purposive or teleological pattern). In all cases of this sort, the intentional idiom can be replaced, without relevant loss, by a nonintentional idiom, simply because, *ex hypothesi,* they are extensionally equivalent. This, of course, is also the reason why the ascription of intentional or teleological properties to computers is thought to be a mere *façon de parler.* But precisely in the case of mental predicates of the sort canvassed, we directly ascribe to persons and creatures said to have minds conditions that are intentionally freighted *and* that are not antecedently marked in purely nonintentional terms. Also, once having fixed these intentional predicates by reference to rules, practices, institutions, purposes, and the like—without assuming that the properties answering to them must be manifested only in some finitely formulable set of physical ways—we are entirely prepared to construe or describe or interpret new physical patterns as manifesting the very intentional property in question and to construe creatures having minds as capable of improvisation, in terms of physical movement, in accord with the rulelike patterns they may be said to follow. It would be questionbegging to claim flatly, on this basis alone, that suitable bodily equivalents (or replacements) cannot be marked for given mental states; but then, this is precisely the problem confronting accounts committed to some version of the identity thesis or eliminative materialism. To say this, however, is not to say either that materialism is defensible or that it is not.

The traditional account of intentionality provides three distinctive and independent criteria applied to mental or psychological phenomena and, with adjustment, applied to sentences purportedly about such phenomena. Roughly, according to this view, (1) sentences are intentional if, employing denoting expressions, neither they nor their contradictories entail the existence of what is purportedly denoted (e.g., 'Gawain searched for the Grail'); (2) sentences are intentional if, containing propositional clauses, neither they nor their contradictories entail the truth or falsity of the contained proposition (e.g., 'Gawain believed that the Grail was in England'); (3) a pair of sentences are intentional if, differing only in codesignative terms, the truth of one does not entail the truth of the other (e.g., 'Peter believes that Cicero denounced Cataline' and 'Peter believes that Tully denounced Cataline'). Since the last distinction introduces the intensional as well (the nonextensional) —that is, that sentential contexts are intensional if codesignative terms cannot be substituted for one another, *salve veritate*—it is also frequently maintained that every intentional context is intensional as well. But there are a number of confusions regarding these views.

For one thing, contexts that are intentional on the first criterion may behave extensionally, though it does not follow that intentional sentences may be replaced by extensionally equivalent sentences employing only physical terms where required. For example, 'Paul is reading about the adventures of Merlin the Magician' is intentional (on the first criterion) but behaves extensionally. Furthermore, 'reading' is a verb that has psychological import, but it is not clear that, in context, any purely physical process could suitably replace the process of reading. In any case, it is a separate question and cannot usefully be conflated with that of nonextensionality. For a second, contexts in which no mental or psychological considerations obtain may behave intensionally; hence (by the third criterion), such contexts would be intentional as well— for instance, contexts of temporal reference ('In 1942, Frank sat next to Richard Nixon at dinner,' but since 'Richard Nixon = the President of the United States,' we might conclude: 'In 1942, Frank sat next to the President of the United States,' which is false). It must be said, however, that it is not obvious that sentential contexts in which so-called tense operators function are genuinely intensional. At least two considerations (that may be tested against our illustration) count against the claim. For one, in sentences involving temporally determined roles, changes in tense must be duly accommodated (if Nixon *is* the President, he *was* not, on the occasion, the President); for another, the descriptions

that, in context, seem to be referentially opaque are really elliptical and need to be amplified in temporally relevant terms (if
Nixon is the President, he is actually *the President-since-1968*).
The intensionality alleged, therefore, may merely be due to an
equivocation and not to the use of tense operators. (It is often
thought, also, that modal contexts behave intensionally—which, if
true, would strengthen our second point. But I take the claim to
be false. For instance, if 'Necessarily $9 > 4$' is true, then if '$9 =$ the
number that numbers the major planets,' then 'Necessarily the
number that numbers the major planets > 4' is also true—on pain
of contradiction—though the number 9 be specified *per accidens*
and though it be contingent that the major planets number nine on
count.) But thirdly, intentional contexts need not concern the mental or psychological directly, though they must at least presuppose
the causal influence of mental or psychological factors. For example, 'Jackson's painting represents the rape of Leda' is intentional
on both the first and third criteria, but paintings have neither mental nor psychological attributes—though whatever attributes *they*
have presuppose the efforts of entities that have minds. But this
shows at a stroke that an analysis of the mental or the psychological cannot be provided satisfactorily in terms solely of the traditional criteria of intentionality.

It is most hazardous, therefore, to theorize about the nature of
the intentional. But it must be attempted since it appears that persons or creatures said to have minds behave in intentionally significant ways or are in states or conditions or undergo episodes and
the like that are intentionally significant. To be able to specify
some essential strand among intentional phenomena seems, therefore, to be able to specify an essential feature of what it is to be a
person. I suggest, then, the following as an approximation to this
strand: the intentional is what is rule-governed or rulelike, a
property of things. Correspondingly, a person is a particular that
acts or behaves in rule-governed or rulelike ways at least—
characteristically, in employing concepts and linguistic distinctions
in judgment, cognition, action, and the like. On this view, the in-

tentional may be present in the absence of (intentional) *action*. Also, by a rule, I mean a formula governing such normative distinctions as between what is permitted and forbidden, correct and incorrect, appropriate and inappropriate, such that given uniformities may be construed (intentionally) as embodying the rule and as subject to assessment in terms of the norm. Furthermore, rules need not be fixed or unchanging, or provided with necessary and sufficient conditions, or merely constitutive in nature, or even formulable or able to be *used* by every one and every thing thus subject and so governed. By whatever convention some creature, phenomenon, state, action, object, or the like is judged to be rule-governed or rulelike, it is thereby judged to have an intentional property. Phenomena exhibiting empirical uniformities, of course, are also subsumable at times under natural laws; but natural laws, unlike rules, require invariant uniformities, do not relevantly invite assessment, and do not presuppose sentience and intelligence.

We must now apply these distinctions to the analysis of persons and of creatures that have minds. Consequently, the independent complexities regarding the nature of persons will affect our account and keep us, not unreasonably, from drawing prematurely simple conclusions.

It will, for instance, make no difference—save a verbal one— to hold, at this point, that persons are bodies of a distinctive kind that behave in rule-governed ways or to hold that they *have* bodies. (There remains, always, the possibility of equivocating on the use of 'is,' as, say, between expressing identity and composition.) The fact remains that mental and physical predicates may be assigned on distinctly and systematically different grounds *and* that there may be types of entities to which mental attributes may be exclusively assigned. To be a materialist, it is essential that it be shown only that the admission does not entail the existence of non-material entities. The radical dualist, by contrast, is committed to disembodied existence; but therein, precisely, lies the difficulty of his view. For, there is an enormous number of mental conditions that are quite unintelligible if not ascribed to embodied systems (sentience, desire, emotions, and the like) and it is not at all convincing, though it has been disputed, that the rest are intelligible (for instance, reason or thought in the narrowest sense, or memory, including memory of perception and perceptual images) if assigned to mere disembodied minds or souls. Problems of reference and identification inevitably arise, without embodiment and bodily continuity. The difficulty with idealism, on the other hand, is that it either succumbs to solipsistic problems or exhausts its claim precisely in preserving a public world (making it a part of God's mind, for instance, but without necessarily attempting to account for the distinction between the mental and the physical).

Where behavior or dispositions to behave, or actions, are directly involved (as in searching for food), the thesis respecting the intentional and the nature of a person seems easiest to defend. But where, for instance, sentient-like states are concerned (like dreaming or perceptual delusion) or states of awareness of a non-sentient sort (believing or thinking that something is the case), the thesis —construing the intentional as the rule-governed—seems at first rather less than likely. Yet we need only consider that, in addition to admitting the so-called intentional inexistence of the object of such conditions (for instance, of unicorns that we may believe exist), persons are particulars that behave with respect to such "objects" and in accord with such beliefs or are disposed to behave (or would behave), under suitable circumstances, in rule-governed or rulelike ways (for instance, by hunting unicorns). It is perhaps foolish to speak of having emotions as of following rules, if for no other reason than that emotions are not actions; but it is not foolish to speak of behaving with respect to one's emotions (both consciously and unconsciously) in rulelike ways, that is, in ways that may be explained in terms of one's intentions, purposes, social practices, conventions, or to hold that the very ascription of emotions depends on the evidence of suitably institutionalized behavior—possibly linguistic. But this is to confirm at the very least the central role of action—and, most particularly, the role of the use of language—in the concept of a person. It is not to say that having emotions is not characteristic of persons—it is, after all, not uncharacteristic of numerous lower animals as well, incapable of stating that they have the emotions they have. It is only to say that it is not (thus far analyzed) fundamental to the most economical concept of a person.

Still, to be capable of emotion *is* to be capable of seizing, in some sense, the significance of events against the background of rule-governed practice. Again, to understand or know (in particular, to know by perceiving) or to believe that something is the case is to be in a state that entails applying, or having the capacity to apply, the rulelike regularities of language to the brute world (or, by an understandable extension to infants, animals, possibly even machines, behaving in accord with rulelike regularities that are analogues of linguistic regularities or incipent forms of them). It is in this connection, precisely, that we speak, heuristically, of entailed mental acts, as of judging or understanding and the like. And it is in this connection, therefore, that we construe mental *states* in terms of a model of *acts,* of following rules even where no explicit behavior is involved, in virtue of which, significance, purposiveness, intentional reference, and the like are assigned as properties of the conditions of living systems. Here then, we notice the differences and similarities embedded in speaking of the intentional as a property of things, of mental states, and of the explicit behavior of sentient organisms. That, for instance, a tree lies in some sentient creature's visual field, that he "sees" the tree without being aware of it, may be duly explained in causal terms without any reference at all to mental acts or to intentional or rulelike factors. But that he sees the tree, in the sense in which he is cognitively aware of *it*—whether human or animal—entails some appropriate capacity, on the creature's part, to characterize it in linguistic terms or to behave with respect to it in ways suitably analogous to such a capacity. Where the capacity involved is advanced enough to count as the capacity to use language, we have before us a *person*—though not necessarily a human person.

Briefly, then, the thesis about intentionality comes to this. Persons are distinguished by their ability to use language, but language use is a rule-governed activity; consequently, persons are intentional beings, in the sense in which, using language, they follow and are governed by rules. But mental states (beliefs and emotions, for instance) are, as we saw earlier, analyzable in terms of a model of mental acts that, even in the absence of the ability to use language, enables us to construe given mental states as analogues of linguistic acts. Hence, mental states are construed in rule-governed ways. *A fortiori,* the same is true of sentience and non-sentient knowledge. The traditional forms of intentionality, therefore, merely constitute prominent forms of rulelike phenomena, particularly closely related to language use itself. And the distinction of sentient beings as opposed to artifacts lies with their capacity to *use* or *follow* rules. The ascription of sentience, then, is the ascription, on theoretical grounds, to a suitably complex organism (or android or the like) of certain central states analyzed on the model of mental acts—which, incidentally, pinpoints the inappropriateness of ascribing in the literal sense *innate linguistic* dispositions to physical *bodies* that, under suitable cultural conditions, will *evolve* as persons.

4. The Nature and Individuation of Persons

To proceed, then, with the analysis of a person, we may concede that understanding, knowledge, belief, thought are characteristically construed as entailing the use of language or processes perspicuously analyzed on the model of linguistic acts, *for* creatures capable of using language. Where (not unusually) belief or knowledge is attributed to animals lacking a language, we do not view them as persons but only as creatures having minds of such an order that certain mental attributes normally ascribed to persons may be ascribed to them as well. A dog, for instance, is said to anticipate his master at the door, but never by the use of language. The critical difference is this: that to be able to use language is to

be able to reflect on the world experienced and on experience itself to the extent of being able to make reference to, and to make
predications of, selected elements in the world and in experience
(including reflexive reference and reflexive predication). Mind,
therefore, is attributable to whatever organisms or systems exhibit
discriminative powers that are at least analogues of the capacity to
use language, that is, in their being describable as rule-following
(or rule-improvising) beings. Sentience, appetite, affect, intelligence are merely alternative manifestations of mind; and persons
are rule-following organisms or systems, or organisms or systems
capable of intentional states, whose mental powers extend to the
use of language. These need not, of course, be human persons unless they exhibit both physical and mental traits of a familiar sort.

   With these distinctions in mind, we may, drawing in another—
initially tangential—issue, coherently hold that a person may exist
discontinuously, as for instance according to the popular doctrine
of reincarnation. It is not even necessary, in conceding this, to
admit the possibility of disembodied existence. For, *if* persons
might be said to be individuated in terms of a certain set of memories (or similarly distinctive personal traits) attributable to suitably "embodied" entities—where the bodies in question may be
independently individuated in terms of bodily continuity—then if
the set of memories in question attributed to a particular person
having a particular body may, at another time, be attributed to a
person having another body (let us suppose, for simplicity's sake,
appearing several centuries later), then it need not be incoherent
to hold that the same person had one body in one incarnation and
another in another. An entity "embodied" and exhibiting the capacity to use language is a person and a person, on the specification of *suitable* mental traits, may be one and the same although
serially "embodied" in different physical bodies. The thesis could
be strengthened, for instance, by introducing suitable causal continuities (bearing on memory and the like) where bodily disconti-
uity obtains; and a kind of memory (not requiring unique assignment to an embodied entity that cannot survive bodily

discontinuity) could be (and would have to be) introduced. But these adjustments are not inconceivable. In fact, if, as is often argued, memory causally depends on certain modifications of physical cells, then it is obviously possible to speak of memories being transferred from one creature to another and of the memories of individuals persisting through distinct incarnations.

This shows at least the intelligibility of a widespread doctrine, though not of course the causal conditions on which it could actually be true. The adjustments regarding identity and continuity, then, do not appear to be insuperable. The bodily continuity of persons, furthermore, is subject to all the puzzles that may arise regarding identifying and individuating mere physical bodies— fission, fusion, transplants, and the like resurrect all of these with a vengeance. And memory, it must be admitted, is a defective criterion for other reasons, for a person may be reidentified who has suffered enormous losses of memory regarding his own life, and his experiences remain his though he has forgotten them: he is said to be numerically the same person (however greatly changed, qualitatively) over an interval in which *he* has lost his memory. Here, clearly, bodily continuity is taken to be decisive or at least more fundamental. In any case, certain psychological continuities are more decisive than particular memories and these may be invoked, if we wish, in claims of reincarnation. Also, memory itself —that is, true memory as opposed to memory claims or the impression of remembering—presupposes some criterion of personal identity and continuity, for to know what is true is not, as such, to remember, and to speak of remembering is to speak elliptically of *someone's* remembering. But where bodily continuity is itself lacking (as with reincarnation), suitable causal continuities linked to a novel kind of "memory" (as not involving bodily continuity) whose content matches the original memory and experience (or, is suitably continuous with them) may justify our speaking of one and the same person and of *his* memory (*if* we wish); and where, though bodily continuity is present (as in separating the hemispheres of the brain in a way that may support the ascription of traits belonging normally to independent persons), anomalies will result that cannot be resolved by appealing to bodily continuity alone.

What these considerations show is that persons are, conceptually, entities distinct from bodies (though not, for that reason, separable from bodies) in a sense not unlike that in which a Mozart sonata is distinct from physical sound but not separable from physical sound or like that in which a tooth is distinct from the silver amalgam that, now that it is repaired, is part of its composition but not separable from that substance or some suitable substitute. That is, the conditions of the survival of a person are, arguably, distinct from those of the survival of some particular physical embodiment. And this suggests that a person is identified by identifying *some* body by reference to which we may appropriately control the ascription of whatever suitable mental traits distinguish persons from creatures having minds (but inferior to persons) and from creatures having no minds and from objects that are not living systems at all; it suggests, also, that persons may, in principle, be reidentified even if serially embodied in different bodies or (as with clones) multiply embodied in different bodies—by way of purportedly uniquely identifying constellations of mental properties. Once again, rather as with works of art, persons would have to be construed as type objects (*not* classes) either uniquely instantiated in single embodiments (even if only serially) or multiply instantiated in clone tokens. But this converges surprisingly well with the fact that persons—as essentially capable of language—are entities identifiable only in cultural contexts and are creatures that cannot, introspectively, discern what answers to the 'I' that has the mental states they can discern. Personal identity—like existence itself—is not a sentiently discernible property of any kind. The concept is theoretically controlled and, in order to maximize coherence, may and must be adjusted in the face of evolutionary and technological novelties.

Three interdependent considerations are crucial here: first, that the identification of persons is necessarily linked with, though not equivalent to, the identification of physical bodies (the question of embodiment); second, that token instantiation of persons is a matter quite distinct from construing bodies as persons (the question of identity); third, that token persons (whether as uniquely or serially embodied or as clones) instantiate persons and not merely properties (the question of ontic commitment)—for, clearly, to speak of the *instantiation* of persons (or other cultural entities) is to speak of a *sui generis* use of 'is' (roughly, 'embodied'). Persons are not abstract entities—certainly not classes—since they are embodied; but given the relative ease with which physical bodies (on which they depend) may be identified and the distinction between the nature of bodies and the nature of persons, we are at liberty to entertain any of an enormous variety of ways of individuating persons. For instance, we may even consider whether what are normally regarded as the phases or stages of a person (given some simple form of bodily continuity) may be coherently reinterpreted as a set of overlapping but distinct (and perhaps briefly surviving) persons: on such a view, not only is reincarnation and multiple embodiment intelligible but it is not even necessary to insist that no more than one person may be embodied in one body. It is precisely because what it is to be a person is an issue distinct from that of the individuation and reidentification of persons that we may entertain these conceptually intriguing possibilities or even others like the transformation of one person into, or replacement by, another (as in science fiction and horror stories) and the continuity of persons (or personlike entities) in serial embodiments that allow for distinct personalities (for instance, as with the Dalai Lama). The advantages of such alternatives are at least debatable and, of course, the alternatives themselves clearly bear on questions of personal responsibility and the like.

There is, however, a further qualification that must be made respecting the intentional that bears on the analysis of persons. For, not only are there creatures that have minds but there are particulars produced by or involving such creatures, themselves lacking minds though exhibiting a wide range of intentional properties

(ineliminable by reference to extensionally equivalent nonintentional properties, if those regarding minds are ineliminable). Such
particulars are of at least two distinct kinds, that I shall call *deposits* and *referred individuals*. Deposits include, prominently,
works of art, machines, and the elements of language. In being
produced by creatures having minds but not (unlike natural off-
spring) themselves having minds, they may still be said to be cultural entities. Their identification depends on physical objects (in
which they are embodied) but they cannot be identified with bare
physical objects and may even involve curious puzzles of identity
that cannot arise for non-rule-governed particulars like mere physical objects: for instance, a Mozart concerto, whose identity depends on scores, cannot be identified with scores and may be manifested in, may be one and the same concerto in, variable
performances. Their distinctive properties presuppose the purposive activity of creatures having minds. Referred individuals are
not independent deposits. They are, rather, collective but fictional
entities, identified by means of the referred, projected interests of
aggregates of individual persons (or creature surrogates) upon
such fictions. They lack minds in the sense proper to persons but,
in being assigned certain "collective interests" (formulable, for instance, in terms of ideologies and doctrines shared by aggregates),
they are treated as if they had minds by creatures that actually do,
and assigned responsibilities, rights, and the like. Prominent
among them, of course, are political states, corporations, commun-
ities, societies, and clans. This shows that the intentional, when
construed merely as the rule-governed or rulelike, cannot satisfactorily distinguish between the mental and the artifactual. In this
respect, alternative forms of sentience and of non-sentient awareness satisfactorily provide a sufficient (and, indeed, a necessary)
mark of the mental.

We may collect our scattered remarks a little more neatly. Intentionality promises to serve as a useful mark of the mental. But
it proves to be unsatisfactory not only because of the distinct and
multiple senses in which we speak of the intentional but also be-

cause, on obvious grounds, a great many things that cannot be said to have minds must be characterized (non-eliminably) in intentional terms. Sentience, consciousness, awareness effectively provide the essential mark of the mental: the ascription of mental and psychological attributes imply consciousness and the like at some level of development; and the cognitive features of the very forms of consciousness may be said to be intentional in nature, in the sense that discrimination is made in accord with some conceptual scheme (that need not be linguistically formulated)—assigned sometimes, as with the lower animals, solely on the strength of suitable patterns of behavior. In this respect, the range of the mental is homogeneous despite the heterogeneity of its manifestations; and in this respect, also, the intentional—in the sense specified—is an essential feature of the cognitively relevant aspects of mental phenomena. Persons, then, are privileged creatures having minds and the capacity to use language.

Furthermore, cultural entities like persons, works of art, words exist as distinct entities only as embodied in particular physical objects or physical systems. Since they are themselves particulars (of the peculiar sort specified as type objects), they may be contrasted with classes or sets (that have members and that are identical with given classes or sets having the same membership) and may be contrasted with kinds or universals (instantiated by whatever we may make corresponding predications of). A given etching, for instance, may be a member of the class of Picasso's etchings; may be of the kind, that of being admired at the moment; and may be the very same etching, though not the same copy of the same etching, as that one over against the wall. At least initially, these may be taken as grammatical distinctions that inform our usual ontic commitments.

5. The Identity Thesis

To return once again to the identity thesis, we must admit that supporters of the thesis normally press their claims for certain quite restricted central cases (though, in principle, they could not be satisfied with less than a comprehensive enumeration of detailed mind-body identities or a comprehensive rule for constructing such identities). In any case, in fairness to the strenuous difficulty of posing the thesis in a debatable form, we should look more closely at its defensibility. A standard way of putting the claim is this: if what is identified under one description or name or the like is, contingently, the same as what is identified under another description or designation, then whatever is true of it under the one remains true of it under the other. There is an obvious ambiguity that arises here, already suggested, respecting intentional (and intensional) contexts. For our own purposes, it is enough to note that, in challenging the mind-body identity thesis persuasively, we must not rest the counterargument on the merely referential and predicative puzzles of intensional contexts. Nevertheless, there are difficulties enough confronting the thesis.

For one thing, if two putatively independent things (x and y) are strictly identical, then, barring overriding considerations, if some essential property may be truly predicated of x ('Fx'), then Fy must also be true; but if this is so, then 'Fy' must be intelligible, must have a clear sense. Yet it is often the case that what appears to be essentially predicated of the body cannot be meaningfully predicated of the mind and vice versa. For instance, an emotion or wish cannot be said to be located at the base of the skull; *if* of course the identity thesis obtained, the predication would be admissible. But that is the very issue at stake and rests, presumably, on such equivalences—*a fortiori,* on their intelligibility. The problem of location (and certain related problems) may be considerably attenuated (though not, perhaps, entirely eliminated) by insisting on speaking not, say, of the identity of emotions or wishes and of certain physical processes but rather of the identity of a person's having an emotion or wish and of his body's being in a certain physical condition. If we bear in mind, however, the syntactical suppleness that we require for purposes of reference and attribution, we shall have to admit that the seeming elimination of troublesome asymmetries is really more camouflage than the resolution of the puzzle. Also, whether the having of an emotion may be located in the same way as the having of a physical condition is not altogether a promising question. The changing location of the body and locating changes in the body are, clearly, distinct issues. Consider, too, that the felt location of a sensation —a felt *quality* of the sensation, however expressed in the idiom of spatial location and however related to spatial location, cannot as such be construed as the spatial location of the sensation *had* by a sentient creature. In any case, it will not matter, for the elimination of such problems is invariably attended by the provision of others of even greater difficulty.

The crucial problem is simply this: when the identities are cast in terms of attributing properties to persons (or minds) and properties to bodies, it is normally assumed that the predicative expression 'having . . .' or 'being . . .' is univocal for persons and bodies. But, though it is true that, *qua* predication, to say that a person *has* an emotion and a person's body *has* a certain physical condition is to use 'has' univocally, actually ascribing the having of an emotion and the having of a certain physical condition invariably raises what may be called the ontological problem of possession or attribution (which is regularly and misleadingly conflated with the merely syntactical problem of predication). To say that a person has an emotion is, from the point of view of mere predication, to say only that some formula will capture relevant syntactical features; but to say that a person has an emotion is also to say that an attribute like having an emotion is, on relevant conceptual grounds, an admissible attribute *for such particulars as persons; whether* the body may be said to *have* an emotion—in the possessive sense—is just the issue of the mind-body identity thesis (is, in fact, just the issue of intentionality, in the comprehensive form proposed). So, it will never be resolved merely by reference to there being a univocal sense in which, predicatively considered, a body is said to *have* a certain physical condition when a person is said to *have* an emotion.

The identity theorist must show that the use of the possessive sense of 'have,' if asymmetrical for persons and bodies, does not upset the thesis or is, indeed, symmetrical for persons and bodies or is symmetrical at least for ranges of predicates that the thesis must accommodate. It appears that all attempts to the present to defend the identity thesis, unless they are downright questionbegging in the manner suggested, founder either because they cannot account for asymmetrical restrictions on the scope of certain predicates (where equivalence is or seems required) or because the equivalences they posit would be decisive (as favoring the identity thesis) *only if* it were shown that predicative expressions like 'having . . .' and 'being . . .' and the like are not only univocal in the purely predicative sense, but univocally employed in the possessive sense as well. But, of course, this *is* the mind-body identity problem and not a resolution of it. Again, the sense in which a person *has* an emotion, a thought, a belief, a pain, or the like is, characteristically, the sense in which he is aware of it; and the sense in which he is aware of it is, normally, the sense in which he is able to characterize it in linguistically appropriate ways or to behave with respect to it in ways that justify the imputation of suitable rulelike analogues. But to say this, is, once more, to focus the problem, not to resolve it. The move to block the difficulty, by identifying the *states* of having, say, an emotion or belief or pain with physical states fails, for, as has been noted, it ignores entirely the subaltern status of such particulars as states and events. The expression 'have' that conveys the appropriate form of possession linking emotions to persons and brain states to bodies need not be univocal or rest on the same criteria (or even, perhaps, remain a relevant consideration) *if* the indissoluble particulars, the paired states in question, are construed in terms of cross-category identity. But if this is disallowed, the identity claim can only go through *if* persons are satisfactorily reduced to bodies *and* the use of 'have' proves, both predicatively and in the sense of appropriate possession, to be univocal or to entail the same criteria of application. We must, then, distinguish carefully between contexts in which 'have' has a purely negligible function in idiomatic phrases and contexts in which it serves as an ontological index of the appropriateness of linking certain entities and certain attributes predicatively. Treating subaltern particulars as particulars characteristically reduces 'have' to the insignificant function of appearing in certain fixed expressions, and exposing the grammatical dependency of subaltern particulars restores 'have' to its function as an index of a certain attributive adequacy.

In fact, the argument may be construed much more affirmatively by way of the following consideration. If it is the case that physical objects like trees or teeth are not identical with their composition or constitution, because at least the conditions of survival for each are different, then we may perhaps say that persons are composed of, or constituted of, physical materials, at the same time that we deny that they are identical with those materials and that their distinctive properties are nonintentionally identifiable. This, then, would provide a line of argument in terms of which materialism (a materialism of composition, let us say) could be rendered compatible with dualism (a dualism only of properties —or states and events—ascribed to particulars, let us say). Thus, if we deny that persons or other creatures having minds are constituted of "mental stuff," the fact that intransitive sentience, intentionality, the property of being rule-governed, and the like cannot be extensionally replaced by suitable nonintentional counterparts is then simply a way of explaining what we should mean by speaking of the *emergence* of the mind and of creatures of different abilities that possess minds. In fact, compositional materialism and a grasp of the distinction of culturally emergent entities are sufficient to accommodate all of the puzzles we have explored regarding the nature and identity of persons. Also, of course, if the systematic and central role of persons be conceded through the entire range of questions that we have explored, and if the critical problem of attribution or possession be admitted (regarding what may appropriately be ascribed to bodies and persons), and if the subaltern status of states, events, and actions be admitted (so that the problem of attribution cannot be obscured), then eliminative materialism will be seen to be even weaker than the identity thesis. For, it cannot possibly be vindicated without demonstrating how to proceed without all the usual ascriptions that we properly make only of persons or of creatures having minds. But the demonstration is just what we lack.

There are other difficulties that may be mentioned (particularly those concerning epistemic asymmetries regarding intransitive mental states and, consequently, concerning at least minimal skepticism, that do not arise for bodily states); for, if the identity thesis obtained, then the sentient discrimination of pains, for instance, would (as in having location) have to be construed as a form of perceptual discrimination and all the asymmetries usually admitted would have to be denied. But these considerations are enough to demonstrate the weakness of identity theories, on internal grounds alone.

In sum, if we are to support materialism, we must do so compatibly with the admission of persons. Logical behaviorism is the crudest form of materialism in that it fails to accommodate internal states of sentience and fails, even in accounting for behavior, to posit formal or functional or intentional central states in terms of which alone bodily movements may be construed as significant behavior. Identity theories fail because they cannot provide for extensional equivalences even where properties critical to the identity thesis—on any view—are specified. Eliminative materialism fails because, at the very least, the cognitive role of persons cannot be eliminated, can at best only be reduced in physicalistic terms—which itself founders on the problem of attribution. Central-state materialism fails because the ascription of intentional content or significance to central physical states presupposes the ascribability of mental states to persons and other sentient creatures. It very much looks as if only a form of compositional materialism is viable, since it is able to accommodate, where necessary, the analysis of properties along behavioral or functional lines or in accord with reductive identities or eliminative views, at the same time that it provides for any and all asymmetries between physical and psychological predicates without insisting on ontological dualism. Compositional materialism, in short, is nonreductive and committed to the emergence of mind and of culturally distinctive entities.

IX

FACTS & VALUES

Disputes about the value of something characteristically threaten to be indecisive, for puzzles are bound to arise about the possibility of confirming relevant claims. Value judgments, accordingly, are contrasted with factual judgments and doubts are raised about the prospect of actually discovering the "proper" values answering to alleged interests, needs, norms, practices, institutions, and the like. The contrast between factual and value judgments is misleading, however, since they cannot be construed as coordinate species of judgments distinguished in terms of a common principle. Factual judgments are simply judgments to which truth values may be assigned; and value judgments are simply judgments whose predicates designate attributes of value. Consequently, there is no reason whatsoever why a given judgment should not be at once a factual judgment and a value judgment—for instance, the judgment that Peter murdered Paul. Nevertheless, it is true that there are value judgments that are not factual judgments, that depend for their justification jointly on the particular tastes, preferences, convictions of the person making the judgment and the discernible attributes of whatever is judged (whether those attributes are at-

*tributes of value or not). But then, these two sorts of value judg-
ments are quite as different from one another as value judgments
of the first sort and factual judgments that employ no valuational
predicates. Furthermore, the sense in which value judgments may
be a species of factual judgment concerns only the logical properties of the judgments involved—in particular, that they may be
true or false—and not the conditions on which we may be said to
know that this or that actually has this or that value. Again, if
these claims hold for value judgments in general, then it is clear
that so-called 'ought'-judgments (for instance, 'Jack ought to pay
his rent') can readily be derivable from so-called 'is'-judgments
(for instance, 'The rent is due' or 'Jack contracted for the room')
simply because 'ought'-judgments may well be factual judgments
and, therefore, 'is'-judgments. And, correspondingly, 'ought'-judg-
ments do not as such entail 'can'-judgments (for instance, 'He can
pay his rent') simply because 'ought' and similar terms may be used,
without change of meaning, in contexts of belief, that is, where no
questions of the ability to act arise (for instance, as in saying 'The
sun ought to rise today at 5:15').*

*Deeper difficulties may be raised regarding the objectivity of
value judgments because there is no straightforward sense in
which allegedly normative values can be discovered. The usual
strategies are all suspect. For instance, the thesis that the meaning
of critical value terms is such that attributions of goodness, say,
are equivalent in truth to attributions of being pleasant or satisfying desire or the like (so-called naturalism) merely raises unresolved disputes about what really is worthwhile to a seemingly
higher level of unresolvable dispute about the meaning of key concepts. Similarly, the thesis that men possess a distinctive faculty
for discerning normative values as such (for instance, so-called in-
tuitionism) combines the weakness of the preceding view with additional and dubious claims about an uncertain faculty. Other
strategies fare no better. Also, in speaking about human beings, it
is at least not necessary, in classifying creatures as human beings
or persons or men, to make reference to norms of excellence or*

perfection or the like; all that is required is resemblance to admitted specimens—not themselves necessarily excellent in any particular regard. And, the very concept of a person as a culturally emergent entity confirms the sense in which the normative values to which given persons are likely to subscribe are just those that belong most firmly to the environing culture in which they develop.

Questions also arise about the kind of consistency that may be required of a rational man who believes that such and such may be valuable to him or who believes that, given that he desires such and such, that he believes that this or that would satisfy his desire in some suitably preferred way. Consistency here—what may be termed consistency in practice—does not directly concern the compatibility of propositions but rather the compatibility of beliefs, desires, and actions. Consequently, there is a strong temptation to speak of practical reasoning (that concerns, precisely, the linkage among beliefs, desires, and actions) as fundamentally different in its logical features from reasoning about relations among propositions (so-called theoretical reasoning). But this is quite unnecessary. For one thing, we have only to think of consistency in practice as a matter concerning the relationship between action and whatever reasoning we may engage in. For another, we may enlarge our account of models of reasoning where—as in practical contexts—imperatives, infinitives, tensed distinctions, and the like are centrally employed and generate novel logical puzzles. Thirdly, the requirements of consistency in practice are bound to vary from one context to another—for instance, from prudential to moral to purely technical and enabling considerations. What may count as consistency in practice respecting entertaining a jewel robbery and assassinating a tyrant may very well depend on the terms of reference of moral and non-moral dispute (entailing, therefore, theories about moral obligation and the like) and not merely the allegedly formal properties of so-called practical reasoning. And finally, failure to act in accord with the requirements of such consistency need not itself betray an inconsistency and need not

be incompatible with the admission of sound and relevant argu-
ments: this is, in fact, just the significance of the phenomenon
known as weakness of will.

In general, then, there is no prospect of a science of values, if
what is wanted is a procedure for determining not only which
value judgments are true and which false but also for determining
such truth-values on the basis of an independent discovery of the
actual norms by which human beings ought to govern their lives,
that is, by a discovery that depends on an examination of human
nature as such. On the other hand, there are a great many disputes
about values that, presupposing the prevailing practices and tradi-
tions of a people, do not require that the stringent constraints of a
science of values be satisfied. And, in particular, if such normative
values as those of consistency, validity, confirmability, and the like
—essential to our empirical and formal sciences—be admitted as
normative values, the limitations acknowledged will have no unto-
ward import. For, the norms relevant to such values are strictly
enabling rather than substantive norms (like health or virtue), in
the sense that they facilitate neutrally the collection of any infor-
mation at all and without regard to the ulterior use to which such
information may be put.

1. The Fact-Value Dichotomy

What are the prospects for a science of values?

It seems reasonable to suppose that value judgments may be
objectively confirmed if values answer to our interests. Thus, if we
suppose that maintaining a certain metabolic equilibrium is in our
interest, we may formulate corresponding value judgments (that is,
medical judgments, judgments regarding health and illness) that
may be confirmed or disconfirmed with whatever success normally
attends the testing of judgments of fact. But the maneuver is altogether too simple. For one thing, legal judgments are, putatively,
as objective as medical judgments and yet they often go contrary

to our interests—at least to the interests of those whom the law penalizes. For another, no one who subscribes to the view that value judgments are objective would admit the thesis to be undermined if, relevantly, the parties involved had, severally, conflicting or incompatible interests or if their interests changed. Again, we regard it as an eligible matter to question whether our actual interests are the interests we ought to have, which—on pain of a vicious regress—could not be settled by consulting our interests. Again, we sometimes christen whatever normative values we take to be binding on men as those which answer to our "real" interests—which is to say that the matter cannot be settled by consulting our interests in the straightforward sense in which people simply declare what their interests are. Finally, although it may be granted that men have an interest in moral matters, for instance, or in questions regarding beauty, it remains true, nevertheless, that controversy and puzzlement may still ensue regarding the objectivity of relevant judgments. The difficulty is clearly pervasive and cannot be eliminated by substituting for the notion of interests wants, needs, desires, purposes, ends, or the like. Alternatively construed, values that *are* institutionalized in some tradition or practice may be said to "answer to our interests"; but then, trivially, the objectivity of our interests will be decided by consulting what values there are, not that of our values by our interests. The matter calls for a fresh start.

The objectivity of value judgments rests on considerations of two quite different sorts, namely, whether such judgments are logically similar to judgments of fact and whether normative values are open, in any sense, to cognitive discovery. If the first may be answered in the affirmative, then—by institutionalizing, routinizing, regularizing our values, or by positing them by way of convention or even arbitrarily—the objectivity of value judgments can be ensured, but at the price of radically relativizing such objectivity to the adoption, implicit or explicit, of particular conventions. If the second consideration may be answered in the affirmative, then we can go beyond the merely conventional or pro-

visional objectivity of values and objectively judge whether these
or those conventions are themselves consonant with values discovered to be "proper," "appropriate," "natural," "normal," "normative," or "real" for human beings. I should say that the answer to
the first is Yes, with qualifications; and that the answer to the second is No, without qualification.

It is also often thought uncertain whether value judgments play
a prominent role in the pursuit of science—even in such disciplines as physics and mathematics; for if they do, and if the conclusions just posited hold, then it would appear that the objectivity
of these disciplines is placed in serious jeopardy. But this fear is
due, as we shall see, to a profound misunderstanding of the nature
of value judgments. It is, in this context, often supposed that such
concepts as those of validity, consistency, confirmation, knowledge, and justified belief—obviously crucial to the pursuit of the
empirical and formal sciences—are inherently value-laden. It
turns out that it is not as serious a matter as one might suppose, to
hold either that they are or are not value-laden concepts. But to
say this is not to say, as we shall see, that to classify other concepts as value-laden (or as not value-laden) is also not of crucial
importance—for instance, such concepts as health and illness, justice and injustice, normality and abnormality, maturity and imma-
turity, virtue and vice. The reasons will need to be canvassed.

It is a mistake to classify judgments as factual or value judgments, as if the distinction held between exclusive alternatives. For,
it is entirely possible that a judgment be both factual and
valuational—at least as far as the first consideration broached
above is concerned (affecting a science of values). The reason is
elementary. To characterize a judgment as factual is to characterize it as a judgment to which truth values may appropriately be
assigned; and to characterize it as a value judgment is only to
characterize its predicates as valuational predicates. Consequently,
the distinction between the two sorts of judgment depends on a
mixed classification for which there is no fundamental principle of
division—that is, with respect to which they might be considered

distinct species of a common genus. But if this is so, then the much-debated fact-value dichotomy falls to the ground and pertinent questions about the nature of human values must be reformulated. There may well be alternative methods by means of which distinct factual matters may be settled, but the sense in which statements about all such matters may be said to be true or false remains univocal though the criteria for such ascriptions vary. Thus, the differences in detailed method affecting the confirmation of claims that concern what is observed and unobservable, what is present and what is past, what is episodic and what is lawlike, what is causal and what is not, what is identified in intentional terms and what is not (and what depends on similar distinctions) do not, as such, affect the very meaning of 'true' and 'false' as assigned to relevant statements. But if this is so, then there is no reason to suppose that the confirmation of valuational and non-valuational claims will require an adjustment in the meaning of 'true' and 'false' either—merely, rather, a careful specification of the criteria on which relevant claims may be decided.

To come to cases, if there is a schedule of distinctions for the grading of apples (that, ulteriorly, answers to the interests of consumers collected in terms of market practices), then if the distinctions may be empirically applied, the judgment that a given lot of apples is a fancy lot will be true or false and, ordinarily, decidable. Also, to say that to say the apples are fancy is to make a value judgment is to say that the predicate 'fancy' may, for theoretically appropriate reasons, be taken to be a valuational one. It is important to see that the question of characterizing the predicate as valuational need not in the least affect the procedures by which determining the truth or falsity of the claim will be decided. This, broadly speaking, is the reason that nothing damaging to the stability of science hangs on whether validity or consistency and the like are or are not construed as valuational concepts. The methods for determining formal consistency, for instance, are entirely independent of any conclusions we may draw regarding whether, without altering the meaning of 'consistent,' it should be construed as a value-laden term or not—though, to be sure, alternative theories about this matter will affect our conception of the very nature of science and may, therefore, affect our practice as well. We may put the point of the neutrality urged here in another way. The interests of science are not, in any sense, binding on men; they are at best characteristic of men and relatively stable and explicit, quite apart from questions of social fashion and cultural orientation. The very notion of information that may be used, if it is usable, for any partisan enterprise whatsoever, suggests that the "values" of consistency, validity, confirmability, knowledge, and the like are merely such as obtain hypothetically, that is, *if* men wish to collect information, to collect what is reliable in a sense answering to any and all possible projects that may be pursued. This neutrality emphatically does not obtain when questions are raised of legal, political, economic, religious, moral, aesthetic, medical, educational values. For then, the values alleged to hold are *not* construed in a purely formal or enabling sense but are themselves quite characteristically thought to be able to be asserted (perhaps in a number of distinct ways) as binding on men. We shall return to this distinction.

To say that predicates are valuational is to say that the ascription of the properties they designate logically depends on reference to norms of excellence, perfection, achievement, fulfillment, and the like, in terms of which the set of particulars over which they range may be graded and ranked. It is, therefore, not in the least necessary that, for instance, to say that Peter is tubercular (or that certain apples are fancy) is to require distinctly different empirical tests, whether we hold that 'tubercular' (or 'fancy') is a valuational predicate or is not. It may be quite sufficient to *construe,* by way of reference to our theories about the properties designated, particular empirical discriminations and tests as value-laden or not. If the meaning of 'tubercular' is explained in terms of norms of health, then to attribute being tubercular to Peter, itself based on testing for the presence and activity of certain microorganisms, will be construed as attributing a value-laden property to Peter (and, correspondingly, one will have made a value judgment). It is also, of course, entirely possible to render evaluations of whatever has been, antecedently, identified in value-neutral terms. The point is that differences of this sort do not necessarily affect the propriety of ascribing truth values to value judgments or the empirical standing of such judgments. Consequently, the claim that the extension of given valuational predicates cannot be equivalent to that of non-valuational predicates—since, if they were, the "open question" could not be asked, viz., whether anything of *that* description had merit or was good or was worthwhile—falls to the ground; the required distinction may be supplied by contrasting the theoretical roles of valuational and non-valuational predicates, whatever their equivalence respecting truth values may be. (We have only to distinguish between questions of meaning and questions of truth.)

It needs also to be borne in mind that there are value judgments that cannot plausibly be construed as factual judgments. To say this is not to undermine what has already been claimed; it is, rather, to draw attention to the fact that value judgments are not, as such, of a logically uniform sort. In particular, when the ascription of a value to something logically depends on one's liking or disliking or preferring this or that—on one's tastes or convictions, as we may say—then anomalies arise if we insist on construing the relevant judgments as factual judgments. If I claim, "The steak at Barney's is nice," where the grading intended depends on my personal taste, then even if you admit that my claim is in some sense justified, you need not be obliged (supposing your taste to be different) to concur (implicitly) in the judgment. Now, my taste cannot be offered as a reason bearing on the truth or falsity of the claim—that you might consider; it cannot, normally, serve to justify the claim, though it may well explain it. In the limit, insisting on such trivial "justifications" reduces an apparent judgment to a mere expression of preference and the like (which is to say that such an utterance no longer has any evaluative function at all). These judgments of taste ("appreciative judgments," as I should term them) obtain only when there is an appropriate congruence between an utterance construed as such a judgment and certain psychological states and attitudes on the part of the would-be claimant; but construing an utterance as an appreciative judgment entails attention to rather special supporting grounds—grounds, in fact, that would allow us to admit judgments, otherwise incompatible if read in accord with the model of factual judgments, to stand as jointly confirmed. To treat value judgments as factual judgments (let us call this sort of judgment a "finding") is to hold to all the usual constraints on truth claims—incompatible claims cannot jointly be true. But to hold that value judgments are appreciative judgments, that is, logically depend on one's having certain tastes, preferences, convictions, or the like—though reference need never be made to these in positing supporting evidence—is to hold that we make value judgments of a sort logically weaker than findings. In the case of appreciative judgments, we do not concern ourselves with whether what is claimed is true but only with whether what is claimed or affirmed is justifiably claimed or affirmed ("reasonable" or "fair" or the like); that is, we concern ourselves only with whether the claimant is justified in *saying,* for instance, that the steak at Barney's is nice. I am so justified if, say, the steak has properties (that factual judgments, whether valuational or not, may mark out) that are both congruent with my taste and preference and relevant to the ascription of the value in question. Where findings are concerned, as with factual questions, we distinguish what is the case from what merely appears to be the case or from what is not the case; where appreciative judgments are concerned, these matters are waived and we consider only whether what is said may reasonably or fairly be said, whether it falls within the tolerance of what will be admitted to support such an affirmation consistently with there being variable and even incompatible tastes or convictions. I find someone to be "bright" and can offer what you recognize to be considerations relevant to the ascription, that is, to so saying; but not sharing my taste, you will not construe the properties offered in evidence as compelling reasons for your affirming the same judgment. The logical weakness of appreciative judgments is unmistakable, though we must realize that they form only a part of a very large range of judgments reasonably characterized as value judgments.

Affirming what one likes or dislikes, then, is not yet to make a judgment or, in particular, a value judgment; and, in making a value judgment, one may be making a judgment of either of at least two distinct sorts. For either of these sorts, supporting reasons may be demanded and are always relevant: those that bear on findings function evidentially in precisely the same way as does evidence for ordinary factual judgments—the difference having to do solely with the characterization of the predicate expressions involved, in particular, with their conceptual linkage to norms of excellence and the like; and those that bear on appreciative judgments essentially concern certain linguistic proprieties, given the speaker's tastes and convictions, of collecting (as supporting reasons) whatever properties things actually have—in a way that concedes alternative judgments to be confirmable, that, construed in terms of findings, might otherwise prove to be incompatible.

These considerations allow a conditional objectivity to value judgments. Indeed, there is a small irony here that may be noted. For, the objectivity of findings, is, as far as we have gone, relative to whatever conventional or traditional or routinized or posited set of institutions (embodying norms) that we admit; whether such judgments may exceed a merely conditional objectivity depends entirely on whether the norms, with respect to which these judgments function as they do, may, on independent grounds, be cognitively confirmed as the "proper" or "true" or "natural" or "ideal" or "real" values that human beings ought to pursue. We shall turn to this matter shortly. But appreciative judgments cannot, because of their very nature, be expected to be freed of a certain relativity: *their* (full) objectivity lies, precisely, in the degree to which they may be confirmed consistently with personal taste or conviction and with prevailing linguistic practices. Hence, in a sense, appreciative judgments do not depend on (and cannot pretend to be supported by) any ulterior cognitive claims respecting the values one places on things—though they pay the price of a certain inherent logical weakness. On the other hand, findings achieve formal parity with non-valuational factual judgments; but, in effect, the parity is conditional on further epistemic considerations, on whether the very normative values in terms of which such judgments are rendered are open to discovery by some cognitive means.

2. Cognitivism and Values

There are many strategies by which, intentionally or not, a stronger sort of objectivity—one with cognitive pretensions—is added to the conditional objectivity already admitted. The incentive is plain: reject the prevailing institutions (embodying normative values) either from within or without—either by challenging the right of such institutions to be authoritative or by exposing the historical accident by which the distinct practices of different societies have arisen—and one is bound to ask whether there are any cognitively compelling reasons for subscribing to these or those particular norms. The answer, I think, is No: there are no such reasons. The upshot, if true, is that, with respect to values that we suppose to be binding on men—that we suppose to have a categorical claim upon the allegiance of rational agents—we are no more than partisans; and that, as partisans, we seek out supporters and generate ideological justifications that we pretend confirm independently the very norms to which we subscribe.

There are, at bottom, two distinctive strategies by which such norms are taken to withstand assault or rejection (that is, of course, on rational grounds). One (often called naturalism) holds that the very meaning of fundamental valuational terms—'good' or 'right' or 'ought,' for instance—may rightly be explicated only in terms of certain (preferred) conditions, arrangements, relationships, qualities, and the like. The trouble with this strategy lies with an embarrassment of riches; for, partisans of every persuasion could (and do) adopt the view, merely producing thereby a linguistic version of every substantive quarrel about values to which they were already prone. The other strategy (often called non-naturalistic) insists on a distinctive faculty for "perceiving" or "grasping" or "intuiting" the actual values that inhere in the real world. The trouble, here, lies both with the admission, on the part of a great many otherwise sensitive men, of being utterly unaware of such a faculty and with the impossibility of confirming the existence of such a faculty; for, if it could be tested (rather like telepathy), there would have to be some other widely available sense by which relevant features of the public world (the very values in question) could be discriminated *and* by reference to which the privileged claims of this distinctive faculty could be independently appraised. But since it is just the confusion of competing claims about normative values that raises the problem, we cannot rightly claim that there is any well-established faculty for determining values, by reference to which the claims of a privileged moral or aesthetic or religious sense may be assessed. Alternatively put, it seems impossible to show that the advocacy of a privileged faculty is anything but the advocacy of partisan values—said, by way of a doctrinal adjustment, to be objectively confirmed by its exercise.

There seems, therefore, no remotely promising way in which to demonstrate that there is some cognitive means for discovering the normative values to which men are, by nature or reality, bound, or to which, for such a reason, they ought to subscribe. Classification (even of men as men) may depend on resemblances merely, not necessarily on norms of excellence or the like; so the cognitive grounds of any eudaimonistic, natural law, teleological, or related model that may be proffered can, fairly, be contested. Again, semantical inquiries having substantive consequences (as of the meaning of 'good' or 'right' or of promising) are demonstrably infected by a preference for the very values that are magically confirmed thereby; the very categories by which we pretend to describe human behavior neutrally, with a view to evaluation, presupposes certain governing values; and even the provision of

admissible data (for instance, "moral facts") that competing justificatory theories are expected to accommodate is, transparently,
partisan. For example, to construe promising as a purely linguistic
act—rather than as a morally significant act that is normally performed by means of using language—is to be tempted to suppose
that whatever substantive rules governing promising can be extracted from an analysis of the institution of promising is, somehow, nothing but a linguistic discovery: hence, a discovery not
controlled by ideological or doctrinal convictions or social practices that would otherwise be subject to ready revision.

The reason the untenability of a cognitivism with respect to values is of decisive importance lies with the nature of the very
claims we make respecting morality, prudence, health, the law, re-
ligion, political allegiance, education, and the like. For values of
these sorts are often said to be binding on men in various ways;
and if they are so said, the normal justification proferred will be
that they are known or discovered to be the "true" values that
ought to bind men. Clearly, the argument moves in a circle if the
discovery alleged cannot be independently confirmed.

But consider, also, the ways in which values are said to have a
categorical claim on men's allegiance. For one thing, given that a
rational agent pursues whatever he takes to be his interest (consulting his own drives, desires, convictions, and the like), a rational man is bound to consider the ranking of his interests and
goods; consequently, he is bound to consider whether there are any
overriding values, that is, values that take precedence over all alternative values, objectives, endeavors, and the like. If such values
were discoverable, then, on discovery, the rational man would be
bound to prefer them to all others. If we call such overriding values *moral* values, we shall understand something of the zeal and
import of the efforts of would-be reformers and guardians of the
various kinds of life so strenuously advocated for entire societies.

On the other hand, it is often supposed that there are certain
values that rational men as such will be disposed to pursue—for
instance, survival, increase in effective power, increase in plea-

sure, gratification of desires, perfection of one's talents, increase in happiness, contribution to the lives of all along any of the scales relevant for oneself. Different theorists select different values from such a set, which—without the support of a suitable cognitivism—is a conceptual (and even practical) embarrassment. If any selection of these sorts is made and if the values selected are claimed to be overriding values as well, then the resulting theory is a kind of egoism or utilitarianism, that must provide a suitable justification for such selection; for it is entirely conceivable that the values sampled be admitted to be characteristically preferred by men but not necessarily to be overriding values. One may, for instance, admit that self-preservation is a normal concern of human beings—rational, in the sense that acting to preserve one's own life does not require ulterior justification—and yet admit also that sacrificing one's life for a high cause need not be irrational and may actually be in the interest of some putatively overriding value. Similarly, maximizing some alleged good may be admitted to be rational (in the sense just given), though distributing that good equitably or justly (even if it involves a reduction in the quantity of the good that may be had) may well be both not irrational and in accord with an overriding value. In the latter sort of case, a distinction will be required between *moral* (that is, overriding) values and what we may term *prudential* values, that is, values said to be proper to man, given his natural drives and inclinations (medical and economic values are perhaps the least controversial specimens). When moral and prudential values are conflated, the rational man cannot go counter to his prudential interests and must pursue them as his overriding concern; where they are distinguished, it is *prima facie* rational to pursue one's prudential interests and it may yet (with justifications supplied) be rational to go counter to them. Hence, on the second view, to act in a prudentially relevant way is not, as such, to act morally: doctrines supporting this view are often said to be deontological. Also, prudential values are "proper" to man only in a non-tendentious sense, that is, statistically. Hence, it seems clear that the admission of

prudential values as rational values *prima facie*—not initially requiring justification—is itself a not negligible source of persuading
or indoctrinating men to regard such values as normative (and
even overriding) in a more substantive (and more dubious) sense.

In any case, cognitive evidence is wanted. For both where prudence and morality are equated and where they are not, we are
bound to demand a justification for whatever overriding values are
posited; and where prudential values are thought to be binding on
men *qua* rational—whether conditionally, on there not being any
relevant overriding values that might take precedence, or uncondi-
tionally, as overriding values themselves—we are bound to demand an account of how an inquiry into human nature may be
made to yield such selective values. Since, as has been argued,
there simply are no compelling ways in which to support cognitive
claims with regard to norms of excellence, perfection, maturity,
and the like, we are obliged to fall back to the conditional objectivity already tendered, that is, to the view that findings may be
objectively confirmed relative to some given system of institutionalized practices. "Rationality," then, is simply the general kind of
merit that corresponds to the forms of admissible rationalization,
or explanation by reasons—that vary from the informal and
merely statistical regularities of prudence to the categorically
binding codes of different societies.

3. Consistency and Practical Reasoning

The point at stake may be put in another way. The importance of
the distinction between factual judgments that employ valuational
predicates and those that do not rests primarily with considerations bearing on the actions of rational agents. The distinction itself does not depend on this—depends rather, as we have seen, on
whether the sense of given predicates is or is not to be explicated
in terms of norms of excellence and the like. But *if* certain values
are admitted to be binding, either prudentially or morally, then a
rational agent, believing them to be so, will be bound (as a matter

of consistency) to intend to act in accord with such values: he will not, therefore, be able to escape such a commitment merely by altering his particular projects, goals, interests, endeavors. A rational thief will, understandably, pursue whatever relevantly contributes to his objectives *qua* thief; but if he is reformed, he will (rationally) both discard the old objectives and no longer be bound to pursue suitable means to those ends. On the hypothesis, however, that one knows what the real moral and prudential values confronting men are, it is irrational to pursue any objectives that go counter to overriding values and it is irrational to pursue any objectives that go counter to prudential values (even if they are not overriding values), unless for the sake of relevant overriding values.

So the importance of the distinction lies principally with questions of consistency, that is, of a consistency between belief (or knowledge) and action (or intention). For, with respect to prudential and moral concerns, the consistency in question affects *all* conceivable actions on the part of rational agents. To classify certain predicates as prudentially or morally significant and to admit that proper values of these sorts are actually open to discovery is, very clearly, to say something that has a profound import for human beings. On the other hand, even if consistency, validity, confirmation, and the like are construed as normative notions, statements and arguments meeting relevant norms will have a neutral bearing on any and every formulated objective said to be prudentially and/or morally binding. Consequently, the thesis that notions like validity are normative does not have the same import (on the ends that men pursue) as do theories about moral and prudential values; the quarrel regarding the valuational import of the former notions, therefore, is decidedly benign. As rational agents, we pursue consistency, validity, justified belief, and the like adverbially, so to say: whatever goals we pursue we pursue compatibly with these norms; but as rational agents believing that certain values are true moral and/or prudential values, we pursue, say, health, justice, happiness, and the like substantively.

These distinctions, then, facilitate a comprehensive account of the logical properties of value judgments; for, by construing the action-guiding role of value judgments (and, in particular, of moral and prudential judgments) in terms of a certain consistency between belief and action, it becomes entirely otiose to construe such judgments (in the face of strong conceptual difficulties) as imperatives or emotive expressions or the like. For that reason, for instance, it becomes relatively easy to construe such a central term as 'ought' as (normally) univocal through the widest range of specimen sentences—covering belief as well as action, and non-moral and non-prudential concerns as well as the moral and the prudential. Thus, 'ought' (which normally appears as, and is normally taken as, a copula) may be characterized rather as a predicative expression designating whatever takes precedence in some ranking order (rendered more perspicuously, perhaps, by 'oughtful'). If, say, X is oughtful (that is, if X ought to be believed or to be done), then if S believes that X is oughtful, then S will, in the relevant circumstances, intend to act in accord with X—even if, as often with beliefs, only hypothetical circumstances for taking action may be assigned. If I believe that the swallows ought to be returning shortly to Capistrano, then I believe that that event has a higher likelihood of occurring than any other of a certain set of relevant events; and I shall (rationally) guide myself accordingly *if* any relevant interest occupies me. And if I believe that, overridingly, I ought not to murder my neighbor, then it would be irrational of me to do so (that is, to choose or intend to do so or the like). Clearly, the sense and criteria of application, for such terms as 'good,' 'right,' and 'ought,' will need to be distinguished: in this way, the sense of the terms may be held to be univocal while their criteria vary; and in this way, too, the question of their sense and criteria of application may be distinguished from that concerning the consistency of belief and action. The upshot is that our theory regarding findings will be sustained and such problems as that of deriving 'ought' from 'is' or of the eligibility of 'ought' without 'can' are quite easily resolved—the first, by reminding ourselves of the mixed classification of judgments as being judgments of fact and judgments of value; the second, by reminding ourselves of the difference between judging and acting consistently with one's beliefs (which, merely in being distinguished, entails the conceivability of the rational akrasiac).

Also, to treat the action-guiding function of judgments (which cannot, it should be noted, be restricted to moral judgments alone or even to value judgments alone) as concerned with a certain kind of consistency between judgment and action obviates the need for a distinctive kind of reasoning—for instance, for the so-called practical syllogism, in which the conclusion is alleged to be an action and the premises, interests or desires and beliefs. For, the practical syllogism will either be an analogue of the theoretical syllogism, in which the usual formal properties of the argument will be assignable to the "content" of relevant psychological states and behavior; or else, given certain desires and beliefs, it will merely concern the consistency of acting or intending to act in accord jointly with those desires and beliefs and with some relevant theoretical syllogism. Where an argument is wanted, there will, so far forth, be no (novel) logical considerations that cannot be accommodated among the usual argument forms; and where questions of psychological and behavioral consistency are raised, the issue will concern an *external* relationship between an argument (whatever it may be) and an agent's *intentions* and *behavior*. Furthermore, and decisively, where practical reasoning is premissed on desires or wants and *beliefs* about one's own capacities and skills, it becomes necessary to distinguish between the validity of arguments and the consistency between behavior, intended behavior, and the conclusions of valid arguments themselves. To suppose that practical as opposed to theoretical reasoning invariably depends on knowledge—not merely belief—about one's capacities (and, correspondingly, the adequacy of the capacities involved) is inherently implausible and fails to provide a suitable parallel to the notion (relevant to theoretical reasoning) of a valid argument from false premisses.

These distinctions deserve to be summarized a bit more trimly. Questions of consistency *between* belief and action are problematic because relevant appraisals cannot be made straightforwardly of a set of mere propositions. The intentional features of believing and of action as well as the obvious differences between propositions and psychological states and behavioral episodes oblige us to consider the difference between (theoretical) reasoning construed entirely in terms of relations between propositions and (so-called practical) reasoning said to hold between beliefs and desires (viewed as psychological states) and the performance of actions. For one thing, the question of consistency in practice cannot arise solely in terms of belief and action; provision must be made for intervening interests, desires, needs, and the like, for only on that condition can normative and justificatory issues of any sort arise. Hence, if cognitivism is defective, questions of consistency will have to be restricted to the putative values of individual agents and of aggregates of agents. For a second, the question of practical consistency cannot be restricted to any particular sector of human interest and behavior—say, the moral—for if practical reasoning is to be construed as a suitable analogue of theoretical reasoning, its canons would have to be formulable for all contexts of practice. Hence, if, as has been argued, valuational predicates (for instance, 'good,' 'right,' 'oughtful') are, in the relevant respects, univocally used across different contexts of practice (for instance, moral, medical, legal, prudential, scientific) and play a central role in practical reasoning, and if the criteria for their ascription vary from context to context, it will be unnecessary to construe the logical properties of practical reasoning (as distinct from its psychological properties or from considerations of merely contextual relevance) as different in any regard at all from those of theoretical reasoning. All that would be required perhaps would be an enlargement of alternative models of (theoretical) reasoning (for instance, regarding imperatives or temporal relations or the like) and an explication of external questions of consistency between action and *whatever reasoning* we may engage in.

A third consideration is this. The ability to follow an argument is utterly different from the ability to act in accord with a conclusion drawn from premises conveying one's own beliefs and desires, and the first ability does not entail the second. Hence, even if practical reasoning were alleged to be distinct from theoretical reasoning, failure to act in accord with what would be required by consistency between belief and action (on the hypothesis, construed in terms of a distinctive model of reasoning) would not necessarily entail a logical (practical) inconsistency; for the agent, competent enough to judge, may not be competent enough to act, may suffer from a weakness of will. Finally, it must be said, regarding intentionally qualified mental states, there is no exclusive model obviously appropriate to the analysis of the content of such states. Hence, there is no obvious grammatical model for detailing the putatively distinctive properties of practical reasoning. For instance, in analyzing having intentions, we may convey intentions by the use of infinitives ("my intention was 'to mate his king in three moves' ") or by the use of propositions ("my intention is 'that Mary will receive her fair share' ") or by the use of imperatives ("my intention is: 'Let Ruth prepare the dinner' ") or by other devices. Similar alternatives arise, obviously, for states of desire and the like. But such distinctions suggest, precisely, the need for widening our account of theoretical reasoning, not for supposing that practical reasoning is fundamentally different. Also, the entire exercise depends on the use of a heuristic model of speech acts—a consideration obscured by speaking of the distinctive logic of practical reasoning.

To return to our main theme, then, and to sum up: the prospects of a science of values will be nil, if what is wanted is a defense of the thesis that normative values are, as such, open to discovery. The primary locus of disputes about values concern human persons—individually, in relationships with other individuals, or in aggregates. But if persons cannot be identified with physical bodies, are culturally emergent entities that are at least linguistically competent and that are variably indoctrinated, it is impossible to resolve the deeper cognitive questions regarding values by an inspection of human nature itself and it is impossible, beyond minimal limits of consistency (what may be termed "rationality," without being tendentious or partisan), to set constraints on alternative ideals and practices compatible with human abilities. In this sense, the ascription of belief in terms of a model of rationality—itself presupposing normal desires and objectives —may be justifiably challenged on the grounds of the untenability of cognitivism. Hence, though, admittedly, it is not necessary, the doctrine of practical reasoning is readily linked to the independent doctrine of the putatively natural (and "rational") desires and needs of man. On the other hand, if we subscribe to the principle "similar things must be similarly judged in similar respects," we are doing no more than committing ourselves to formal consistency —regardless of what substantive values we may prefer. Or, if we insist that wherever distinctions are introduced that, once granted, justify a difference in judgment where none would otherwise be allowed, a justification for their introduction must be supplied, we are doing no more than committing ourselves to an avoidance of arbitrariness—regardless of what substantive values we may prefer. Or, if we insist that whenever men believe that given values are overriding or take precedence in a given context of (their own) action they must intend to act accordingly, we are doing no more than committing ourselves to consistency between belief and action—regardless of what substantive values we may prefer. These and similar constraints are fairly construed as rational constraints; but, of course, they are entirely formal. The same kind of vacuity attends such principles as "Prefer the greater good to the lesser," "Do what is right," and the like. Internal coherence, whatever its own merit, can hardly decide the relative merit of all competing proposals; also, by introducing temporal considerations, would-be inconsistencies may be resolved by an honest change of mind; also, the congruence between belief and action viewed in accord with a favored principle is readily challenged from the vantage of another.

The point may be differently focused. If persons are culturally emergent entities, then *their* values, on whatever basis ascribed, cannot be convincingly drawn from an examination of the properties of their bodies. But if they are cultural emergents, distinguished minimally in terms of their linguistic competence, there can be no discoverable rules or norms by reference to which their conduct ought to be governed or favorably appraised—if what is wanted are rules and norms other than those embedded in the very culture in which they have emerged or, given such norms, that they can project as possible alternatives. There are no natural laws in accord with which cultures evolve from their physical embodiments; and whatever lawlike regularities we may provide concern the behavior of creatures already habituated in accord with some set of rules or other—that, for reasons of conviction, they may supersede. Men do not have antecedent natures that flourish or fail in given cultures; they have whatever nature their culture actually breeds, permits to develop among the living systems that they groom. Still, on the argument given, there are a great many normative considerations that do not themselves need to be cognitively grounded in order to support an entirely objective practice of grading and ranking with respect to their distinctions; and, with regard to those values that may, if adopted, be supposed to have some categorical claim on the allegiance of their own partisans, it is entirely possible to admit at least a certain conditional objectivity. The trouble, of course, is that it will never satisfy the zealots. But that is a matter not of theory but of engineering.

EPILOGUE

I have favored a number of controversial doctrines that have seemed to me both to fit perspicuously the data usually admitted in philosophical controversy and to cohere together in a gratifyingly unforced way. For the sake of summary, I should like to list some of the key views I support and reject. They may perhaps serve as a checklist of sorts.

I reject a cluster of powerful theories bearing on cognition and understanding—the causal theory of knowledge, the causal theory of perception, the causal theory of meaning, and the like—without denying the relevance of causal factors in the analysis of knowledge, perception, inference, memory, grasping meanings. I take the latter concepts to have normative import and to depend on the application, characteristically informal, of rules or rulelike considerations in virtue of which ascriptions of knowledge and the like are rationalized and justified. Correspondingly, I deny that rationalization and justification are, as explanatory patterns, species of causal explanation. Without holding such a view, of course, it would be a relatively simple matter to outflank attacks on the causal theories mentioned. But in saying this, I do not wish to deny that what may serve as a cause may serve as a reason, and vice versa. More generally, I hold that causal contexts are extensional, in that causal connections hold regardless of changing designations of what is thus connected, though contexts of causal explanation are nonextensional; and I hold that ascriptions of reasons and contexts of rationalization are nonextensional as well. If these doctrines hold, then it is a straightforward matter to support the rejection of the causal theories mentioned. I also deny that intentionality means what nonextensionality (intensionality) means or is a species of nonextensionality.

I treat actions as a species of events and treat both (as well as states and similar distinctions) as what I call subaltern particulars, whose admission depends on a grammatical liberty regarding whatever may antecedently be predicated of particulars like physical bodies and persons. This enables me to demonstrate certain key weaknesses in mind-body identity theories, without denying the continuing eligibility of such theories; I merely hold that there is no clear way, among the extant versions of these theories, to overcome the difficulties isolated. I do not, however, construe the uncertainty or indefensibility of identity theories or of eliminative materialism as equivalent to the uncertainty of materialism as such. Also, the admission of subaltern particulars does not, on my view, entail any particular ontology, only the relative independence or dependency of given concepts. The rejection of the causal theories mentioned is particularly suggestive of promising ways of analyzing the concepts of mind and person compatibly with some forms of materialism.

I reject, on independent grounds, claims of incorrigible and indubitable knowledge, often taken as sufficient marks of the mental; and I also explore the possible adequacy of the intentional as the mark of the mental—that minds only and always are "directed upon" an object. Here, distinguishing between what "has a mind" and what lacks a mind but depends on creatures that have minds (like art or language produced by men, or national states that collect men in a distinctive way), I exhibit a deficiency in the thesis that intentionality, on any familiar interpretation, is the mark of the mental. Also, I construe the intentional in terms of the rule-governed (or rule-following or rule-improvising), which permits me to link the mental and the cultural, to link the analysis of language, belief, and action; the thesis suggests, also, a promising conception of what it is to be a person or a creature inferior to persons but possessing a mind. Intransitive or transitive sentience I take, then, to be a necessary and sufficient mark of a particular's having a mind; graded mental achievements on the part of such a particular are marked by advanced forms of intentionality; and, in particular, the capacity to use language is taken as the mark of a person. The critical importance of persons in the cognitive setting indicates, in my opinion, the difficulty of rejecting persons as particulars basic to any viable ontology. I do not defend disembodied existence, but I do defend the coherence, for instance, of reincarnation, with whatever attendant modifications may be required regarding ascriptions of memory and the reidentification of particulars under conditions of discontinuous existence. I also defend the tenability of materialism (a materialism of composition—that precludes mind-body identity, central-state materialism, eliminative materialism, behaviorism, physicalism) and a dualism of properties. The latter depends directly on the admission of persons as culturally emergent entities. Here, the puzzles of identity and individuation need to be considered. I hold that, where spatio-temporal continuities and forms of decomposition are involved, reidentification needs to be informal, in the sense that anomalies arise regarding all putatively necessary and sufficient conditions of identity under such conditions and in the sense that an element of decision is inescapable. I treat persons as cultural entities not reducible to physical objects but physically embodied; and I hold that the concept of a person is compatible with radically divergent criteria for individuating and reidentifying persons, rather along the lines of instantiating such cultural entities as works of art.

I adopt a realist theory of perception, argue that sense-datum theories are avoidable, and distinguish sharply between perception and forms of (intransitive) sentience, as of pain—which difference is also critical to the defense of mind-body identity theories. I distinguish between veridical perception and what resembles, or may be phenomenally confused with, perception (hallucination, dreams, images, and the like) chiefly in terms of syntactical ambiguities in the use of expressions employing semantically univocal terms. This permits a clear distinction between such intentionally qualified forms of sentience and such forms as of the discrimination of pain (which, I argue, is nonintentional, in the relevant sense); it also allows an important similarity to be brought out between intransitive (and intentional) forms of sentience (for instance, hallucinations and dreams) and non-sentient forms of intentional awareness (for instance, beliefs and thoughts), that undercuts the plausibility of construing knowledge and belief along essentially isomorphic lines. I reject the isomorphism, treating knowledge in terms of the status of beliefs and treating beliefs themselves as psychological states. I argue that ascriptions of knowledge are, in general, informal and only informally related to the conditions on which we determine what is true. And I treat belief-states in terms of a heuristic model of mental acts, based on linguistic acts. Also, to accommodate cognitive and ontological questions, I distinguish two senses of 'exist' (relating to referents and existents) and hold that we may refer to what does not exist; correspondingly, I hold that it is neither anomalous nor self-contradictory to say that something (to which we are referring) does not exist or that there is a such-and-such that does not exist. This forces all questions of what actually does exist to be explicated in terms either of perception (or of other cognitive sources) or of ontological analyses of whatever is antecedently provided by perception (or other such sources) without denying that ontological commitments infect our perceptual discourse. Also, I hold that 'exists'—in the sense in which we speak of what exists in the actual world—is a predicate of a special sort. This permits us to see more perspicuously whatever semantical alternatives we wish to consider in providing a minimal interpretation of any formal logical calculus.

About language, I chiefly argue, in the same spirit, that sentence and term (and similar distinctions, including speech act) are correlative distinctions that may be marked out for given concatenations of noises or marks or the like only within some linguistic theory and that, therefore, the analysis of language—admitting that we normally use language to speak about the world—itself depends on ulterior assumptions regarding cognitive conditions in general. I indicate how this bears on preserving the analytic/ synthetic distinction and on the testing of ontological alternatives; and I question the sense—given the fragmentary and improvisational nature of actual speech—in which, though natural languages are said to be rule-governed, necessary and sufficient conditions of meaningful discourse can be formulated for them (without denying that open, rulelike regularities may be statistically supported). I also subscribe to the correspondence theory of truth, but in a form that makes it incapable of supplying working criteria for appraising particular cognitive claims. The theory, in fact, is merely a corollary of the rejection of skepticism and the assumption of a public world: it fixes the timelessness of truth, without assuming its eternity; accommodates reference and predication, without ineffable connections; and imposes the constraint of coherence on all of our cognitive resources, without pretending to any privileged access of its own. Correspondingly, I adopt a skeptical view about ontologies, holding that, at most, we may construe candidate ontologies as defeasible and that, given putatively necessary conditions, alternative, non-converging ontological systems can always be successfully generated. For related reasons, I stress the difficulty of separating syntactical and semantical considerations, particularly where the difference bears on nonextensional contexts and the semantic theory of truth. I also hold that sentences are cultural entities embodied in physical marks and sounds; that speech acts are similarly embodied in physical events; and that propositions need not be construed as mental entities, may merely be embodied in sentences that are physically and even culturally diverse.

Finally, I hold that the fact-value dichotomy is a conceptually mixed distinction and that, on formal grounds alone, it is entirely possible that a proposition be both factual and valuational. The development of this consideration explicates the neutrality—in the face of the implausibility of claiming that substantive values are open to straightforward discovery—of speaking of knowledge, confirmation, validity, and the like, in normative terms. Also, I argue against the necessity of admitting a distinctive kind of practical reasoning; I press instead the concept of consistency between relevant forms of reasoning and practical action, chiefly in terms of the analysis of value judgments and the analysis of the phenomenon of weakness of will. And I link the indefensibility of cognitivism to the fact that man is a cultural entity.

INDEX

act-ascriptions, 155-56, 159, 178
action(s):
    and effort of will, 149-50; and causation, 150-55 *passim,* 160, 167; and agent-causation, 151-52; and persons (agents), 152, 160, 178-79; and freedom, 153, 166-67; complexity of, 150-51, 154-56 *passim;* individuation of, 150, 155, 158, 159; description (redescription) of, 156-57, 160-62 *passim;* reidentification of, 156, 158, 159; elision of, and consequence, 156-59 *passim,* 161-62; explanation of, 161-65, 170
agent-causation, 151-52
akrasia (weakness of will), 169-70, 274, 276
analytic/synthetic, 198-201 *passim*
appreciative judgments, 264-65, 266-67

bare particulars, 228-29, 234
behavioral sciences, 192
behaviorism, 231-33 *passim,* 254
belief:
    compared with knowledge, 5-10 *passim,* 17-21 *passim;* as determi-
nate psychological state, 8-23 *passim;* in animals, 10-13 *passim,* 17; as or not normatively ascribed, 12-14 *passim,* 18; and assertion, 12, 17, 21; as monadic or dyadic, 18-23 *passim;* reasonable $_{val}$, 25; and justified claims, 25-27 *passim;* as caused, 31-32, 67-68, 70; and incorrigibility and indubitability, 78-79; and self-intimating states, 82-83; informality of ascriptions of, 10-12 *passim;* heuristic model of, 17, 21, 23; intentional nature of, 17-18, 22, 23

causal contexts, as extensional, 164-65
causal explanation, 163-65 *passim,* 178
central-state materialism, 232, 254
certainty:
    and knowledge, 32-33, 45, 80; principal forms of, 73-75; empirical, 76-83 *passim,* 86; logical, 77-78, 86
choice, 168
cloning, 145, 246
coherence theory of truth, 208

285